WHAT MAKES CLUSTERS COMPETITIVE?

What Makes Clusters Competitive?

Cases from the Global Wine Industry

Edited by
ANIL HIRA

McGill-Queen's University Press
Montreal & Kingston • London • Ithaca

© McGill-Queen's University Press 2013
ISBN 978-0-7735-4259-4 (cloth)
ISBN 978-0-7735-4260-0 (paper)
ISBN 978-0-7735-8955-1 (ePDF)
ISBN 978-0-7735-8956-8 (ePUB)

Legal deposit fourth quarter 2013
Bibliothèque nationale du Québec

Printed in Canada on acid-free paper that is 100% ancient forest
free (100% post-consumer recycled), processed chlorine free.

This book has been published with the help of funding from
Genome British Columbia and Genome Canada. Genome BC
funding was sourced from the British Columbia Provincial
Government and Genome Canada funding was sourced from the
Government of Canada.

McGill-Queen's University Press acknowledges the support of the
Canada Council for the Arts for our publishing program. We also
acknowledge the financial support of the Government of Canada
through the Canada Book Fund for our publishing activities.

Library and Archives Canada Cataloguing in Publication

    What makes clusters competitive? : cases from the global
wine industry / edited by Anil Hira.

Includes bibliographical references and index.
Issued in print and electronic formats.
ISBN 978-0-7735-4259-4 (bound). – ISBN 978-0-7735-4260-0 (pbk.). –
ISBN 978-0-7735-8955-1 (ePDF). – ISBN 978-0-7735-8956-8 (ePUB)

    1. Wine industry – Case studies. 2. Competition – Case
studies. 3. Industrial clusters – Case studies. I. Hira, Anil,
author, editor of compilation

HD9370.5.W43 2013   338.4'76632   C2013-905695-5
                                            C2013-905696-3

This book was typeset by True to Type in 10.5/13 Sabon

Dedicated by the editor to
Robert and Jean Hardwick
for serving as great role models of magnanimity,
selflessness, sacrifice, and hard work.

Contents

Figures and Tables

TABLES

Acknowledgments

We would like to thank first and foremost the funding agencies and contributors who made this study possible, namely, Genome Canada, Genome British Columbia, Simon Fraser University (SFU), University of British Columbia (UBC), Universidad de la Extremadura (Spain), Universidad Alfonso Ibañez (Chile), Università di Pisa (Italy), and University of Technology, Sydney (Australia). The province of British Columbia and SFU provided invaluable research support through a direct grant as well as the work-study program. Our scientific partners at UBC, Hennie Van Vuuren and Steve Lund, were incredibly collegial and supportive through a large number of challenges throughout the process. The Scientific Board of our grant, particularly Peter Phillips, was very helpful in giving feedback throughout the process. We also received feedback from a Genome Canada interim review that took place with an international scientific board in Calgary in 2011. We would like to thank our editor, Kyla Madden, for her sage advice in guiding us through the preparation, and two anonymous reviewers for their help in considerably improving the manuscript.

An early version of chapter 1 was presented at the 2011 Industry Studies Association meeting. We wish to thank colleagues there for feedback, particularly Howard Wial and Ron Hira. In addition, Elisa Giuliani made very helpful comments on chapters 1 and 8. The funders noted above as well as the BC Wine Grape Council supported the culminating two-day conference in Penticton in 2011 at which the authors presented all of the case study findings and enjoyed a very interesting dialogue with the wine industry. Findings from the BC chapter were delivered again to the BC Wine Law Seminar in February 2012. Patty Hira did most of the copyediting, helping to bring this project to fruition.

WHAT MAKES CLUSTERS COMPETITIVE?

Explaining the Success of Clusters: A Framework for the Study of Global Wine Industry Dynamics

ANIL HIRA, SARAH GIEST, AND MIKE HOWLETT

INTRODUCTION TO THE PROJECT

Understanding Sources of Global Competitiveness

The guiding research question for our project is: What makes some late-developing industries competitive in global markets, while others fail? The question is of great interest given the challenges faced by Northern countries – to restart long-term economic growth as manufacturing retreats and services seem to generate less employment – and those faced by the Southern, or developing, countries who seek new ways to generate economic growth, particularly those that might generate export revenues and act as growth catalysts.

For much of the twentieth century, the "battle of ideas" has been one of polarised views of economic management decisions being dominated either by the state or by the free market (Yergin and Stanislaw 2002). The battle was largely won by free market forces and the idea that global market liberalisation agreements for finance and trade would both level the playing field and render state support of industries ineffective and wasteful, given their global nature. The primary conclusion of most mainstream economists, and the underlying logic behind economic strategy in much of the West over the last three decades, has been that markets are (spontaneously) self-created and organised, and that comparative advantage determines who produces what, where (R. Anderson 2004; Klein and Hadjimichael 2003, 155–6). With the onset of the financial crisis, from 2008 to the present, the idea that the state could play a complementary role in aiding markets has begun to gain some attention. For example, US President Obama has mentioned the importance of supporting innovation in new industries, such as clean energy, throughout his term. Nonetheless, the effectiveness of direct subsidies to the energy and other innovative industries has been severely questioned. Therefore the second overall guiding question for our research is: What role, if any, can the public sector effectively play in supporting new industries, given globalisation?

In order to start to move past the century long battle of ideas, we need to acknowledge that the world is not dialectical; there are many shades of gray between state direction and laissez-faire free markets. Thus, the objective really becomes to understand what types of roles states are presently playing in supporting their industries, and how successful are they in their strategies. Since there are a limited number of states, this suggests a comparative strategy to examine state support over space and time.

In order to answer this question, we believe that one has to control for industry. The types of support for one industry may not be suitable for others. Information Technology (IT), for example, seems to be thriving in the US with minimal direct ongoing intervention, though indirect support such as defence contracts and support for basic research are apparent, as well as intervention in strategic periods, such as the saving of the semiconductor industry in the 1980s. Other industries, such as renewable energy, are receiving more direct intervention and support. As documented elsewhere (Hira, Wixted, and Arechavala 2012), these examples demonstrate that the type of industry and the timing of entry into it matter greatly for developing competitive advantage. These aspects suggest a research design that controls for industry, but also looks at different cases that have entered into markets at different periods, and therefore represent different stages of maturity. Moreover, if we can compare cases that represent a spectrum of different levels of success and failure in global markets, then we can see not only if different state policies are associated with levels of success, but also how those policies evolved in tune with local industry developments. The cluster approach gives us a useful empirical referent by which to study these questions.

Why the Cluster Approach?

The idea of economic clusters, since it was popularised by Michael Porter (1986), has caught fire, and countries and regions are now expending huge efforts and resources to try to develop new clusters that could be new sources of employment and growth. Clusters have been noticed for a long time, going back to the "industrial districts" noted by Alfred Marshall (1890) at the turn of the twentieth century. Clusters are often defined by (geographically) densely linked firms, services, and labour pools working in a common industry, with close agglomerations of firms engaged in the same product chain, sharing mutual benefits from proximity. Regions are sometimes marked by foundational industries, such as the automobile industry in Detroit, and the IT industry in the Silicon Valley. The traditional image of clusters, as in the fashion industry in Milan and New York, has given way to a more advanced image of clusters, as in the IT industry in the Silicon Valley. There has been a plethora of attempts to create clusters in emerging industries such as biotechnology around the world (e.g. Singapore's Biopolis project), with the hope of capturing a concentration of value-added employment and revenue-creating businesses that can compete in global export markets. Studying clusters is the key, therefore, to understanding if innovation and industrial organisational policies can help countries and regions to "capture" industries within their territory. Thus, the cluster approach is one apparently important strategy to create jobs and improve standards of living in a globally competitive world.

The underlying idea of supporting industry through cluster policy seems sound in that it represents a move away from lobbying for or favouritism shown to particular firms and towards the economic well-being of a region or country, and it supports entrepreneurship and specialisation among firms (Cortright 2006, iv, 24). As Martin and Sunley (2003) point out, the issue in practice is far more problematic. Cluster theory is still in an early stage, and there is no consensus around a precise set of causal concepts. For example, there are disagreements about whether they are *sui generis* and of spontaneous development or whether they can be created, and whether in fact they (and the advantages of geographical concentration) are becoming less relevant given globalisation. Therefore, as we discuss below, clusters lend themselves to ongoing contention precisely because there is no well-defined theory by which to test out clear causal propositions. Even defining basic variables – whether a cluster is defined by geographical proximity or simply by supply chains, for example – becomes problematic given such conceptual confusion.

Therefore we have a paradoxical situation of in-motion cluster-based policies that have not been tested for their effectiveness. We really do not know if the Silicon Valley success can be re-created, whether it is largely a product of timing and market forces, or whether policies play(ed) a fundamental role in the creation and maintenance of its competitive advantage. In sum, we know very little with any degree of certainty about what explains the success or failure of clusters, and, in turn, the effectiveness of the growing policy support and financial support for them. Moreover, we are still not clear about whether the globalisation of supply chains renders the idea of local agglomeration a less relevant strategy over time.

Our response to this confusion is to suggest a slightly different approach, one that borrows perspectives from industrial policy and innovation theory and combines them in a four-pronged explanatory framework that takes an evolutionary and a public-private partnership view of possible sources of the success of clusters. Again, our focus is to better understand the sources of global competitiveness (or lack thereof) of clusters. The four key issues considered in our approach are: firm adaptability to market shifts, state policies to promote adaptability and collective cluster goods, the quality and flexibility of institution-firm and firm-firm networks, and the ability to adapt to global supply chains. In the rest of this chapter, we defend our choice of these four perspectives as a reasonable approach to explaining cluster success. Because of the lack of theoretical consensus, we take a more inductive approach to developing case studies in order to ensure that we are not merely confirming what we want to see.

Why the Wine Industry?

The wine industry is a particularly apt one for studying clusters, as reflected in recent literature (Giuliani, Morrison, and Rabellotti 2011). As we discuss in chapter 2, there are several key prerequisite agricultural conditions required to make quality wine, related to climate, soil, and water. Thus, wine production naturally tends to concentrate in certain geographic locations, and different types and qualities of wine naturally result from the particular conditions of the location where it is produced.

The wine industry is also compelling as a case study from the point of view of global competitiveness. Wine has been around for centuries, but in recent years a major shift has taken place in global markets, with upstarts such as Australia and Chile capturing increasing market share, as we demonstrate in chapter 2. Such developments suggest that late entry into markets is not a death sentence. Rather, they suggest that barriers to entry related to timing can be overcome.

Such developments are particularly interesting because we do not usually think about wine as an industry subject to continual technological revolutions. While there is innovation in the wine industry, it is certainly not as dynamic as the IT, automotive, or aerospace industries. Rather, the innovation has tended to be incremental and oriented towards developing nuances in the flavour of particular varietals, as slight improvements in taste can make the difference between a highly recognized and a generic wine. The basic techniques of winemaking remain the same. Since this industry experiences few exogenous shocks, we would expect that it should experience more stability in markets, as incumbents garner market share and extend it through their advantages in marketing and incremental knowledge specialisation.

In sum, we have seen a major shakeup in wine markets over the last two decades. The burning question is why has this occurred. Our particular interest is in what role, if any, public policies played in developing the competitive advantage that allowed new challengers to begin to take on the Old World producers that had centuries of advantage.

Methodology

The logic of our research methodology, as noted above, suggests that a comparative study that considers the development of different clusters is most appropriate. That leaves the question of whether to conduct such a study as a large statistical one or a small comparative one. We choose the latter because of the lack of clear variables, data, and measurements for clusters. Given the lack of clarity of cluster theory, and the fact that winemaking techniques depend on developing unique, differentiated, but consistent tastes, we believe that an inductive if systematic approach is most appropriate. This allows us to recognise that there may be conditions unique to particular wine industries, such as the historical discovery of Champagne in France, that give a cluster a unique advantage. These are, to some extent, now enshrined in the appellation system of identifying wines (including Champagne) by their region of origin. Therefore, we want to be open to the possibility that policies do not really figure into the success of wine industries, thus leaving open the possibility of inimitability.

For the most part, wine research has been focused on one-off local studies, or collections of them, as well as general market trends, with no real systematic international comparison of what makes them competitive. While there are some important exceptions, notably K. Anderson (2004), Giuliani, Morrison, and Rabellotti (2011), and Jenster et al. (2008), we try to improve upon them by using a common research methodology for each of our cases. Thanks to the generosity of Genome Canada and Genome BC, we were able to use a pool of resources to try to attract the top wine researchers in the field to this project, by helping to defray survey costs and subsidising in-person meetings. Anil Hira therefore contacted a number of top researchers with track records in examining the question of wine industry competitiveness throughout the world during the Fall of 2009. Unfortunately, some cases that would have been of great interest, particularly Argentina, New Zealand, and South Africa, did not yield ready partners.

To create an international team of experienced researchers in an industry required some degree of flexibility in the research methodology. Thus, while we have three case studies of particular regional clusters (BC, Extremadura, and Tuscany), we also have two cases done at the national level (Australia, Chile), still using the same conceptual approach. In sum, we were able to assemble an experienced team with in-depth expertise of particular wine clusters that cover different levels of timing, maturity, and overall success. By gaining commitment of the team to a common research methodology, we hope to move forward knowledge about our key theoretical questions concerning competitiveness and clusters, but more importantly, we seek to develop knowledge that will be useful and applicable to policymakers working with the wine industry. Our case studies alone will provide interesting insights into the workings of each cluster for local policymakers. The comparative and theoretical components add to this value, and, hopefully, make a more lasting contribution.

Our case studies are based on intensive field research of wine industries in Canada, Australia, Italy, Chile, and Spain from 2009 to 2011, in which a common survey was distributed to wineries, support institutions, and supply chains. The survey was developed by Hira and Aylward, based on Hira's theoretical framework of global competitiveness, other surveys of innovation such as that of the OECD, and other surveys of the wine industry, including Aylward's surveys of the Australian wine industry. A copy of the survey is available in the appendix of this book. The survey contains three basic parts, and throughout, where importance was measured, we used a six-part Likert scale, with a range starting at 0 for not important, 3 for neutral, and 5 for extremely important. The first part of the survey consists of a set of demographic questions about each participating winery – intended to control for variables such as size that could confound conclusions, but also to track dependent variables of performance, particularly revenue changes over the past year. We also asked winemakers what they think are the sources of competitive advantage for their firms. The second part asks about wineries' opinions of their local support institutions. Here we build upon the "triple helix" approach (Etzkowitz 2003) that sees a partnership among researchers, industry, and government as key to success. The third part asks how often respondents network with other winemakers in the local cluster. In both the second and third parts, we use the social network mapping approach to test the importance of relationships. We developed this part of our methods by consulting with veterans of the approach, Kathryn Ibata-Arens (forthcoming) and Camille Ryan and Peter Phillips (Phillips et al. 2008). We used UCINET software to develop our network maps. Network maps measure the numbers of connections that a firm (or other actor) has with other firms as well as how important those connections are. These, in turn, are reflected in two measures – extension and strength, both measures of "social capital." The extension of a network shows how many actors in an area have ties to each other. The strength is how important those ties are. Social capital or social ties, are widely considered to be important sources of competitive advantage (Putnam 1993), as we discuss below. In the fourth part of the survey, we asked wineries for their opinions about the sources of innovation (new ideas, techniques), and in which areas of their business they implemented them. Innovation is a particularly important area, as it is often the main focus of policymakers seeking to support local industries.

Besides the common survey, we also developed a set of interview questions around competitive strategy. Interviews lasted 30–60 minutes. The survey was tested out in pilot cases in British Columbia (BC) and Australia before finalising it. Over the three years of the project, we shared findings and ideas, and debated the implications of our comparisons. We also sought out comments from experts in the industry along the way. The culmination was an in-person discussion and presentation of our findings in July 2011 in Penticton, BC, at an all day workshop and at the annual BC Wine Grape Council industry conference, which included the participation of over one hundred members of the local industry and other experts. Our study has also been reviewed in its various stages by wine industry experts around the world – from Australia to Canada – in various policy reports, working papers, and conference presentations.

Recognising that markets change and interact with social and political contexts (Polanyi 1944), as reflected in our case study approach, is a far cry from understanding how they change and what this means for industrial location. We focus on industrial clusters as the object for testing how success in globally competitive markets can be achieved through producers' interactions with support institutions and each other, thus allowing us to examine what types of relationships and policies make sense. We balance the systematic approach with recognition of the importance of the context of socio-economic-political relations within each cluster. Following the presentation of our theoretical approach in the rest of this chapter, and a chapter on market trends within the global wine industry, we present case study chapters. Each chapter begins with a brief history of the evolution and key events of the specific wine industry cluster under discussion. We then examine the key factors we have identified as being most likely to be behind the relative success or failure of each cluster, based on the common survey and our theoretical framework. But we have also encouraged each author to highlight the path-dependent nature of the development and present challenges of his/her cluster, using his/her deep knowledge to tease out the nuances and provide a deeper explanation than a simple deductive or inductive approach would allow.

In the final chapter, this study concludes that countries and firms within them can develop certain types of deep but flexible governance around clusters that, with an understanding of the cycles of innovation and market evolution, can allow them to improve their chances of creating successful global industries and maintaining their position within them. Needless to say, the stakes are high: the countries that succeed in gaining global market share and increasing profits will have new and dynamic sources of export revenue, employment, investment, and extremely valuable spillovers in knowledge, global marketing chains, and innovation. Such success could help to transform the institutional and social capital of a country, and would have profound effects throughout the economy, including the transformation of other sectors.

WHY FIRMS ALONE DON'T DECIDE INDUSTRIAL COMPETITIVENESS

The predominant market-based view of economics sees competition among firms as the driving force for innovation focused on efforts to find ways to improve efficiency of production. The competition for customers drives firms to be responsive to consumers' developing demands, including for new products and services. The well-known problem with economic doctrine is that there are frequent violations of the basic assumptions needed for these economic principles to hold in practice, problems that go well beyond the acknowledgement of externalities and common or public goods. As one moves away from undifferentiated commodities, quality, rather than price, becomes a key trigger. Quality might therefore lend itself to complementarity of products, rather than direct competition. For example, one may be inclined to buy a certain type of wine for a large informal dinner, and another for a formal business setting. Moreover, barriers to entry and information asymmetries often mean concentration, rather than perfect competition, prevails among suppliers. Certainly the recent financial crisis also shows that herd-like behaviour can exist among both suppliers and customers, contributing to bubbles that are motivated by imitative, rather than rational utility-maximising behaviour. While the insights of basic economic theory still explain some of the dynamics of the overriding logic of suppliers to respond to customers, and thereby the motivations behind competitive improvement, it is insufficient to explain a number of aspects related to the overall dynamics of industries and their location.

On the micro level, business competitiveness literature provides some insights but equally daunting limitations. Indeed, the business literature (Kanter 1997) has created vast volumes on firm advantage, including the importance of encouraging change; flexibility, networking, and culture; information and marketing systems that create intelligence about customer needs and potential markets; virtuous (with breakthroughs making possible future breakthroughs) cycles of innovation and product development; and willingness to take risks. Core strategy revolves around differentiating products, understanding customers, taking advantage of geographic locations, and developing core competencies and a core culture (Saee 2007).

The literature on corporate strategy revolves around two paradigms of competitiveness that depend upon superior management of resources, and environmental opportunities and constraints, respectively. The resource paradigm focuses on the internal assets and liabilities of a company, including human and financial capital, which create a competitive advantage and specialisation for a company. The environmental paradigm includes regulatory, competitive, and production and technology factors that companies compete to take advantage of. Both views are, in reality, compatible – firms begin from different initial conditions, and respond with different degrees of effectiveness to changing market contexts (Cockburn, Henderson, and Sterm 2000). Competitiveness is also affected by the element of strategy, namely the organisation's ability to add value (Lynch 2006). However, the ability to define and measure competitiveness, in practice, is quite problematic (Cockburn, Henderson, and Sterm 2000). The problem with these views is that changes in the environment are effectively relegated to a background condition, when in fact companies and governments very much affect environments.

Resource-based theory suggests firm advantage can derive from a number of sources. Some are more intangible, such as leadership and culture. Yet, there is limited consensus about what makes leadership or management effective. Leaders create a sense of purpose and vision; help to create a core set of values such as efficiency, trust, co-operation, loyalty, entrepreneurship, and attentiveness; and create a sense of teamwork that works along with incentives (Barney and Clark 2007, 6–7). Some are based on proprietary knowledge, experience, research and development, finance, better knowledge and servicing of customers, communication and other ways to reduce transaction costs, and the like. In short, one of the main things the literature points out is that firms need advantages that are not readily replicable.

Michael Porter's work lays out the foundations for much of the literature on environmental factors for firm competitiveness. Porter's work derives from the industrial–organisation literature's structure, conduct, and performance models that look at the level of concentration (monopoly, oligopoly), etc., that set out the constraints within which firms make decisions on how to maximise profits (Barney and Clark 2007, 12–13). For example, an oligopoly is more likely to lead to emphasis on product differentiation rather than cost differentiation. Porter suggests five forces that inform business strategy environments. The first is the level of rivalry among existing firms. The second is the threat of potential new entrants. Both of these depend on barriers to entry, such as economies of scale, product differentiation, capital requirements, switching costs, access to distribution networks, and other proprietary advantages, including those related to favourable public policies. Entry barriers naturally could also include the exertion of market power. The third and fourth are the bargaining power of suppliers and buyers. The fifth is the threat of product substitutes. For Porter, a successful firm embodies dynamic capabilities to deal with industry and product innovations, as well as changes in supplier and buyer segments, government regulation, and new entrants. Porter and others point to the need to understand a company in the context of the particularities of the sector in which it operates, which led to his use of the term "cluster" to describe the linked activities of a sector, as we discuss below (Porter 1998a).

Firm strategy does seem to follow the Porterian formula of cost or product differentiation. Cost differentiation would reflect a strategy where products tend to be similar, while product differentiation might entail the ability to create differences in the quality, upgrading attributes, or a "niche" strategy whereby a particular customer segment's preferences are catered to (Walker 2004, 20). Obviously, a combination of strategies is likely. More important still is that a cost-differentiation strategy is more likely to reflect wider levels of competition between commodity types than would be seen in a niche strategy.

Like the measures of sources of firm competitiveness, measures of firm innovation tend to come up short in explaining the reality of how industrial success can be achieved. Much of the research on innovation discusses patent creation, and captures neither the timing of innovation, nor the complexity or breadth of the different aspects of innovation. As Unger (2005, 31–2) points out, surveys of companies usually reveal exaggerated claims of inventiveness, such as company statements that their activities and products are first-mover innovations. Moreover, much of the innovation consists of new combinations and adaptations that are considerably harder to track and ascribe than general purpose innovations. The problem is further complicated when we consider services as well as products. There is no easy way to measure knowledge intensity in the way that we measure capital or labour intensity.

What does the firm literature say about changes in markets? In terms of the dynamic nature of all industries, companies must be continually ready to re-invent themselves, simultaneously changing the industry and institutional environments while being shaped by them (Hamel and Prahalad 1994, 21). Historical studies of the introduction of innovation at the firm level have refuted the idea that demand forces create innovation. Demand comes into play in terms of modifications, but only after a general technology has been introduced (Unger 2005, 25). Path dependency can create very strong first mover advantages where industry evolution is predictable. Therefore, continual innovation is required and Schumpeterian (Barney and Clark 2007, 53) market or technological shocks always come. Innovation may occur at the firm or industry level. An example of the latter is the introduction of Voice Over Internet Protocol (voip) and cell phones, which has undercut telephone companies. The competitive dynamics of an industry are often described as "slow" and "fast" cycle, depending on the rate of innovation and disruptive change in the industry. In slow cycle industries, proprietary advantage, such as that held by Disney theme parks, is more easily protected. In fast cycles, new launches are met with quick counterattacks, reducing time for exploitation of proprietary advantages, as seen in the marketing of iPods and mp3 players (Hitt et al. 2006, 194–6).

Leoncini and Montresor (2008) suggest that there are four ways to understand learning on a firm level. First is learning from strategic management of environmental opportunities and constraints. Second is technologically based or induced learning. Third is organisational learning from internal interactions. Last is the evolutionary perspective that suggests an interaction between the firm and other firms as well as the environment, including institutions.

Despite the strong points of the economics and business literature, we can see from our brief review that both offer rather limited answers on how industries, rather than individual firms, learn to compete. While recognising the importance of proprietary resources within firms, the business literature also acknowledges the importance of changes in the operating environment, a factor that is largely exogenous to economic theory. In fact, the operating environment itself helps to create, determine, maintain, and reduce firm resources within certain industries.

In the rest of this chapter, we review the four explanatory perspectives drawn from the industrial policy and innovation literature that underpin our theoretical approach towards cluster competitiveness. We assert that no one strand of the literature is sufficient, however, combined they begin to provide insights into why industrial clusters succeed in certain locations. We then explain why clusters are an optimal vehicle for testing out how the four strands of theory combined together can explain competitiveness.

EXAMINING FOUR POTENTIAL SOURCES OF CLUSTER COMPETITIVENESS

The first perspective of our approach is based on Schumpeter's (1939) evolutionary framework for innovation. This literature begins to explain how markets change by pointing to the disruptive nature of technological breakthroughs and economic growth. It includes historical studies showing the revolutionary changes in industrial and economic organisation that follow the introduction of a new general purpose technology, from the internal combustion engine to the Internet (Lipsey, Carlaw, and Bekar. 2005; Hirooka 2006). We extend the idea of windows of opportunity (Hira, Wixted, and Arechavala 2012) to include those created by any major market disruption, not just innovative ones. We suggest that such disruptive life cycles also help to explain success and failure at the industry level, and that firm adaptability is a key factor of long-run success. In the case of automobiles, Detroit manufacturers have gone through several cycles, including most recently attempting to develop a new generation of hybrid and electric vehicles, such as the Chevy Volt, in response to rising petrol prices.

The second perspective is based on the literature that studies state policies in late industrialising nations and within industrial policy. According to this literature, comparative advantage can be dynamic, and the state can develop and guide new industries to success (Wade 1990; Amsden 1989). The developmentalist state literature (Johnson 1982) worked hand in hand with a resurgent literature on industrial policy and strategic trade that emerged in the 1990s to suggest that states could and should engage in strategic interventions to build, improve, and save industries (Cohen and Zysman 1987). The example of cellphones (Hira 2012) shows that state support was crucial for the remarkable success of Finnish company Nokia and South Korean companies LG and Samsung to succeed in the market.

The third perspective is derived from Granovetter (1985) and Putnam's (1993) seminal work on the correlation between high levels of social capital and economic wealth. This literature notes that the depth and number of interactions between social actors help to build levels of trust that are, in turn, behind successful public and private institutions (Lascaux 2005). Such institutions are key to the creation of public goods and shared capital needed for the success of advanced industries. For automobiles, we see that the automotive industry historically developed close ties to the Detroit area, including a plethora of auto parts suppliers, universities, research centres, and public sector support institutions. Part of the unraveling of the automotive industry during the last two decades was related to the lack of coordination between automotive sector management and unions – a breakdown of social coordination in which both parties ended up losing.

The fourth perspective requires a consideration of the globalisation of supply chains. In every industry, there is a growing sense of loss of control of industrial location. Revolutions in reducing transportation and communication costs, in line with the liberalisation of economies around the globe, have led to increasing movement of segments of production lines to various parts of the world. Multinational corporations have merged and sprung up with the perception that they are not beholden to any particular state or location. This brings into question the efficacy of any state policy intended to capture or maintain local employment. In the case of Detroit, operations in the auto industry have been scaled down and outsourced, leaving the city a shell of its former self. Promising markets and cheaper labour have moved many of the supply chains to China.

SCHUMPETER-BASED THEORIES
OF EVOLUTIONARY ECONOMICS

Joseph Schumpeter's seminal work (1939) gives us some of the key dynamic factors that help to explain the rise and fall of industries. Schumpeter clarified the difference between innovation, a new way of doing things that leads to a new production function (58–62), and invention, a new product or service. Innovation leads to disruptions of the existing economic order, and opens the way for "new men" (entrepreneurs) to create new organisations that will produce better goods and cheaper prices, increasing the overall wealth of a society (69–70). The beneficial aspect of these cycles is what Schumpeter referred to as "creative destruction." Schumpeter offers the term "lumpiness" (67) to explain the cyclical nature of such changes – a new innovation will lead to rapid industrial change through the loss of sunk costs by existing businesses in rapid, rather than gradual, fashion. Lumpiness is also related to the fact that innovations tend to come in "bunches," with concentration in certain sectors at first (75). This lumpiness leads to temporary excess profits that motivate entrepreneurs to undertake risky investments (80–1). Thus, Schumpeter captures two key elements of long-term technological innovation. The first is the long-term movement towards continual improvement through continual innovation, a cumulative self-propelling process. The second is the cyclical and disruptive nature of such evolution, where, as environmental conditions change, it is unclear exactly which innovation/mutation will best adapt. The fluidity and uncertainty of the process is what opens the way for new ideas to enter and create new realities.

Nelson and Winter (1982, 308–51) expand upon and update Schumpeter's ideas somewhat, drawing on Schumpeter's concerns about "mode 2" innovations occurring as research and development become concentrated in large enterprises. For most technologically advanced industries, such as pharmaceuticals, as we elaborate below, there are huge entry and exit barriers, including massive financing for ongoing research and development. Therefore, lumpiness may have a tendency to prevail over entrepreneurship, underlining again the possibility that the state may facilitate firms' abilities to overcome these barriers to entry.

A new study by Hira (2012) extends the implications of Schumpeterian theory further by melding it with Vernon's product cycle theory (1966), using a comparative cross-national study of the wireless industry as an example. The key points of this study are, first, that Schumpeter's theory does not say anything directly about the role of the state; the state may accelerate, impede, or remain neutral to the evolution of innovation. Second, there is a strong path dependency that over time leads to lumpiness in the form of increasing barriers to entry. The cumulative, if disruptive, nature of innovation means that late-developing countries will have a hard time, for example, entering into the automotive industry when innovation in the North has been occurring for the past century. This suggests, thirdly, that new products or sectors are the most open to new entrants.

Despite these observations, the implications of evolutionary theory leave us quite mixed in terms of what can be done to enter industries in mid cycle, keeping in mind that the innovation cycle for advanced products such as automobiles or computers could last for decades. Many evolutionary economists argue that the role of the state must be inherently limited to "generic" interventions, so that the mutation and natural selection process will not be interfered with (Dopfer and Potts 2007, xv).

Key Strengths and Weaknesses of Evolutionary Perspectives

The evolutionary economics perspective points to the importance of timing and lumpiness in terms of barriers to entry, economies of scale, and scope in industrial organisation. It also brings to our attention the importance of innovation at points when product cycles are beginning or being re-formed.

As McCarthy (1994) and other business historians point out, the grand multinationals were not created in a vacuum, but within the context of their location and time. For example, it is well known that the oil industry in North America evolved from Standard Oil, which was based on John Rockefeller's early monopolisation of the oil industry in the US (Yergin 1991). Similarly, the production line innovations of Henry Ford were the precursors for the domination of the US multinationals in the automotive industry. In every case of major industrial development, from aerospace to steel, US government procurement and support have played a major role. It is inconceivable to think of the emergence of the dominant US aerospace giants such as Boeing and McDonnell Douglas without wartime procurement contractors when the industry was in its infancy. Companies formed later, such as Royal Dutch Shell in oil or Airbus in aerospace, followed the general model of the pioneers, adapted for their national reality. Thus, we see that there is a time- and location-specific aspect to the rise of successful industry giants. In effect, institutions, and regulations, industries, and firms co-evolve, thus complicating any attempt to isolate actors or causal factors. This suggests the importance of comparative case studies while controlling for industry and trying to look particularly at the specific industry's infancy in terms of global industrial evolution.

While giving us a general long-term shape of opportunity structures and path dependencies for industrial innovation, it does not allow us to make much more than macro-level observations. So, it leaves us unable to make any specific observations or policy prescriptions about which industries and/or firms to favour and which instruments to use. In fact, one interpretation of Schumpterian theory could veer towards a sense of fatalism, in that new firms and "new men" are needed, therefore the only policy prescription is to level the playing field for entrepreneurs. The approach is easy to validate in hindsight, but does not really allow us to understand who will be the winners and losers (including which nations) of industrial competition in the long run. The question of whether and how states should intervene in evolutionary innovation cycles is thus a key one.

The Role of State Policies in Creating Competitive Industries

In his famous *The Competitive Advantage of Nations* (1990), Michael Porter lays out the archetypical environmental conditions for country competitiveness in his basic diamond model of competitiveness. He suggests that key factors include demand conditions, related and supporting industries, and firm strategy, structure, and rivalry. Furthermore, he suggests that the existence of national factors such as a skilled workforce, a large local market with sophisticated customers, and related industries make up the necessary environment for competition. The last factor, firm strategy, structure, and rivalry, relates to how the industry is organised and governed within a country, and is the focus of this study.

Porter's pioneering work is the basis of the World Economic Forum (WEF)'s annual *World Competitiveness Yearbook* and *Global Competitive-*

ness Report. This data set measures a variety of factors that are supposed to determine national competitiveness, including: openness, how low taxes are, how low government spending is, quality of infrastructure, spread of information technologies, and number of patents. While the WEF typology includes some of the key elements of comparative advantage, reflecting differences between Northern and Southern business environments, the validity of the studies is questionable in that the factors are not tested and the rankings depend on surveys of international business executives, missing the perceptions of all the other stakeholders as well as concrete measures, though recent efforts such as those of the World Bank have sought to improve these studies. More importantly for our discussion, they discuss neither if nor how comparative advantage can be changed, nor how the combination of supposedly necessary factors can be built up. All good variables seem to be present in the North, while and multiple deficiencies converge in the South.

The most promising work on innovation stems from the national innovation systems (Nelson 1996) and the related triple helix (Etzkowitz 2003) literature. Both agree that there are complimentary roles for academics (basic research and accountability), government (support and guiding action towards collective goods), and the private sector (production and efficiency). The triple helix nicely captures the dynamic nature of the process, and covers the logical roles for different actors, from basic to applied research, to product development and production. However, this literature has focused thus far at the level of the national economy, when global production and related innovation decisions are made at the sector level (Malerba 2005). Thus, there is a general heuristic that needs further testing and elaboration.

Much of the work explaining East Asia's miraculous development during the postwar period rests upon the further reification of the market as the source of all things good and the state as the ultimate villain of development (World Bank 1993). According to these analysts, the only thing East Asia did was to have institutions that could "get markets right." It was sound macroeconomic management, low interest rates, and stable fiscal policy that allowed markets to work in the region. Mainstream economic faith lies in competitive markets and comparative advantage related to natural factor endowments, however such notions are clearly outdated in an age of knowledge-intensive products, as demonstrated in the industrial policy literature.

This literature dates back to the early work of Friedrich List (1856) who brought forth the idea that late industrialisers such as Germany needed to protect infant industries. Gerschenkron's (1962) historical studies of industrialisation suggest that the later one industrialises, the more intervention will be needed. Recent work helps to explain why the East Asian state is ubiquitous in almost every aspect of successful industries (Hira 2007). Chalmers Johnson's (1982) work on the developmentalist state suggests that state leadership of the private sector is most appropriate for economic and sectoral transformation. Alice Amsden's (1989) seminal work on South Korean development introduced a new term, "dynamic comparative advantage," to describe Korea's success in developing shipbuilding, electronics, steel, and automotive industries despite not initially having any advantage in those areas.

As Porter himself states, "traditional sources of comparative advantage can be very elusive sources of competitive advantage ... because comparative advantage frequently shifts." He cites the example of Japanese postwar growth as beginning by occupying less desirable segments of the world economy: "the Japanese translated these beachheads into world leadership by broadening their lines and reaping advantages in scale and proprietary learning" (Porter 1986, 38). Amsden also emphasises the importance of learning in her studies of late industrialisation. She notes that Korean success in new industries was based on advantages in improving process technologies and management, rather than product innovation. Robert Wade notes that developmentalist policies are market-governing, that is, aimed at shaping the direction and evolution of markets rather than controlling or directing them, thus destroying the now meaningless dichotomy between market and state.

In sum, the role of the state in creating an appropriate operating environment and guiding firms in new industries is strongly supported by the literature on East Asia. Our review thus far allows us to move us beyond the market-state dichotomy, yet we are still lost in the vast spectrum of positions in between.

Strengths and Weaknesses of the State Policy Perspective

One of the key issues is what determines the productivity of the state-firm relationship. Some authors point out that a healthy relationship can be "growth-oriented," while others are "rent-seeking." Yet what determines these outcomes? The answer is not clear by simply finding correlated variables that are also either growth-oriented or rent-seeking. For instance, Evans's work on embedded autonomy suggests that state autonomy to direct business towards productive collective ends depends on the state's ability to discipline as well as co-operate with business networks towards a common goal. He suggests that the success of East Asia relates in part to its cohesive, competent Weberian bureaucracy and the level of institutionalised relations with business. This seems logical, but nowhere does Evans tell us how such institutions can be created in environments of strong historical path dependency (Evans 1997).

Atul Kohli (2004) follows the same path, producing a different typology to explain disappointing outcomes in development. He suggests that there are three types of states: neo-patrimonial, corresponding to Evans's rent-seeking category; cohesive-capitalist, reflecting the purposive-oriented bureaucracies of Evans's growth-oriented category; and fragmented-multiclass, which represent another source of failure, namely lack of coherence or unity. Like Evans, Kohli does a very good job of pointing out that successful states have "deep centralized and purposive authority structures that penetrate deep into society" (10). Leaders in fragmented states, by contrast, are more worried about whether they will have stable support, and therefore be unable to pursue long-term agendas based on "broad class alliances" (11). Following Evans, he points to colonialism and other long-term path dependencies that help to determine the type of state, but does not explain if or how the type can be transformed. Kohli provides an important contribution in that he helps to explain why state intervention sometimes succeeds and sometimes fails. In a neo-patrimonial setting, state intervention will likely be disastrous, while in a cohesive-capitalist setting, it can lead to long-term growth and diversification. In fragmented states, progress is marked by stop-start volatility.

In sum, we do not really know when or why state policy becomes functional (East Asia) or dysfunctional (Latin America). More importantly, we do not know how state-industry relationships can be transformed. To better understand embedded autonomy and state-firm relationships, we need to turn to social networking theories.

Social Networks as the Backbone for
Industrial Success and Failure

One key problem of economic theory is that it ultimately rests on reductionist thinking that posits individuals as the only appropriate unit of analysis, and that rational utility maximisation is the only mode of decision-making (Grinberg and Rubinstein 2005), when in fact we know that individuals operate within a collective political, social, and economic context. Two foundational authors for social network theory as applied to economics are Mark Granovetter (1985) and Harrison White (1992). Granovetter made the term "embeddedness" the core concept of the theory. Embeddedness refers to the fact that we as individuals are all enmeshed in different networks of relationships that are the basis of social actions. White's seminal work, *Identity and Control* (1992), suggests that identity is constructed through both our own volition and the types of networks we engage in. Like units (e.g. the geeks) tend to mesh well with each other, leading to a sense of reinforcement. "Stories" are events retold from a certain point of view, such as the heroic venture, that bring larger groups together in a common sense of identity and purpose. White points out that there is a constant flux in networks, a congealing and forming, as well as closure and breaking apart, thus pointing to the ever creative and unpredictable ripple effects of action on a social scale. In sum, both Granovetter and White give us a sense of an ever-changing set of social networks that move well beyond atomistic views at the heart of traditional economic theory.

Social networking theory is foundational, therefore, to how individuals and organisations link together to form collective action. The basis of collective action theory reflects the fact that small, well-organised and dedicated groups, such as the National Rifle Association, show strength over disorganised groups with larger numbers and facts on their side (the anti-gun lobby).

Other concepts from social networking theory can help us to understand the dynamics of social groups over time. The idea of networks entails a finite number of connections that each individual or organisation can make. Some ties are strong (frequent, deep interactions), while others are weak. The nature of the ties and their history allow for informal mechanisms of trust to prevail, thus reducing transactions costs, including costs of enforcement. Ties therefore have a dual nature – both enabling and constraining. Thus, this approach suggests that strength lies in those who have access to deep ties and more networks, and the flexibility to move within and among those networks with lower constraints.

What makes for a successful network? Aldrich posits integration, differentiation, and ambiguity as three variables that help to explain outcomes. Integration speaks of a tight organisational culture, where there is a strong sense of solidarity and therefore high levels of effectiveness in the use and/or procurement of collective goods based on consistent expectations. These cultures have a rich set of integrating tools, such as narratives, rituals, and artefacts. Differentiation suggests a culture where clusters of activity are effective, but also suggests the possibility of inter-group conflict. Ambiguity suggests a lack of consistent ties, and/or ties which may fluctuate and/or are weak. In this case, the units of analysis are more likely to be individuals and small groups (Aldrich 1999, 151). Burt suggests the terms "bandwidth" and "echo" to posit that integrated networks can be effective by reinforcing information flow, leading to conformity and group-enhancing individual behaviour. Strong ties are characterised by repeated transactions, thus the shadow of the future (potential gains/losses) as well as the past reinforce the gains from reciprocity. The concept of "bandwidth" emphasises the importance of transparency in increasing trust as third parties' (peers) judgements create informal enforcement mechanisms that lead towards conformity (Burt 2001).

The literature also suggests the importance of both diversity and "bridges" among networks. Diversity creates tensions that lead to new outcomes. Networks that are closed may be stronger, but could result in groupthink, thus missing opportunities for creative improvement. Bridges are important in order to access new ideas and possibilities for interaction with other networks. Without such connections, there could be "structural holes," that result in the breakdown of collective action. On the other hand, such holes also provide opportunities for new entrepreneurs to step in and provide new types of services (Aldrich 1999, 81–2).

Strengths and Weaknesses of the Social Networks Perspective

Our lengthy discussion up to this point about industrial competitiveness and innovation has led us to ask the question of how state-firm and firm-firm relations are best governed for competitiveness in the context of emerging new markets. The literature on this topic is still emerging. As we have seen, there are a number of interesting ideas and frameworks, but few clear paradigms as of yet. There seem to be tangible and intangible factors that allow a (production) network to succeed; as Van Alstyne (1997) notes, there must be a common sense of identity and shared purpose around collective assets and means of joint control of them.

One strand of the literature on clusters attempts to create typologies of clusters, such as the common three patterns: atomized industrial districts connected by labour market pooling, supplier specialisation, and knowledge spillovers à la Marshall; the hub and spoke industrial complex model, whereby a large firm creates subcontractor systems that feed off of it; and the network or "Italianate" model whereby strong bonds of trust and associational activity among relatively equal firms lead to flexible specialisation (differentiation of suppliers by market niches) à la Piore and Sabel (Cortright 2006, 6, 8, 12). Recognising the importance of possible architectures is a useful starting point, but it does not really allow us to move towards any concrete propositions. We do not find a compelling reason for mapping out architectural types along these lines, as the policy implications of different types are unclear. Another basic problem with this literature is again that we can identify them post-hoc, but we cannot explain how they are created or change over time. In addition, we have the heterogeneity problem discussed earlier. For example, Japan has been highly successful in a number of sectors, yet, has not developed a strong petrochemicals sector. Moreover, Japanese automotive production companies, such as Toyota, are managed differently than European or American ones such as Mercedes, yet both are successful. In cases such as Saturn, where an American company has tried to reproduce a Japanese production system, the results have been limited.

There is furthermore a lack of consideration of dynamic factors. Similarly, in many of the currently in-vogue geographic studies of cluster location, a mapping exercise reveals locational and functional ties, but without a clear explanatory framework. We simply do not have good ways to understand or measure governance mechanisms in embedded networks (Meeus and Oerlemans 2005b, 172). Nor do we have good measures of inter-firm knowledge sharing. The point is that the mainstream economic approach of rational utility maximisation on an individual unit level is an extremely limited instrument for understanding the tacit and interactive nature of knowledge construction in unpredictably contingent ways. Therefore, we should think of technological development as marked by relations among punctuated equilibria in different product lines, such as the cassette recorder being deleted by the mp3 player, where the costs and benefits of sharing information evolve over time.

A weakness is pointed out by critics of the value chains literature – the lack of grappling with relative power variables. We are still in the dark as to a clear policy framework that is politically as well as technically feasible because the policy network approach lacks a clear sense of agency and lacks content (Rowley and Baum 2008, xix). In fact, White's 1992 work suggests that agency comes in part from the ability of individuals to negotiate with others using their connections to network chains. However, this underemphasises the evolutionary learning perspectives of feedback loops and the importance of resource allocation, as embedded in the state policy perspective.

Meeus and Oerlemans (2005a, 63–4) suggest an interesting typology for beginning to understand how power could shape supply chains. The first is "the imposition of organizational structure," where a dominant actor(s) imposes structure, such as a hostile takeover. The second is "the authorisation of organisational structure," where a subordinate agent seeks out the attention and approval of a more powerful actor, such as a small company seeking to sell modular products or services to a large one (e.g. Walmart's suppliers). The third possible system of power relations is "the inducement of organisational structure," where there is no clear concentration of power or authority in the system. This might be an example of stressful principal-agent problems, such as the US government's attempts to understand and regulate the asset structure of the financial industry. Finally, there is "the acquisition of organisational structure," that reflects the voluntary choice of structural models. An example would be the adoption of sustainability standards by the Forestry Stewardship Council.

Therefore, it is clear that the evolutionary economics (timing) and state policy (power) perspectives must be combined with the network approach to really explain industrial competitiveness. We believe that the cluster approach is a perfect vehicle for accomplishing this. However, first we must address to one more question: whether globalisation influences industrial location preferences.

How Globalisation Affects Competitiveness Policies

The question of industrial competitiveness must grapple with the shift towards a global production economy, accelerating over the last two decades, and also whether and how locational advantage can be created and maintained through state policies. We see through the business literature an identification of the potentially vital environmental variables for corporate success. There seems far less consensus on what internal variables, whether resource allocation or personnel, account for successful corporate strategy. How does globalisation affect the ability of Southern countries to develop new clusters?

Vernon's important work on the product cycle (1966) helps us to begin to address this question. Vernon suggests that as products become standardised, more of the production process will move to the developing world where labour costs are lower. Vernon thus presaged the movement towards globalisation in manufacturing and services that gained speed in the 1980s and continues today. Yet, his model also implies that if there is continual innovation in products, such as automobiles, only the countries with abundant research and development capability will be able to capture the early monopoly or oligopoly rents before the commodification stage when the supply side moves closer to perfect competition. Vernon helps to explain the uneven nature of globalisation, and why developing countries that succeed, such as those in East Asia, have invested heavily in upgrading innovation systems.

What is clear is that we are not living in a borderless, "flat" world (Friedman 2007). While fragmentation and spread of global production has taken place, it has not done so in random fashion; location does matter. All major multinationals in every industry still do have a distinct affiliation with the nation where they originated. As the empirical literature on foreign direct investment (FDI) points out (Navaretti and Venables 2004, 5), almost all FDI (92.9% between 1998 and 2000) emerges from the North, though there are signs of a limited shift through the emerging activities of Chinese companies. In an extensive empirical study, Rugman and Verbeke state that two thirds of the twenty most internationalised multinational enterprises (MNES) are actually based in a triad country (US, Europe, or Japan). "Most of the other 80 of the top 100 internationalized companies are even less global and are either domestic or home-based MNES" (Rugman and

Verbeke 2003, 52). Where internationalisation does occur, it tends to be concentrated in the home region of MNES (Rugman, Oh, and Lim 2012, 230). Linkages between North and South through MNES also follow regional patterns (Rugman and Doh 2008, 4), as do supply chains (Rugman 2005, 240). Most foreign direct investment is concentrated in skill- and technology-intensive industries. As Navaretti and Venables (11–12) state: "The broad sectors in which the presence of MNES is greatest are characterized by large investments in research and development, a large share of professional and technical workers, and the production of technically complex or differentiated goods." These include both goods and services.

Kogut and Zander (1993) point out that global competitiveness for firms depends on a combination of firm- and country-level advantages. Where an industry lends itself to both firm- and country-specific competitiveness, we are likely to see a highly horizontally and vertically integrated industry across borders, such as the automotive industry. Where only the firm advantage is highly specific, we are likely to see a more horizontally integrated industry across borders. Consumer products industries are an example. Where the country advantage alone is specific, we are likely to see a vertically integrated industry across borders. An example is the mining industry. Where neither the firm nor the country advantages are specific, we are most likely to see a nationally segmented industry. There are few examples of these nowadays, but low-level services oriented towards specific population needs, such as funeral services, are the common example (Walker 2004, 179–84). Thus, we could see a Porterian industry diamond occurring across economies, particularly small open ones. But how are such global industries organized? The literature that originally sought to examine global commodities helps to explain this.

Value and Commodity Chains Literature

Commodities have long been of interest to those who study development. Commodity production has been linked to neo-colonial systems of differential production, and cited as a basic source of increasing global inequality. The precise mechanism and extent to which commodity production is a "curse" is hotly contested, though a number of studies seem to verify the long-term trends (Lederman and Maloney 2007; Radetzki 2008, 73). However, the main arguments can be summed up in economic and political terms. In economic terms, the famous Prebisch-Singer hypothesis suggested that income elasticities meant a long-term downward trend for commodities vs manufacturing prices. In political terms, there is the problem of the "resource curse," and "Dutch disease," in which resource rents tend to lead to political concentration and reliance on multinational corporations (MNCs) for resource extraction and external markets, leading to "rentier" states that are captured by a "compradorial elite" (Karl 1997).

Both the value- and commodity-chain literature break up the production process into a series of steps. The firm or country that can capture more steps of that process will gain more revenues from the added value represented therein.

The value–chain literature is derived from business discussions of competitive advantage from a firm perspective. It breaks up the steps of the production process and applies firm advantage theory to each step, to the methods of integrating and coordinating those steps, and to quality and cost control. Steps might include purchasing of raw materials, inventory management, design and engineering, manufacturing, distribution, sales, and servicing and technical support (Grant 2008, 258). Naturally, the specific steps will depend on the industry and product or service involved.

By contrast, the commodity-chain literature focuses more on the global distribution of different parts of production chains, called global commodity chains (GCCs). Gereffi proposes we study GCCs along three key dimensions: the first is the input-output structure, representing the sequence of production and distribution steps; the second is the location where each of those steps takes place, and the governance structure, or power relationships that "determine how financial, material, and human resources are allocated and flow within a chain" (Gereffi 2008, 430–3).

This literature distinguishes between buyer- and producer-driven chains. Buyer-driven chains are ones in which retailers, marketers, and branded manufacturers have the greatest power, as in the consumer electronics, handbags, shoes, and clothing industries, where retailers and brand names are the keys to sales. Producer-driven chains, such as those in the aerospace and automotive industries, locate power more into the integrating producing agent, which needs strong vertical control over suppliers and forward linkages into distribution and retailing (Gereffi and Memedovic 2004, 70–1). Gereffi posits that government intervention is facilitative in buyer-driven chains, but more interventionist in producer-driven chains (Gereffi 2008, 430–3).

The approach to industrial upgrading is also straightforward, with several key elements. The first is that "sequences of export roles are contingent, not invariant, features of industrial upgrading." While it is possible for suppliers of components to move up to the distribution phase of final products, the reverse can also happen. The second is that "industrial upgrading involves organizational learning in global supply chains to improve the position of firms or regions in international trade and production networks." Though learning through interactions with backwards and forwards linkages is possible, there are significant barriers to entry for those wishing to capture the next run of the supply chain. Third, "industrial upgrading requires not only physical and human capital, but also social capital – that is, relevant and effective networks." Lastly, "the upgrading processes of firms in terms of shifts along or between commodity chains is an important, but not sufficient, condition for ensuring positive development outcomes." Upgrading is often uneven across regions and firms within a country (Bair and Gereffi, 2004, 64–5). Commodity chain theorists indicate that capturing more elements of a value chain is increasingly difficult under globalisation. Sturgeon says, "vertical integration is consigned to the dustbin of history." He suggests, instead, that value chain modularity as the more appropriate way to think of the organisation of production networks (Sturgeon 2005, 71–3).

The GCC literature tends to be heuristic, and does not generally generate a clear set of policy propositions or consistent empirical observations. The question of dynamism in the chain and its linkages, including how the chain is upgraded, how units change their position, and how power is distributed can only be understood in descriptive fashion (Morrison, Pietrobelli, and Rabellotti 2008). Sverisson (2004) points out further that the difference between buyer- and producer-driven chains is sometimes elusive. He also notes that the commodity-chain literature treats changes in markets as exogenous to their model, particularly price and innovation, that drive changes to and in the chains. Further, the links between and among chains and the fragmentation of chains related to specialised production functions, such as subcontracting for an MNC, are not well mapped out. Thus, important factors that would help to guide the South towards how to produce more locally are not fully captured in the theoretical framework.

The GCC literature has also adapted to critiques, particularly its neglect of governance. For instance, the school of thought now calls itself Global Value Chains (GVC) rather than Global Commodity Chains as it recognises that there are non-commodity aspects, such as services, that create value in production (Daviron and Ponte 2005, 28). The latest iteration of the GVC literature seeks to improve analysis of governance by bringing in the notions of transactional economics, such as principal-agency, organisational costs, information asymmetries, and asset specificity to understand supply chain governance. They also cite the importance of path dependency in terms of the way institutions shape governance (Sturgeon 2009). Recent authors focus on the possibilities and modalities for upgrading and learning. They suggest upgrading occurs in four areas: process upgrading, product upgrading, functional upgrading (or changing one's role within the chain), and chain upgrading (McCormick 2007, 31). Yet, there seems to be limited understanding about how such upgrading can be accomplished, perhaps reflecting the tacit nature of knowledge and social capital in sectoral networks.

The nature of an industry, and its degree of multinationality, will depend on the nature of the sector and its global market characteristics. Pietrobelli and Rabellotti (2008, 218–19) suggest several categories that match type of sector with type of goods or services. They suggest that natural resource-based clusters will focus on scientific process and product upgrading. Traditional manufacturing clusters are supply dominated, where innovation comes incrementally from machinery and materials producers. There is often concentration and hierarchy in the way the value chain is organised. In complex product systems, the parts and components of a complex product such as electronics are constantly pushing product innovation and quality improvement. In these types of chains, the large assemblers and first-tier suppliers tend to have more power. Customer-oriented services such as software are more demand-driven and depend on customisation and adaptation to client needs.

Recent work by Kimura (2007) moves the literature forward on the question of power in chains. As Kimura points out in his study of Japanese commercial aircraft value chains, the key question implied by the GVC literature is who captures what part of the global value chain? This depends on the relative power of each player in the value chain. Just as firms and countries' have and seek to build specific assets and advantages, so do suppliers in a vc. Thus, globalisation is a game where multinationals outsource modular parts of the production process to lower cost areas, but seek to retain control over knowledge of how to manage the production chain (11).

Kimura begins to shed light on how power is wielded in a value chain. The lead firm may set the key parameters of production (what, how, when and how much is produced); integrate the different components and manage the system; select and monitor all the members of the chain; manage conflict within the chain; position and reposition the chain in response to markets; and continue to build and deepen the structure and culture of the chain (40). While his case study is based upon the aircraft industry, he does also provide some possible categories for understanding the basic roles within the chain (43). In his example, the roles from the top to the bottom are: top system integrator; module system maker (e.g. companies that create aircraft engine systems, from different suppliers); sub-system supplier (e.g. those who produce key elements of the engine, such as the exhaust system); and piece part subcontractors. The obvious implication is that being higher up in the chain reflects more firm- and knowledge-specific assets as well as a greater share of the final rents. Those who design and integrate the system are more powerful than those who build the parts for the system.

This leads Kimura to suggest two possible strategies for late industrialising firms. The first is what he calls the "catch up" strategy, whereby the company seeks to become a lead firm in the value chain, meaning it must compete with system integrators already in the market. The second is "upgrading" whereby firms seeks to capture module components or segments of the production chain and slowly learn how to expand their contribution to other parts of the chain (52–5). While the first strategy is likely to be extremely difficult, the second strategy will also be fraught with potential for failure, as other firms in the chain will be doing the same thing, and the systems integrator will be very careful to isolate and reduce the possibilities for a usurper.

GLOBALISATION ALTERS, BUT DOES NOT LIMIT THE IMPORTANCE OF EVOLUTION, POWER, AND NETWORKS

While globalisation may call into question the applicability of early twentieth century industrial policy, by no means does it obliterate location, geographical advantage, or uneven gains resulting from such advantage. If anything, globalisation increases the stakes for the creation of a successful competitive-creating business governance system. Similarly, we have seen that the problems of emerging markets are not just limited to "governance." Rather, the problem resides equally with how to create innovation systems within clusters, in order to capture and maintain the higher and most lucrative segments of global production chains. This brings us back finally to how to create the appropriate state-firm relationships to achieve these goals.

Testing out the Four Explanatory Perspectives on Industrial Competitiveness Together: The Meso Case of Clusters

Given the limitations we have pointed out at the micro level, where firm-level analyses do not consider enough patterns in changes to the environment, including deliberate efforts at shaping by the state, and the macro level, where states are unable to keep up with the micro-level need for variation, adaptation, and failure in industrial development, the meso level seems to be the most appropriate one on which to focus an industry study of competitiveness. The meso level is able to capture the interaction of individual firms and collective responses, and individual or collective attempts to modify the environment (Dopfer and Potts 2007, 25). It is based on institutional proximity, which stems from "actors' adherence to rules of action and, in certain contexts, from their sharing of the system representation that serves to orient collective behavior" (Gilly and Perrat 2006, 160). Beyond this, co-operation at the meso level is based on a common understanding of organisational and structural aspects for collective behaviour to work. This implies that market and social factors are taken into account, ultimately and ideally leading up to a collective learning modus. These vertical compromises, which can be mainly traced back to proximity, are in flux: "the compromises that stabilize inter-actor coordination are not set at once and for all, and because we always end up with contradiction/conflict whenever actors can no longer solve a given productive problem collectively" (Gilly and Perrat 2006, 160). To solve these conflicts or compensate for weaknesses, actors develop interactions on both a local/vertical and global/horizontal scale, while the relations between the states and linked firms and the network ties amongst the firms remain the hub of the cluster analysis.

Porter's *Competitive Advantage of Nations* formalised the idea of clusters that helps us to begin to tackle this question. His theories push forward a number of claims well beyond Krugman's celebrated ideas that agglomeration is a reflection of economies of scale in production and the desire to reduce transactions costs, particularly to be close to large pools of demand or supply inputs (Krugman 1991, 98). Porter defines clusters as "geographic concentrations of interconnected companies, specialized suppliers, service providers, firms in related industries, and associated institutions (for example, universities, standards agencies, and trade associations) in particular fields that compete but also cooperate ... Clusters are a striking feature of virtually ... every economy" (Porter 1998b, 197–8).

The idea is that there are externalities that help to explain agglomeration in industry. Porter states:

In a healthy cluster, the initial critical mass of firms triggers a self-reinforcing process in which specialized suppliers emerge; information accumulates; local institutions develop specialized training, research, infrastructure and appropriate regulations; and cluster visibility and prestige grows. Perceiving a market opportunity and facing falling entry barriers, entrepreneurs create new companies. Spinoffs from existing companies develop, and new suppliers emerge. Recognition of the cluster's existence constitutes a milestone. As more institutions and firms recognize the cluster's importance, a growing number of specialized products and services become available and specialized expertise responsive to the cluster arises among local financial services providers, construction firms, and the like. Informal and formal organizations and modes of communication involving cluster participants develop. (1998b, 240–1)

Porter emphasises that "organizational relationship-building mechanisms are necessary because a cluster's advantages rely heavily on linkages and connections among individuals and groups" (1998b, 240–1). Porter specifically highlights innovation activity as the distinguishing factor for cluster location. He notes that a company's home base for each product line is a hub for strategy development, core-product and process R&D, and, we could add, the most important human capital, "to create and renew the company's product, processes, and services. Therefore, locational decisions must be based on both total systems costs and innovation potential" (Porter 1998c, 87). It is interesting that Porter specifically rails against industrial policy and government intervention. He states that "the aim of cluster policy is to reinforce the development of *all* [emphasis his] clusters ... Governments should not choose among clusters ... market forces – not government decisions – should determine outcomes" (1998c, 89). Porter (2000, 26–7) states that the best policy is to simply allow new industries and clusters to "emerge," and that all clusters deserve equal consideration.

The vast amount of literature that has sprung up around cluster theory provides several frameworks explaining why clusters exist. The first frameworks are agglomeration theories that explain that the nature of some industries forces close proximity, such as their need for common business services, skilled labour pools, and niche specialisations. The second frameworks are based on industries' goals of reducing transactions costs and increasing tacit knowledge. The third framework is called flexible specialisation (Piore and Sabel 1984) and relates to the need for some companies (such as those in the fashion industry) to adjust very quickly to changes in market demands. Proximity allows for rapid transformation according to new trends as well as reduced transaction costs for linked industries. The fourth framework is related to the benefits of learning through continual interaction and a shared labour pool. The last type of framework relates to evolutionary and institutional path dependency and the locations where industries have been set up (Perry 2005, 24–5).

Clusters have gained special importance in the last two decades with the information technology revolution. Clusters are now often depicted as vehicles for innovation in a wide range of industries, reflecting the gestalt of success in Silicon Valley, the quintessential regional cluster. Clusters are now viewed as "learning regions," in which localised social interactions are required for learning because of the non-linear and interactive nature of knowledge accumulation through research and development (Asheim 2007). Clusters appear frequently in industries where unskilled labour costs are not as important, where economies of scale are generally low, price is not the sole driving factor for sales, and where there is a high degree of uncertainty. These conditions seem to relate well to emerging technologies as well as rapidly changing industries such as fashion.

Histories of clusters point to the importance of chance as well as a lead firm and often several close university partners over long periods of time. For example, Silicon Valley's origins relate to these reasons as well as military procurement during the Korean War. Supplier firms and competitors then come in to take advantage of the propitious conditions established. Stanford University was a leading middleman, using government contracts to create spin-off companies in electronics, such as Hewlett-Packard (Fligstein 2008, 144). The interaction and shared labour pool allow for spillovers and learning between firms. More specialised products and services, such as venture capitalists and intellectual property rights lawyers, develop. As Sturgeon (2000, 47) states in his study of the origins of Silicon Valley, "the fact that the San Francisco Bay Area's electronics industry began close to the turn of the twentieth century should lay to rest the notion that industrialization and urbanization on the scale of Silicon Valley can be quickly induced in other areas. Silicon Valley is nearly one hundred years old. It grew out of a historically and geographically specific context that cannot be re-created." The lesson for planners and economic developers is to focus on long-term, not short-term developmental trajectories. Porter suggests that clusters often take a "decade or more" to develop. He also notes that the intersection of clusters can wield competitive advantage and new products as cross-fertilisation takes place (Porter 1998b, 241). In the Silicon Valley example, the most critical intercluster link is the inflow of skilled workers from all over the world. And at the same time, skilled workers that went back to their home countries from Silicon Valley became key players in the development of new technology clusters (Rosenberg 2002, 33).

This intersection and co-operation of clusters gained more importance in recent years. As Rosenberg (2002) points out, some clusters "have stronger links than others but all to one degree or another interact with other clusters to compensate for the cluster ingredients that they lack at home" (32). Also, when a cluster seeks those global links or expansions, it is usually into a culturally similar market. Here, interaction is based on increased sharing of knowledge and skilled labour between clusters as well as learning from other cluster practices. Several analyses and reports support the advantage of these links (Meyer-Stamer 1998; Porter 1998b; Pyke, Becattini, and Sengenberger 1990; Rabellotti 1995; Schmitz 2000; Simmie and Sennett 1999). They point out that "firms in industrial clusters that present a high degree of knowledge integration and compete globally innovate more, present stronger growth patterns, adapt to changing environmental conditions more rapidly and have a more sustainable economic performance than firms that tend to compete within strictly local geographic boundaries" (Morosini 2004, 316). Therefore, the European Commission encourages "intercluster" linkages by emphasising that "clusters in the EU cannot rely merely on the natural forces of agglomeration to attract talent and other assets in the same way, for instance, as US clusters can. Clusters in the EU can compensate for some of these disadvantages by creating stronger linkages with other clusters offering complementary strengths" (European Commission 2008, 7).

A current ongoing initiative called Europa Intercluster aims to support such linkages through a common platform. Interclustering is understood as different types of co-operation. First, co-operation as sharing of information: "the companies, public organizations, or research centers which make up the clusters get involved in optimizing their knowledge, practices and expertise in their key areas" (Europa Intercluster 2010). This mainly entails co-operation on an informal basis, meaning that it facilitates meetings in which tacit knowledge is exchanged. The second form of co-operation tackles the competitive element of clusters: "the players from the clusters involved decide to engage in co-operation to make use of the full range of competitive weapons for ad hoc projects" (Europa Intercluster 2010). Basically, these efforts supposedly create a critical mass to carry out research and to be innovative. Finally, co-operation is understood as integration. Clusters co-operate in order to pool resources and enter markets, which for each cluster individually would be inaccessible. These co-operation efforts are enhanced by interclustering labs and workshops on how to set up cluster networks.

As global and intercluster links turn into crucial success factors, they are now incorporated in cluster evaluation studies. For example, Germany's Federal Ministry of Economics and Technology (BMWi)'s study, "Initiative Networks of Competence," developed dimensions and indicators which can be used for the benchmarking of clusters. These include predictors such as collaboration with other clusters and internationalisation of cluster members, and indicators related to policy instruments such as output and results of the program (in terms of R&D business development and internationalisation of cluster members). This ties in with the capabilities firms should possess when they want to succeed on a global scale. They need to be "globally efficient, multinationally flexible and capable of capturing the benefits of worldwide learning all at the same time" (Dicken, Malmberg, and Forgren 1995, 30).

Plans to develop global ties or expand on an international level are linked to the maturation stage of the whole cluster or of some of the firms located in it (Todtling 1995, 83). If the gap between maturation stages of different firms grows, a development towards large-firm/ small-firm networks is possible. Then, the large-firm networks are usually connected globally or are planning internationalisation steps, while the small-firm networks remain local, due to economic limitations or their organisational structure (Dicken, Malmberg, and Forgren 1995). At this point, clusters could split up into a general cluster mainly run by a large-firm network, and a sub-cluster organised by smaller firms.

Overall, these processes describe active approaches to globalisation in which the cluster in general or firms and actors in particular reach out to have a wider knowledge base or to be more competitive. But there is also a passive side to the international linkages a cluster can have: "On the one hand, in some districts small firms are ... growing and internationalizing their markets and networks. On the other hand, these regions also get penetrated and dominated by external large firms" (Todtling 1995, 81). In general, the term "globalisation" or "global ties" obscures a rich variety of actual forms and actions. In addressing the question of local developments and transnational co-operation, the existence of such diversity must be kept in mind when analysing and evaluating a technology or a specific cluster – especially in relation to government initiatives and cluster policies (Dicken, Malmberg, and Forgren 1995). Porter's view of government's role in terms of cluster policy is that it should facilitate existing clusters, rather than attempt to create new ones; governments should focus on "removing obstacles, relaxing constraints, and eliminating inefficiencies that impede cluster productivity and innovation." The main areas for government activity are education and training, infrastructure, and providing regulations that do not impede growth (Porter 1998b, 247).

However, this conclusion goes directly against the lessons of the national competitiveness literature we reviewed above, and is clearly contradictory to the public goods aspect acknowledged by Porter himself. As a recent World Bank publication (Kopicki 2002, 161–2) notes,

> supply chains also create positive externalities for competitors and participants in parallel supply chains. Moreover, the costs of developing supply chains typically exceed the benefits realized by any individual participant or any individual chain partnership ... [yet] few governments focus on supply chain development as a policy or investment priority. Most aspects of public policy that affect supply chain operation have accumulated incrementally through accretion. The effects of old policies or regulations are manifested most dramatically in the failure of supply chains to form or take hold in a specific economy. Often a zero-based review is undertaken only on the occasion of a wholesale review of transport, trade, and trade process policy in the context of implementing a regional trade or common market treaty.

European policy documents show that governments in member states try to find a fruitful balance between the reliance on market mechanisms and the role of policy to channel and catalyze lead market initiatives. Regarding specific cluster programs, the key ideas are evidence-based strategies (European Cluster Policy Group 2010, 2), fact-based policy (Graversen and Rosted 2010, 65), and cluster management (European Cluster Policy Group 2010, 5). The goal is to provide "improved mapping and knowledge of the 'real cluster landscape' in Europe [which] would support policymakers' efforts to formulate more evidence-based strategies and evaluate the success of their policy initiatives" (European Cluster Policy Group 2010, 2). This means that data on performance and framework conditions is needed in order to act efficiently on this information. The European Cluster Policy Group (ECPG) further recommends greater levels of disaggregation at a level 3 NUTS.[1] This cluster-related and evidence-based policy is in line with a new type of impact assessment was outlined in European Commission documents[2] in 2002. The so-called "extended impact assessments" (EXIAS) have the purpose to "carry out a more in-depth analysis of the potential impacts of the policy proposed on the economy, society, and the environment; and consult with interested parties and relevant experts according to the minimum standards for consultation" (Lee and Kirkpatrick 2006, 25).

Such new attempts in European policy-making led to discussions in cluster research. Today, researchers are not only trying to derive performance data, such as value-added, labour, and total factor productivity, but also raising questions regarding measurement issues. Basically, empirical studies go back to the basics of clusters, asking how a cluster is identified and how its success and conditions can be measured.

In sum, there are two general versions of cluster policy that are closely related to innovation policy. First, there is the laissez-faire version that emphasises non-interventionism and signals that the focus should be on framework conditions rather than specific sectors or technologies. Second, there is the systemic approach based on the concept of innovation systems. This perspective implies that most major policy fields need to be considered in the light of how they contribute to innovation. "The respective theoretical foundations of the two different versions of innovation policy are (1) an application of standard neoclassical economics on innovation, and (2) a long-term outcome of research on innovation and economic evolution" (Lundvall and Borrás 2005, 612). The relationship between government and the co-operation of firms is crucial, as it can heavily affect cluster development. When clustering projects are initiated and driven by the public sector, there is the danger of the cluster being a pure "government initiative" (Ffowcs-Williams 2000). This makes the private sector a bystander, which leads to less commitment, co-operation, and trust – things that cluster projects aim to create. Also, timing of such initiatives is crucial. To achieve sustainable results, government has to move at an industry pace regarding funding and networking. This usually includes "smart money," meaning that the financing is set up as a private-public partnership in which government invests first to jumpstart cluster activity and then industry follows – moving from public money to more and more private investments (Pamminger 2010). Down the road government actors must be willing to hand over responsibilities to private stakeholders as major funding shifts from the public to the private sector.

The cluster literature also builds upon network and social capital perspectives, emphasising again the public goods nature of such activities. These perspectives look at the depth and number of ties among social actors, with the presumption that the greater the ties, the greater the possibility for co-operation on collective goods. Network approaches map out the ties, their nodes, and their margins, as well as "structural holes," points in the network that are not connected to others. Actors at key nodes can be presumed to have greater (relational) power, however network theory says little about how relational positions change over time. Unfortunately, many of these studies tend to be one-shot snapshots that are applied in idiosyncratic situations (Rowley and Baum 2008, xviii–xix).

LIMITATIONS OF PRESENT KNOWLEDGE ABOUT CLUSTERS

To summarise our discussion on clusters – there still is no consensus about what factors influence business location (Jovanovic 2006, 3). The term clusters itself is conceptually vague. In the classic Marshallian and Porterian sense, it refers to geographically contiguous, linked businesses, but, under globalisation, we now have virtual clusters as part of global production networks that are functionally integrated if locationally distant. In another sense, clusters reflect post-Fordist production patterns where primarily knowledge-based products and services such as IT require deep but flexible specialisation in capital and labour markets, and do not require economies of scale in production. Such products tend to compete more on the basis of innovation and product innovation rather than strictly on price (Malmberg and Power 2006, 54–5, 59).

The fact is that we really don't have any clear answers about clusters, why they emerge and decline, or what generally gives them the edge. Nor is there any clear guide to policies (Borrás and Tsagdis 2008, 1). As Orsenigo states:

> Thus, formal applications of network analysis to the study of innovative clusters as well as an exploding number of case studies have highlighted the extreme diversity in their structure, logic, and dynamics ... clusters are characterized by different highly structured patterns of knowledge diffusion and generation, produced by the interaction of overlapping economic relations ... Hence, clusters might emerge as the outcome – or as a specific subnetwork – of sets of relations which are not necessarily based on spatial proximity, but on other forms or contiguity, like organizational proximity, epistemic communities, or communities of practice.

Conversely, clusters might well result as the effect of the coales-
cence of different networks. (2006, 199)

There are even deeper problems when it comes to understanding
learning in clusters. As Borrás and Tsagdis (2008, 24–26), point out,
the key explanatory approaches – of tacit knowledge and proximate
distance ties through networks to explain cluster learning – reveal
three major blind spots. The first is that such studies tend to treat policy as an exogenous variable, rather than one directly causal of learning. The second is a focus on learning within and among firms, but
not social learning. The third is a methodological focus on case studies, with few using comparative methods.

The idea of a cluster as an industrial ecosystem or a complex adaptive system evokes a sense of spontaneous order, one that is consis-
tently dynamic, non-linear, and chaotic, reflecting movements in
numerous markets, actors, consumers, and operating in an evolving
regulatory environment (Ruth and Davidsdottir 2009, 3; Albino, Carbonara, and Giannoccaro 2005). On the one hand, this suggests that
direct policy guidance can not likely anticipate the actual effects of
any particular state activities upon the cluster, and that, particularly in
a globalised world, such activities are likely to be ineffective.

On the other hand, the idealised view of clusters may mask the
reality of an infinite variety of possible network structures, including hub and spoke and nodes and subsystems, that speak to power
asymmetries among the different actors (Taylor and Leonard 2002,
4). Thus, in many (if not most) network systems, firms will actively
seek to shape the environment rather than be passive recipients
(Boschma, Lambooy, and Schutjens 2002, 32), resulting in heterogeneous performance even among similarly sized units within the
same cluster (Giuliani 2005, 175). This idealised cluster perspective
might also hinder public initiatives to grasp the full business side of
the network. At the firm level, business-to-business (B2B) co-operation and competition are a key factor for the creation and successful
development of a cluster. Acknowledging those inter-firm dynamics
involves knowing the market they co-operate or compete in, making
quick decisions and providing support that maintains the momentum of the cluster (Smith and Brown 2009). But taking the firms
into account while being aware of the bigger picture in terms of the
cluster itself and the regional or even national economy is a difficult

task, especially when the impact of the available policy tools is not yet fully evaluated, or investment money is not available. Indeed, a cluster still must grapple with the ubiquitous problem of resource scarcity, ranging from financing choices among highly risky unknown activities to developing basic spillover R&D knowledge to vehicles for export promotion. The geographically based idea of a cluster bespeaks a shared infrastructure, knowledge base, skilled labour pool, and access to finance, among other possible reasons for locational agglomeration, even where costs are high. Beyond this, and perhaps equally important, lie the ideas that new clusters can be formed and older ones transformed, speaking to "revolutionary" rather than "evolutionary" policies (Boschma and Frenken 2007, 15). These aspects encourage a close relationship between government actors and industry to understand the processes and to learn from other clusters. Histories of clusters seem to lead to varying conclusions. Those of Silicon Valley reinforce heavy government involvement at the outset of the cluster, with interventions ranging from military spending, to infrastructure, to local innovation systems links through university ties, namely Stanford (Markusen 1999; Sturgeon 2000). On the other hand, the prototypical Italianiate cluster seems more sui generis. Fligstein (2008, 147) suggests that the network approach is overblown in regard to how clusters really operate:

But I think that the "network approach" ignores some of the most compelling industrial organization facts about Silicon Valley. There are already high levels of concentration in the main products produced in the information technology revolution. Microsoft (software), Sun (workstations that power the Internet), Cisco Systems (the hardware and switches for the Internet), Intel (computer chips), ATT (cable and long distance), and AOL-Time Warner (Internet service provider and cable) control over 60 percent of their relevant markets. While some of these firms are clear technological innovators, they are also using familiar tactics to control competition ... As each of these new markets has emerged, a single firm has come to dominate.

It is therefore no surprise that cluster policies range from factor promotion (such as subsidised R&D), to specific provision of financing for promotion of a sector to setting up industrial or science parks, to aid in the formation of a cluster. Cluster policies tend to focus on shared resources, but this may ignore the importance and particular needs of a lead firm. Clusters also support existing networks, yet this tends to "pick winners," precluding the development of external relations and new and evolving networks (Blien and Maier 2008, 8). Cluster policies can always be twisted towards pork barrel ends. Wang (2007, 159) notes that Chinese regional policies and state ownership of some firms led to inefficiencies in bulk steel for construction, including overly costly supply chains that ignored cheaper small and medium enterprises. He also notes that many industrial parks are labour-intensive with few linkages to local suppliers, a common problem in the developing world where industries are often more oriented towards labour-intensive export processing. Based on these aspects of co-evolution and contingency, as well as a number of case studies, Breschi and Malerba conclude:

> *Thus, the replicability of successful clusters by public policy is often doomed to failure* ... the identification of single factors ... may not imply necessarily the understanding of a "complete recipe" for the triggering off of a phase of clusters' emergence and growth. And, moreover, this complete recipe is not what public policy should aim at in the first place. In fact, all the policy indications stemming from this book clearly point to the role of accommodating policies and the creation of support infrastructure ... rather than to a well-structured, articulated and complete set of policy interventions aiming to directly affect the dynamics of a cluster. Finally, public policy should be *sensitive to the life cycle of a cluster* ... Public policy has to be supportive (but not dirigiste) in the early stage, outward looking in the mature stage and creatively destructive in the declining stage. (2005, 24–5; their emphasis)

Despite a growing plethora of pro-cluster policies, in short, there is little we know concretely about what does and does not work. Empirical studies of clusters seem to point to a convergence of locational resources, including access to local, demanding, and large markets, high levels of nearby specialised human capital, and lower infrastructure and rental costs (Yusuf 2008, 5–15). Yet, analyses of empirical studies raise a number of doubts that go beyond ambiguous conceptualisation. Evidence for inter-firm interactions may be one source of competitiveness, but it obviously is not the only source, since clusters do decline (for which there does not seem to be any clear theoretical explanation). One suggestion is that clusters that are not open, particularly to global connections and partners, become atrophied by groupthink. A related suggestion is that export orientation is crucial for cluster success both because it creates a sense of dynamism and a means of accumulation that will lead to agglomeration effects. Moreover, there are in fact more isolated competitive companies than there are clusters (Malmberg and Power 2006; and Simmie 2006). Clusters sometimes fade as well. Analysts suggest that a cluster can become congested, have increasing input costs, including labour and real estate, lose competitive advantage, and suffer from groupthink (Brown and McNaughton 2002, 18–25; Leslie 2000). These problems are further magnified by globalisation, which seems to call into question the very notion of locational advantage at the heart of the cluster concept, and thereby whether the state can really play the role of creating an appropriate operating environment for its companies.

We began this essay with an investigation of firm competitive advantage. What we see is that firm competitive advantage depends greatly on environmental and resource factors, which in turn both reflect the quality of public policy. The question remains: what type of policy? Does an activist state policy stifle or nurture emerging market firms? If it is necessary, what type of policies make sense for capturing and maintaining global production, and at what stage of cluster maturation? In order to begin to address some of these questions, we will study wine clusters around the world.

CONCLUSION

The assessment of the theoretical foundations and current knowledge has shown that at least three major puzzles remain in understanding cluster evolution and cluster policy:

1 What explains the competitiveness (or lack thereof) of clusters in globalised markets?
2 What are the sources for levels of adaptability to market changes, and particularly the ability of governments to devise policies to take advantage of windows of opportunity for cluster development?
3 What are the appropriate tools and metrics – for both firms and government, to act and interact within networks – which reduce

transactions costs through routine, and co-operation, consensus, and norms to produce collective goods, while also preserving firm initiative and ability to compete locally and globally?

The case studies that follow, of wine clusters in British Columbia (Canada), Chile, Australia, Extremadura (Spain), and Tuscany (Italy), represent cases at different levels of experience (nascent to long-established), and different levels of density and complexity (from tiny, locally oriented firms, to global, export-oriented ones). They also represent cases from new producers attempting to enter into the industry, to those Old World producers who have established market presence over the past two decades, to old stalwarts. In each of the cases, we place particular attention on the historical evolution of the cluster, and then examine each of the four key perspectives of our study (adaptability to market evolution, state policies, networks, and globalisation), which together form our theoretical framework. We take an inductive case study approach, as our emphasis is on understanding the role of institutional frameworks in creating competitive clusters. This approach allows for a full appreciation of the nuances of each case, without losing the possibility to make reasonable implications for theory from careful comparison of them.

NOTES

1 The Nomenclature of Statistical Territorial Units (NUTS) is a hierarchical system for dividing up the economic territory of the EU for the purpose of collecting statistical data (Eurostat 2010).
2 The new European Commission impact assessment system is outlined in the "Communication on Impact Assessment" (COM 2002, 276; EC 2002) and is elaborated in supporting guidelines. Two closely related communications, issued at a similar time, are the "Action Plan for Simplifying and Improving the Regulatory Environment" (EC 2002b), which identifies the new impact assessment system as one action within the "Better Regulation Action Plan," and the "Principles and Minimum Standards for Consultation" (EC 2002), which, in the first instance, are to be applied to those initiatives subject to extended impact assessment (Lee and Kirkpatrick 2006, 24).

REFERENCES

Albino, Vito, Nunzia Carbonara, and Ilaria Giannoccaro. 2005. "Industrial Districts as Complex Adaptive Systems: Agent-Based Models of Emergent Phenomena." In *Industrial Clusters and Inter-firm Networks*, edited by Charlie Karlsson, Börje Johansson, and Roger R. Stough, 58–82. Northampton, MA: Edward Elgar.

Aldrich, Howard E. 1999. *Organizations Evolving*. Thousand Oaks: Sage.

Amsden, Alice H. 1989. *Asia's Next Giant: South Korea and Late Industrialization*. New York: Oxford University Press.

Anderson, Kym, ed. 2004. *The World's Wine Markets: Globalization at Work*. Northampton, MA: Edward Elgar.

Anderson, Robert E. 2004. *Just Get Out of the Way: How Government Can Help Business in Poor Countries*. Washington: CATO Institute.

Asheim, Bjorn T. 2007. "Industrial Districts as 'Learning Regions': A Condition for Prosperity." In *The Learning Region: Foundations, State of the Art, and Future*, edited by Roel Ruttan and Frans Boekma, 71–100. Northampton, MA: Edward Elgar.

Bair, Jennifer, and Gary Gereffi. 2004. "Upgrading, Uneven Development, and Jobs in the North American Apparel Industry." In *Labor and the Globalization of Production: Causes and Consequences of Industrial Upgrading*, edited by William Milberg, 58–87. New York: Palgrave MacMillan.

Barney, Jay B. and Delwyn N. Clark. 2007. *Resource-Based Theory: Creating and Sustaining Competitive Advantage*. New York: Oxford.

Blien, Uwe and Gunther Maier. 2008. In *The Economics of Regional Clusters: Networks, Technology and Policy*, edited by Uwe Blien and Gunther Mier, 1–12. Northampton, MA: Edward Elgar.

Borrás, Susana and Dimitrios Tsagdis. 2008. *Cluster Policies in Europe: Firms, Institutions, and Governance*. Northampton, MA: Edward Elgar.

Boschma, Ron A. and Koen Frenken. 2007. "Introduction: Applications of Evolutionary Economic Geography." In *Applied Evolutionary Economics and Economic Geography*, edited by Koen Frenken, 1–26. Northampton, MA: Edward Elgar.

Boschma, Ron A., Jan Lambooy, and Veronique Schutjens. 2002. "Embeddedness and Innovation." In *Embedded Enterprise and Social Capital: International Perspectives*, edited by Michael Taylor and Simon Leonard, 19–36. Burlington: Ashgate.

Breschi, Stefano and Franco Malerba. 2005. "Clusters, Networks, and Innovation: Research Results and New Directions." In *Clusters, Networks and*

Innovation, edited by Stefano Breschi and Franco Malerba, 1–28. New York: Oxford University Press.

Brown, Peter, and Rob B. McNaughton. 2002. "Global Competitiveness and Local Networks: A Review of the Literature." In *Global Competition and Local Networks,* edited by Rob B. McNaughton and Milford B. Green, 3–37. Burlington, VT: Ashgate.

Burt, Ronald S. 2001. "Bandwidth and Echo: Trust, Information, and Gossip in Social Networks." In *Networks and Markets,* edited by James E. Rauch and Alessandra Casella, 30–74. New York: Russell Sage Foundation.

Cockburn, Iain M., Rebecca M. Henderson, and Scott Sterm. 2000. "Untangling the Origins of Competitive Advantage." *Strategic Management Journal* 21:1123–45.

Cohen, Steven S. and John Zysman. 1987. *Manufacturing Matters: The Myth of the Post-Industrial Economy.* New York: Basic Books.

Cortright, Joseph. 2006. *Making Sense of Clusters: Regional Competitiveness and Economic Development.* Metropolitan Policy Program. Washington: Brookings Institution.

Daviron, Benoit, and Stefano Ponte. 2005. *The Coffee Paradox: Global Markets, Commodity Trade and the Elusive Promise of Development.* New York: Zed.

Dicken, Peter, Anders Malmberg and Mats Forgren. 1995. "The Local Embeddedness of Transnational Corporations." In *Globalization, Institutions, and Regional Development in Europe,* edited by Ash Amin and Nigel Thrift. New York: Oxford University Press.

Dopfer, Kurt and Jason Potts. 2007. *The General Theory of Economic Evolution.* New York: Routledge.

Etzkowitz, Henry. 2003. "Innovation in Innovation: The Triple Helix of University-Industry-Government Relations." *Social Science Information,* 42 (3): 293–337.

Europa Intercluster. 2010. Interclustering, Definition. Accessed April 2011, http://www.intercluster.eu/index.php?option=com_content&view=article&id=13&Itemid=2&lang=en.

European Cluster Policy Group. 2010. "Consolidated Set of Policy Recommendations on Four Themes." *European Commission.* Accessed February 28, 2011, http://www.proinno-europe.eu/ecpg/newsroom/ecpg-final-recommendations.

European Commission (EC). 2002a. Communication from the Commission on Impact Assessment. Brussels, COM (2002) 276 final. Accessed March 5, 2013, http://eur-lex.europa.eu/LexUriServ/LexUriServ.do?uri=COM:2002:0276:FIN:EN:PDF

– 2002b. Communication from the Commission, Action Plan "Simplifying and Improving the Regulatory Environment." Brussels, COM (2002) 278 final. Accessed March 5, 2013, http://eur-lex.europa.eu/LexUriServ/Lex UriServ.do?uri=COM:2002:0278:FIN:en:PDF

– 2008. "Towards World-Class Clusters in the European Union: Implementing the Broad-Based Innovation Strategy." *Communication from the Commission to the Council, the European Parliament, the European Economic and Social.* COM (2008) 652 final/2.

Eurostat. 2010. "Nomenclature of Territorial Units for Statistics: Introduction." Accessed March 5, 2013, http://epp.eurostat.ec.europa.eu/portal /page/portal/nuts_nomenclature/introduction

Evans, Peter. 1997. "State Structures, Government-Business Relations, and Economic Transformation." In *Business and the State in Developing Countries,* edited by Sylvia Maxfield and Ben Ross Schneider, 63–87. Ithaca: Cornell University Press.

Federal Ministry of Economics and Technology, Germany. 2011. "The Initiative Networks of Competence Germany." Accessed July 4, 2011, http://www.kompetenznetze.de/the-initiative.

Ffowcs-Williams, Ifor. 2000. "Policy for Inter-firm Networking and Clustering: A Practitioner's Perspective." Paper presented at the OECD/Italian Ministry of Industry Bologna Conference for Ministers, June 13–15 2000.

– 2004. "Cluster Development: Red Lights & Green Lights." Regional Science Association International, Australia and New Zealand Section. Accessed July 4, 2011, http://www.desertknowledge.com.au/dka /documents/IFW%20Cluster%20development%20red%20and%20green %20lights%200404.pdf.

Fligstein, Neil. 2008. "Myths of the Market." In *The Institutions of the Market: Organizations, Social Systems and Governance,* edited by Alexander Ebner and Nikolaus Beck, 131–56. New York: Oxford University Press.

Friedman, Thomas L. 2007. *The World Is Flat: A Brief History of the Twenty-First Century.* New York: Farrar, Straus, and Giroux.

Gereffi, Gary. 2008. "The Organization of Buyer-Driven Global Commodity Chains: How U.S. Retailers Shape Overseas Production Networks." In *The Transnational Studies Reader: Intersections and Innovations,* edited by Sanjeev Khagram and Peggy Levitt, 429–45. New York: Routledge.

Gereffi, Gary and Olga Memedovic. 2004. "The Global Apparel Value Chain: What Prospects for Upgrading by Developing Countries?" In *Globalization and Its Outcomes,* edited by John O'Loughlin, Lynn Staeheli, and Edward Greenberg, 67–97. New York: The Guilford Press.

Gerschenkron, Alexander. 1962. *Economic Backwardness in Historical Perspective.* Cambridge: Belknap.

Gilly, Jean-Pierre and Jacques Perrat. 2006. "The Institutional Dynamics at Work in Territories: Between Local Governance and Global Regulation." In *Clusters and Globalisation: the Development of Urban and Regional Economies,* edited by Christos Pitelis, Roger Sugden, James R. Wilson, 159–74. Cheltenham, UK: Edward Elgar.

Giuliani, Elisa. 2005. "Technological Learning in a Chilean Wine Cluster and Its Linkages with the National System of Innovation." In *Clusters Facing Competition: The Importance of External Linkages,* edited by Elisa Giuliani, Roberta Rabellotti, and Meine Pieter van Dijk, 155–76. Burlington, VT: Ashgate.

Giuliani, Elisa, Andrea Morrison, and Roberta Rabellotti, eds. 2011. *Innovation and Technological Catch-Up: The Changing Geography of Wine Production.* Northampton, MA: Edward Elgar.

Granovetter, Mark. 1985. "Economic Action and Social Structure: the Problem of Embeddedness." *American Journal of Sociology* 91 (3): 481–510.

Grant, Robert M. 2008. *Contemporary Strategy Analysis.* 6th ed. Malden, MA: Blackwell.

Graversen, Andreas Blohm and Rosted, Jorgen. 2010. *Towards Fact-Based Cluster Policies, Learning from a Pilot Study of Life Sciences in the Baltic Sea Region.* FORA: Copenhagen.

Grinberg, Ruslan and Alexander Rubinstein. 2005. *Economic Sociodynamics.* New York: Springer.

Hamel, Gary, and C.K. Prahalad. 1994. *Competing for the Future.* Boston: Harvard Business School Press.

Hira, Anil. 2012. "States and High Tech: Cases from the Wireless Sector." *International Journal of Technology and Globalisation* 6 (1–2).

– 2007. *The New Path: How Industrial Policy Succeeded in East Asia and Can Work in Latin America.* Burlington: Ashgate.

– 1998. *Ideas and Economic Policy in Latin America.* Westport: Greenwood.

Hira, Anil, Brian Wixted, and Ricardo Arechavala-Vargas. 2012. Explaining Sectoral Leapfrogging in Countries: Comparative Studies of the Wireless Sector. *Interdisciplinary Journal of Technology and Globalisation* 6 (1–2): 3–26.

Hirooka, Masaaki. 2006. *Innovation Dynamism and Economic Growth: A Nonlinear Perspective.* Northampton, MA: Edward Elgar.

Hitt, Michael A., R. Duane Ireland, Robert E. Hoskisson, W. Glenn Rowe, and Jerry P. Sheppard. 2006. *Strategic Management: Competitiveness and Globalization.* Canada: Thomson Nelson.

Ibata-Arens, Kathryn. Forthcoming. *Clustering to Win: Firm, Regional and National Entrepreneurship Strategies in the United States and Japan.*

Jenster, Per V., David E. Smith, Darryl J. Mitry, and Lars V. Jenster. 2008. *The Business of Wine: A Global Perspective.* Copenhagen: Copenhagen Business School Press.

Johnson, Chalmers. 1982. *MITI and the Japanese Miracle: The Growth of Industrial Policy, 1925–1975.* Stanford: Stanford University Press.

Jovanovic, Miroslav N. 2006. *Location of Production: Local vs Global Game.* New York: Nova Science.

Kanter, Rosabeth Moss. 1997. *Frontiers of Management,* Boston: Harvard Business Review.

Karl, Terry. 1997. *The Paradox of Plenty: Oil Booms and Petro-States.* Berkeley: University of California Press.

Kimura, Seishi. 2007. *The Challenges of Late Industrialization: the Global Economy and the Japanese Commercial Aircraft Industry.* New York: Palgrave Macmillan.

Klein, Michael U. and Bita Hadjimichael. 2003. *The Private Sector in Development: Entrepreneurship, Regulation, and Competitive Disciplines.* Washington: World Bank.

Kogut, Bruce and Zander, Udo. 1993. Knowledge of the Firm and the Evolutionary Theory of the Multinational Corporation. *Journal of International Business Studies* 24 (4): 625–45.

Kohli, Atul. 2004. *State-Directed Development: Political Power and Industrialization in the Global Periphery.* New York: Cambridge University Press.

Kopicki, Ronald. 2002. "Value Creation through Supply Chain Management." In *Building Competitive Firms: Incentives and Capabilities,* edited by Ijaz Nabi and Manjula Luthria, 149–64. Washington: World Bank.

Krueger, Anne O., ed. 2000. *Economic Policy Reform: The Second Stage.* Chicago: University of Chicago Press.

Krugman, Paul. 1991. *Geography and Trade.* Cambridge, MA: MIT Press.

Kuczynski, Pedro-Pablo and John Williamson, eds. 2003. *After the Washington Consensus: Restarting Growth and Reform in Latin America,* Washington: Institute for International Economics.

Lascaux, Alexander. 2005. "Trust and Transaction Costs." In *Complexity and the Economy: Implications for Economic Policy,* edited by John Finch and Magali Orillard, 151–71. Northampton, MA: Edward Elgar.

Lederman, Daniel, and William F. Maloney. 2007. *Natural Resources: Neither Curse nor Destiny.* Washington: World Bank.

Lee, Norman and Kirkpatrick, Colin. 2006. "Integrated Impact Assessment, Evidence-Based Policy-Making in Europe: An Evaluation of European

Commission Integrated Impact Assessments." *Impact Assessment and Project Appraisal* 24 (1), 23–33.

Leoncini, Riccardo and Sandro Montresor. 2008. "Learning and Firm Dynamics: Theoretical Approaches and Empirical Analysis of Dynamic Capabilities." In *Dynamic Capabilities Between Firm Organization and Local Systems of Production*, edited by Riccardo Leoncini and Sandro Montresor, 17–72. New York: Routledge.

Leslie, Stuart W. 2000. "The Biggest 'Angel' of Them All: The Military and the Making of Silicon Valley." In *Understanding Silicon Valley: The Anatomy of an Entrepreneurial Region*, edited by Martin Kenney, 48–70. Stanford: Stanford University Press.

Lipsey, Richard G., Kenneth I. Carlaw, and Clifford T. Bekar. 2005. *Economic Transformations: General Purpose Technologies and Long Term Economic Growth.* New York: Oxford University Press.

List, Friedrich. 1865. *National System of Political Economy.* Translated by G.A. Matile. Philadelphia: J.P. Lippincott & Co.

Lundvall, B.-Å and S. Borrás. 2005. "Science, Technology, and Innovation Policy." In *The Oxford Handbook of Innovation*, edited by Jan Fagerberg, David C. Mowery, and Richard R. Nelson, 599–631. New York: Oxford University Press.

Lynch, Richard. 2006. *Corporate Strategy.* New York: Financial Times, Prentice Hall.

Malerba, Franco. 2005. "Sectoral Systems: How and Why Innovation Differs across Sectors." In *The Oxford Handbook of Innovation*, edited by Jan Fagerberg, David C. Mowery, and Richard R. Nelson, 380–406. New York: Oxford University Press.

Malmberg, Anders, and Dominic Power. 2006. "True Clusters: A Severe Case of Conceptual Headache." In *Clusters and Regional Development: Critical Reflections and Explorations*, edited by Bjorn Asheim, Philip Cooke, and Ron Martin, 50–68. New York: Routledge.

Markusen, A. 1999. "Fuzzy Concepts, Scanty Evidence, Policy Distance: The Case for Rigour and Policy Relevance in Critical Regional Studies." *Regional Studies* 33 (9): 869–84.

Marshall, Alfred. 1890. *Principles of Economics.* London: Macmillan and Co.

McCarthy, Dennis M.P. 1994. *International Business History: A Contextual and Case Approach.* Westport, CT: Praeger.

McCormick, Dorothy. 2007. "Industrialization through Cluster Upgrading: Theoretical Perspectives." In *Industrial Clusters and Innovation Systems in Africa: Institutions, Markets, and Policy*, edited by Banji Oyelaran-Oyeyinka and Dorothy McCormick, 20–39. New York: UN University Press.

Meeus, Marius and Leon Oerlemans. 2005a. "National Innovation Systems." In *Innovation and Institutions: A Multidisciplinary Review of the Study of Innovation Systems* , edited by Steven Casper and Frans van Waarden, 51–67. Northampton, MA: Edward Elgar.

– 2005b. "Innovation Strategies, Interactive Learning and Innovation Networks." In *Innovation and Institutions: A Multidisciplinary Review of the Study of Innovation Systems* , edited by Steven Casper and Frans van Waarden, 152–92. Northampton, MA: Edward Elgar.

Meyer-Stamer, J. 1998. "Path Dependence in Regional Development: Persistence and Change in Three Industrial Clusters in Santa Catarina, Brazil." *World Development* 26 (8): 1495–511.

Morosini, Piero. 2004. "Industrial Clusters, Knowledge Integration and Performance." *World Development* 32 (2): 305–26.

Morrison, Andrea, Carlo Pietrobelli, and Roberta Rabellotti. 2008. "Global Value Chains and Technological Capabilities: A Framework to Study Industrial Innovation in Developing Countries." In *Dynamic Capabilities Between Firm Organization and Local Systems of Production*, edited by Riccardo Leoncini and Sandro Montresor, 157–80. New York: Routledge.

Navaretti, Giorgio Barba and Anthony J. Venables. 2004. *Multinational Firms in the World Economy.* Princeton: Princeton University Press.

Nelson, Richard R. 1996. *The Sources of Economic Growth*. Cambridge, MA: Harvard University Press.

Nelson, Richard R. and Sidney G. Winter. 1982. *An Evolutionary Theory of Economic Change*. Cambridge, MA: Harvard University Press.

Orsenigo, Luigi. 2006. "Clusters and Clustering: Stylized Facts, Issues, and Theories." In *Cluster Genesis: Technology-Based Industrial Development*, edited by Pontus Braunerheim and Maryann Feldman, 195–218. New York: Oxford University Press.

Pamminger, Werner. 2010. "Clusterland Upper Austria, Innovation through Cooperation. Clusterland Upper Austria Ltd." Accessed July 4, 2011, http://www.clustercollaboration.eu/documents/10147/16788/100915_Overview+Clusterland+Upper+Austria+ENG+short.pdf.

Perry, Martin. 2005. *Business Clusters: An International Perspective.* New York: Routledge.

Phillips, P.W.B., Camille D. Ryan, Jeremy Karwandy, Tara Lynn Procyshyn, and Julie Lynn Parchewski. 2008. "The Saskatoon Agricultural-Biotechnology Cluster." In *Handbook of Research on Clusters: Theories, Policies and Case Studies,* edited by C. Karlsson, 239–52. Aldershot, UK and Brookfield, MA: Edward Elgar.

Pietrobelli, Carlo and Roberta Rabellotti, 2008. "A Sectoral Approach for

Clusters and Value Chains in Latin America." In *High Technology, Productivity, and Networks: A Systemic Approach to SME Development*, edited by Mario Davide Parrilli, Patrizio Bianci, and Roger Sugden, 209–32. New York: Palgrave Macmillan.

Piore, M.J. and C.F. Sabel. 1984. *The Second Industrial Divide: Possibilities for Prosperity.* New York: Basic Books.

Polanyi, Karl. 1944. *The Great Transformation.* Boston: Beacon Press.

Porter, Michael. 1986. "Competition in Global Industries: A Conceptual Framework." In *Competition in Global Industries,* edited by Michael Porter, 15–60. Boston: Harvard Business School Press.

– 1990. *The Competitive Advantage of Nations.* New York: Free Press.

– 1998a. *Competitive Strategy: Techniques for Analyzing Industries and Competitors.* New York: Free Press.

– 1998b. "Clusters and Competition: New Agendas for Companies, Governments, and Institutions." In *On Competition,* by Michael Porter, 197–288. Boston: Harvard Business Review.

– 1998c. "Clusters and the New Economics of Competition." *Harvard Business Review.* Reprint Number 98609 (Nov–Dec): 77–90.

– 2000. "Location, Competition, and Economic Development: Local Clusters in a Global Economy." *Economic Development Quarterly* 14 (1): 15–34.

Putnam, Robert D. 1993. *Making Democracy Work: Civic Traditions in Modern Italy.* Princeton: Princeton University Press.

Pyke, F., G. Becattini and W. Sengenberger, eds. 1990. *Industrial Districts and Inter-firm Cooperation in Italy.* Geneva, Switzerland: International Institute for Labour Studies.

Rabellotti, R. 1995. "Is There an 'Industrial District Flow'? Footwear Districts in Italy and Mexico Compared." *World Development* 23 (1): 29–41.

Radetzki, Marian. 2008. *A Handbook of Primary Commodities in the Global Economy.* New York: Cambridge University Press.

Rosenberg, D. 2002. *Cloning Silicon Valley: The Next Generation High-Tech Hotspots.* London: Pearson Education.

Rowley, Timothy J. and Joel A. C. Baum. 2008. "Introduction: Evolving Webs in Network Economies." In *Network Strategy Advances in Strategic Management,* Vol. 25, edited by Joel A.C. Baum and Timothy J. Rowley, xiii–2. Bingley, UK: Emerald JAI.

Rugman, Alan M. 2005. *The Regional Multinationals: MNEs and "Global" Strategic Management.* New York: Cambridge University Press.

Rugman, Alan M. and Jonathan P. Doh. 2008. *Multinationals and Development.* New Haven: Yale University Press.

Rugman, Alan M., Chang Hoon Oh, and Dominic S.K. Lim, 2012. "The

Regional and Global Competitiveness of Multinational Firms." *Journal of the Academy of Marketing Science* 40 (2): 218–35.

Rugman, Alan and Alain Verbeke. 2003. *Regional Multinationals: The Location-Bound Drivers of Global Strategy*. West Sussex, UK: Wiley.

Ruth, Matthias and Brynhildur Davidsdottir. 2009. "The Dynamics of Regions and Networks in Industrial Ecosystems: Background and Concepts." In *The Dynamics of Regions and Networks in Industrial Ecosystems*, edited by Matthias Ruth and Brynhildur Davidsdottir, 3–5. Northampton, MA: Edward Elgar.

Saee, John. 2007. *Contemporary Corporate Strategy: Global Perspectives*. New York: Routledge.

Schmitz, H. 2000. "Does Local Co-operation matter? Evidence from Industrial Clusters in South Asia and Latin America." *Oxford Development Studies* 28 (3): 323–36.

Schumpeter, Joseph A. 1939. *Business Cycles: A Theoretical, Historical, and Statistical Analysis of the Capitalist Process*. Toronto: McGraw-Hill.

Simmie, J., and Sennett, J. 1999. "Innovative Clusters: Global or Local Linkages?" *National Institute Economic Review* 170: 70–81.

Simmie, James. 2006. "The Role of Clusters in Knowledge Creation and Diffusion: an Institutional Perspective." In *Clusters and Regional Development: Critical Reflections and Explorations*, edited by Bjorn Asheim, Philip Cooke, and Ron Martin, 188–98. New York: Routledge.

Smith, Madeline and Ross Brown. 2009. "Exploratory Techniques for Examining Cluster Dynamics: A Systems Thinking Approach." *Local Economy* 24: 283–98.

Sturgeon, Timothy J. 2009. "From Commodity Chains to Value Chains: Interdisciplinary Theory Building in an Age of Globalization." In *Frontiers of Commodity Chain Research*, edited by Jennifer Bair, 110–35. Stanford: Stanford University Press.

– 2005. "The Future of Manufacturing: The Implications of Global Production for Environmental Policy and Activism." In *Environmentalism and the Technologies of Tomorrow: Shaping the Next Industrial Revolution*, edited by Robert Olson and David Rejeski, 71–9. Washington: Island Press.

– 2000. "How Silicon Valley Came to Be." In *Understanding Silicon Valley: The Anatomy of an Entrepreneurial Region*, edited by Martin Kenney, 15–47. Stanford: Stanford University Press.

Sverisson, Árni. 2004. "Local and Global Commodity Chains" In *Linking Local and Global Economies: The Ties that Bind*, edited by Carlo Pietrobelli and Árni Sverisson, 17–35. New York: Routledge.

Taylor, Michael and Simon Leonard. 2002. "Approaching 'Embeddedness.'"

In *Embedded Enterprise and Social Capital: International Perspectives*, edited by Michael Taylor and Simon Leonard, 1–18. Burlington: Ashgate.

Todtling, Franz. 1995. "The Uneven Landscapes of Innovation Poles – Local Embeddedness and Global Networks." In *Globalization, Institutions, and Regional Development in Europe*, edited by Ash Amin and Nigel Thrift. New York: Oxford University Press.

Unger, Brigitte. 2005. "Problems of Measuring Innovative Performance." In *Innovation and Institutions: A Multidisciplinary Review of the Study of Innovation Systems*, edited by Steven Casper and Frans van Waarden, 19–50. Northampton, MA: Edward Elgar.

Van Alstyne, M. 1997. "The State of Network Organization: A Survey in Three Frameworks." *Journal of Organisational Computing and Electronic Commerce* 7 (3): 83–151.

Vernon, Raymond. 1966. "International Investment and International Trade in the Product Cycle." *Quarterly Journal of Economics* 80 (May): 190–270.

Wade, Robert. 1990. *Governing the Market: Economic Theory and the Role of Government in East Asian Industrialization.* Princeton: Princeton University Press.

Walker, Gordon. 2004. *Modern Competitive Strategy.* 2nd edition. San Francisco: McGraw Hill Irwin.

Wang, Jici. 2007. "Industrial Clusters in China: The Low Road Versus the High Road in Cluster Development." In *Development on the Ground: Clusters, Networks and Regions in Emerging Economies*, edited by Allen J. Scott and Gioacchino Garofoli, 145–64. New York: Routledge.

White, Harrison C. 1992. *Identity and Control: A Structural Theory of Social Action.* Princeton: Princeton University Press.

Williamson, John. 2000. "What Should the World Bank Think About the Washington Consensus?" *World Bank Research Observer* 15 (2): 251–64. Washington, DC: International Bank for Reconstruction and Development.

World Bank. 1993. *The East Asian Miracle: Economic Growth and Public Policy.* New York: Cambridge University Press.

Yergin, Daniel. 1991. *The Prize: The Epic Quest for Oil, Money, and Power.* New York: Simon & Schuster.

Yergin, Daniel and Joseph Stanislaw. 2002. *The Commanding Heights: The Battle for the World Economy.* New York: Simon and Schuster.

Yusuf, Shahid. 2008. "Can Clusters Be Made to Order?" In *Growing Industrial Clusters in Asia: Serendipity and Science*, edited by Shahid Yusuf, Kaoru Nabeshima, and Shoihi Yamashita, 1–38. Washington: World Bank.

2

Development of the
Global Wine Industry

ANIL HIRA AND HUSAM GABRELDAR

INTRODUCTION

This chapter provides background to readers unfamiliar with the
wine industry. It focuses on the contextual factors behind competitiveness in the global wine industry as exposed in the current literature. The most important development to explain is the phenomenal
growth of New World wine producers at the expense of Old World
producers. We examine existing explanations for this phenomenon in
order to set up our study of factors behind competitiveness in the
industry.

BACKGROUND TO THE WINE INDUSTRY

Technical Aspects

Wine is made naturally when crushed grapes of the species *vitis vinifera*
are left for a few days. Yeast cells collect on the outside of the skin and,
when exposed to the natural sweetness inside the fruit, ferment the
sugar into carbon dioxide and ethyl alcohol. Dry wines are those with
no appreciable sugars remaining. Sparkling wines are made from table
wines that are partially re-fermented to capture the carbon dioxide gas
that is generated, leading to effervescence (sparkling qualities), as with
Champagne. Dessert wines are made by adding grape brandy (distilled
wine) which inhibits the growth of yeast at some point, leaving natur-

al sugars unfermented. Aperitifs are infused with combinations of herbs, spices, and essences (Vine 1981, v–vi). Wine is stored in wood, generally oak, barrels, which affects the overall taste of the wine through little understood chemical reactions (Paul 1991, 346).

Evidently, the climate, soils, and subsequent quality of the fruit directly impact the quality of the wine. Wine is best grown where temperatures are mild year-round, with dry summers and cool winters. Table wines do better in cooler regions, natural sweet wines in warm regions, and dessert wines and raisin wines in moderately hot regions. Key minerals needed in the soil include nitrogen and potassium (Weaver 1976, 45, 160).

As with other plants, weeds are a common problem for grapes, and have traditionally been treated with herbicides. Common problems with wine grapes include downy and powdery mildew and moulds, such as collar, armillaria root, and brown and black rot. These are usually treated with fungicides. Some moulds such as *botrytis cinerea* are helpful as they lead to higher sugar concentration. Grapes also suffer from virus infections, such as grape leafroll (white emperor disease), fan leaf, yellow mosaic, vein banding, yellow vein, corky bark, yellow spectacle, and asteroid mosaic. The viruses are transmitted by insects. Harmful insects to fruit include fruit flies, the aphid *phylloxera*, and nematodes. There are numerous insects that pose threats to roots, leaves, and stems as well. Birds, deer, gophers, and rabbits also eat the plant or fruit, or create problems by digging into irrigation systems, leading to water loss. There are also concerns with acidity related to *acetobacter aceti*, a bacteria that changes ethyl alcohol into vinegar, and is often transmitted by fruit flies or other insects. Certain types of *lactobacillus* bacteria can also cause spoilage, as can *leucconostoc mesenteroides* (Vine 1981, 270, 273 and Weaver 1976, 251–90).

Wine yeasts are unicellular organisms belonging to the kingdom Fungi. They are mobilized by natural forces in water and wine and are carried by the air to different sites to bloom. Different strains of yeast have different effects on wine. The strain of the genus *saccharomyces cerevisiae* is used for wine fermentation. The genus *dekkera*, *candida*, *kloeckera*, and *pichia*, among others are called wild or apiculate yeasts, and spoil wine. Wine makers treat wine with 50–75 ppm of SO_2 to kill the wild yeasts just prior to crushing. *Saccharmyces* is available commercially in dried form for the fermentation process (Vine 1981, 265–70).

· Wine cultivation has included active efforts to select breeds for tasting, and fungus and disease resistance. Hybrids have also been long cultivated by grafting vines onto different roots. For example, in response to a phylloxera outbreak in the late nineteenth century in France, winemakers grafted French vines onto more bug-resistant American roots, but hybrid wines supposedly were less tasty. The same concerns arise in regard to fruit clones, which are bred to be higher in fruit content and more disease resistant (Paul 1996, 16–17).

HISTORICAL EVOLUTION
OF THE GLOBAL WINE INDUSTRY

Key Forces in Wine Industry Evolution

The evolution of wine can be understood through the interplay of geography, climate, and natural conditions; changes in demand and supply markets; state policies, and technological improvements. Evidently, quality wine requires certain climactic and soil conditions, thus effectively leading to a natural comparative advantage for certain parts of the world. Transportation costs have also been a key factor, giving locations close to demand centres a decided historical advantage. However, comparative advantage alone, as we saw in the first chapter, can hardly explain why some areas where quality wine is possible, such as southeastern Brazil, have never developed a strong industry, while others that are seemingly less suitable, such as Ontario, Canada, have. Our brief overview of the evolution of the industry points to the importance of human agency in deciding the overall fate of industrial location.

Wine may date back to the beginnings of civilisation, at least from 6000 BCE in Georgia and Iran, while rice wine in China might date back even further. Wine trade began early, with Egyptian wine imports dating back at least to 3150 BCE (Phillips 2001, 17).

Wine has always been an integral part of Western civilisation. The Roman Empire helped to spread wine cultivation throughout Western Europe and developed basic storage techniques, wine presses, and appellations representing specialities of different regions. Wine's importance in Christian rituals led to the development of a wine industry throughout Europe, including vineyards owned by monkish orders. Such orders helped to develop early varieties of Champagne (including

Dom Perignon) and Riesling. They also helped to spread basic viticulture throughout Europe. During the Middle Ages, wine was a common
drink for merchant and noble households throughout southern Europe.
The Carolingian Empire emerging in the eighth century under Charle-
magne also witnessed the first modern proactive state regulations promoting wine production and regarding standards of production.
Drinking, by this time, was deeply embedded in social life, and associated with ceremony, bonding, and manliness (Wikipedia 2009; Phillips
2001, 73, 75–6). Wine had multiple uses and was considered a part of
everyday life, a source of sanitary water, and a widely prescribed medi-
cine for a variety of ailments.

Trade and markets have always played a key role in industry development. By 1000, exports to England and the Netherlands led to
major expansions of vineyards in France, wiping out English production (Phillips 2001, 86, 88). Portugal, a large producer, suffered losses
in the mid-nineteenth century due to declines in English demand for
wine generally, and the development of sherry produced in Spain as a
substitute for port. The development of other spirits, beer, tea, and coffee, as well as concerns about the consequences of high alcohol content all converged to reduce demand (Johnson 1989, 324). Champagne's attribution to ceremonies, celebrations, and solemn occasions
was part of an elaborate marketing effort by producers during the late
nineteenth century (Phillips 2001, 244–5). A pattern is discernible in
the historical development of domestic wine markets, where a shift
occurs when tastes move from cheap, high-alcohol, and generally
sweet bulk wine to more sophisticated tastes and higher prices
focused on differentiation (Johnson 1989, 457).

State policies have had varying degrees of success in establishing
wineries historically. The Thirty Years War of the seventeenth century
and subsequent wars with France helped to decimate German vineyards, driving German drinking habits back towards beer. Spanish and
Portuguese desire to ensure the success of their exports led to their control over wine producers in Mexico and Brazil (to which shipment
without spoilage was possible) during colonial periods (Phillips 2001,
129, 259). Repeated efforts to establish wine production in the US
from the seventeenth century on failed as climactic, pestilence, fungi,
and local vine varietal conditions impeded efforts. Mildew wiped out
the nascent winemaking industry in Ohio in the mid-nineteenth century (Johnson 1989, 357–9). At other points, state policies have greatly

benefited the industry. The French Revolution led to a relaxation of taxes on wine producers and major state demand for wine for troops. Concerns about the inconsistent quality of port wines in England led the Portuguese in the mid-1700s to begin regulating all stages of wine production there, the precursor to the appellation system by which only wines from certain regions can carry certain names (such as Champagne) (Phillips 2001, 188, 212–13). In the early 1900s, France developed the first comprehensive regulations regarding wine production motivated to safeguard the higher price of quality vintages. Such efforts culminated in the interwar period with the Appellation d'Origine Contrôlée (AOC) defining regions, grape varieties, and wine characteristics for wine produced from them (Phillips 2001, 293, 300).

Campbell and Guibert note the ubiquitous effect of state policies in developing New World wine industries. The spread of the phylloxera louse devastated wineries across the world during the later part of the nineteenth century. While it wiped out Peru's industry, Chile was exceptionally spared (a precondition to its current success). The grafting of Old World vines onto New World root stock helped to revive the industry after a long downturn. However, the social and medical evils of alcoholism created a new challenge, culminating in the Prohibition period in the US in 1918. World Wars I and II and related events such as the Spanish Civil War contributed to a downturn in the industry. Wine was no longer a necessity, with the advent of safe drinking water and other more effective painkillers and medicines (Johnson 1989, 179). The Argentine government founded the national wine industry in 1853 through the import of French wine expertise, technology, and grape stock. In Ontario, Canada, following the Prohibition era, the provincial government set up the Liquor Control Board of Ontario, and promoted a reduction of the number of producers, from 63 to 6. However, only poor quality ports and sherries resulted. The provincial government also hurt the local industry. A 1973 Wine Content Act allowed for 75% imported content, and in 1975, the quasi-monopoly in production was lifted. The adoption of the Canada-US Free Trade Agreement (CUSFTA) in 1989 led to a flooding of imports from the US (Heien and Sims 2000). However, the development of new technologies and the establishment in 1997 of the Brock University Cool Climate Oenology and Viticulture Institute, reflect the newfound success of local producers, with a growing specialisation in icewine. In California, the restriction of sales of land helped to preserve areas for vineyards, and this policy was instrumental to the development of the Napa cluster, starting in the late 1960s (Campbell and Guibert 2007, 6–9).

Technological innovations are another key evolutionary force. Concerns about the spoilage of wine during long ocean passages led to the development of local vineyards in Peru, Chile, Argentina, and South Africa by the seventeenth century. From the fifteenth century, beginning in Germany, experimentation with the addition of sulphites prolonged the preservation of wine. Concern about this led to early proscriptions on the amount of sulphur that could be added to a barrel (Johnson 1989, 126). During the sixteenth century, the Dutch development of brandy that could be transported more cheaply, stored longer, and had a higher alcohol content, created a challenge to wine. Dutch entrepreneurs became active in France and Spain in setting up new areas for developing wine and brandy for consumption and re-export. The seventeenth century also saw the development and spread of other distilled spirits, including whiskey, vodka, and gin, which could be produced in the northern climates, and rum from sugar cane in the New World (Phillips 2001, 123, 125–6). In the seventeenth century, long glass bottles were first used for horizontal storage, and corks were first used to seal bottles. This allowed for the development of Champagne and port. Port was first developed in Portuguese vineyards, spurred by English importers' priorities to find alternatives to France for their wine supplies (Phillips 2001, 136–9, 173). An important innovation that spurred wine growth in more remote areas including California and Mendoza, Argentina, was the development of railways in the later half of the nineteenth century. Steam-powered ships also spurred the development of wineries in Australia. The mid-nineteenth century also witnessed the development of improved quality standards for production in France, Italy, and Germany particularly as new techniques, such as paying more attention to the particular qualities of certain varietals, spread. The development of stronger bottles and reliable methods of Champagne production also came through experimentation leading to the technique of "remuage" to remove sediment without losing fizz. The need for labour-intensive efforts in Champagne made it the first industrial-based drink, pushing out smaller producers (Johnson 1989, 337–9). Other techniques, such as pasteurisation, were slower to spread. Refrigeration only began to catch on in the 1950s (Johnson 1989, 451).

The movement towards more sophisticated wines, generally with the development of the New World wineries attaining global status (us in the 1960s, Australia and others in the 1980s), has been accompanied by a technological revolution in wine making. California's success led the way with the pioneering use of quantitative analyses and techniques geared towards improving quality and consistency. The California wineries also developed the business model around wine tourism in Napa, which not only supplements revenues, but also helps to increase the sophistication of consumer demand (Porter and Bond 2004, 2–3).

In terms of more recent revolutions, Giuliani (2007b, 145) suggests that the introduction of mechanics, electronics, and information technology can be seen in four key categories. The first is vine planting, where plant genetics and understanding of different terroirs have led to increasing ability to design new flavours. The second is canopy management, in which practices such as "precision viticulture" have allowed for the collection of data that allow for more appropriate and timely interventions, such as pest management, that allow for better long-term management. The third is the development of more advanced chemical and microbiological fermentation processes using steel tanks, allowing for greater control of temperatures, enzymes, and yeasts, and again feeding into an information system allowing for greater precision over time. The fourth is sensory analysis, including the codification of different practices, allowing for greater understanding of the chemistry of winemaking. In this process, a corps of specialised agronomists and oenologists, often linked to specialised research universities or institutes, has brought a more technical rigour to winemaking. They also act as a link to other specialists around the world, serving as an information bridge to developments in the industry (150). Giuliani (148) also points out that "this has not resulted in dismantled tacit knowledge, which rather gains in importance supporting the generation of new knowledge, complex decision taking and operational routines." This relates of course to the unique aspects of each terroir as well as the desire to create differentiated products.

Statistical Analysis of the Evolution of Global Wine Industry

Using the Food and Agriculture Organisation (fao) stat program, we were able to create a historical profile of the global wine market, as

Table 2.1
Historical evolution of global wine exports – dominance of the Old World

1961–1970

Rank	Countries	1961	1970	10-Year Average	Average Growth Rate (%)	Average 10-Year Market Share (%)
1	Algeria	1,309,000	1,231,060	971,256	6.02	39.75
2	France	400,361	387,923	364,000	0.50	14.90
3	Spain	152,958	324,428	225,984	9.10	9.25
4	Italy	155,839	482,066	213,573	17.11	8.74
5	Morocco	138,216	88,388	132,847	−2.04	5.44
6	Bulgaria	73,548	194,098	127,986	12.15	5.24
7	Tunisia	133,467	83,397	110,456	1.60	4.52
8	Hungary	41,088	97,458	65,066	11.14	2.66
9	Greece	21,915	116,157	55,645	23.05	2.28
10	Yugoslav SFR	39,022	42,253	42,219	4.07	1.73

1971–1980

Rank	Countries	1971	1980	10-Year Average	Average Growth Rate (%)	Average 10-Year Market Share (%)
1	Italy	844,251	1,466,930	1,216,831	10.04	31.97
2	France	473,634	887,266	682,463	7.90	17.93
3	Algeria	550,776	226,103	480,532	−5.40	12.63
4	Spain	357,361	545,881	460,111	8.30	12.09
5	Bulgaria	206,748	271,005	232,587	3.51	6.11
6	Hungary	108,796	209,215	165,887	7.97	4.36
7	Germany	44,997	185,084	103,871	17.46	2.73
8	Greece	88,776	25,502	78,121	−3.77	2.05
9	Yugoslav SFR	57,039	112,408	77,918	9.34	2.05
10	Tunisia	23,777	22,844	57,922	22.66	1.52

seen in table 2.1, in which we analyse the top ten wine-producing countries.

What we see in the first two decades of data is the dominance of European producers. What is often overlooked, as revealed by these data, is the early importance of North African producers. The reason is that these producers as well as Eastern European ones largely sell in the bulk wine markets. The rapid increases in German and Italian production from 1971 are also remarkable. In table 2.2, we examine the two most recent decades of statistical data, including Canada though it is a slight producer.

Table 2.2 reveals a remarkable transformation in the global wine market – with the USA entering the market first, in the early 1980s, followed by Australia and Chile in the 1990s. The most recent stats reveal the entry of other newcomers – South Africa and Argentina. The Eastern European and North African countries – with the exception of Moldova, also a bulk wine producer – has been displaced from the market. With the exception of Spain, we also see a general decline in the absolute amounts produced and market share held by the Western European (Old World) producers. We turn now to explaining these broad trends.

EXPLAINING THE RISE OF NEW WORLD PRODUCERS

Mechanisation, new insecticides and pesticides, and improved control and use of varieties have all improved and spread production during the later part of the twentieth century. The rise of new producers, as we describe below, has further increased competition. These improvements led to a wine surplus in the late 1980s, leading the European Union to offer some incentives to producers to pull out vines. The anti-alcohol campaign by Gorbachev in the Soviet Union in the 1980s led to major declines in wine production there. The fall of the Soviet Bloc also freed up Eastern European producers to start producing for global markets. Further, the end of apartheid-related sanctions on South Africa in the 1990s also freed up its producers to begin flooding global markets. Recent stories about wine's restorative effects are sources of hope for increases in demand. The popularisation and growing knowledge of wine has also led to increased competition in terms of quality (Phillips 2001, 314–6, 328–9, 332).

The wine industry is relatively small in global terms – accounting for only 0.4% of global household consumption and about 0.17% of global cropland. Yet this industry is also an intriguing case of globalisation at work. In the last three decades new producers from Oceania, the Western Hemisphere, and Eastern Europe have usurped the

Table 2.2
Global wine market exports, 1981–2008 – rise of the New World

1981–1990

Rank	Countries	1981	1990	10-Year Average	Average Growth Rate (%)	Average 10-Year Market Share (%)
1	Italy	1,896,570	1,206,890	1,434,441	–3.00	32.49
2	France	886,760	1,230,760	1,153,924	3.91	26.14
3	Spain	564,476	442,998	517,122	–1.61	11.71
4	Germany	205,763	277,622	265,246	3.87	6.01
5	Bulgaria	272,361	122,331	235,261	–7.45	5.33
6	Hungary	225,141	128,702	210,707	–4.32	4.77
7	Yugoslav SFR	132,639	95,448	119,357	–3.07	2.70
8	Algeria	239,276	26,412	102,233	–2.28	2.32
9	Greece	22,335	93,005	63,140	36.98	1.43
10	USA	39,457	94,918	45,399	13.21	1.03
	Canada*	0	608	304	–41.62	0.01

1991–2000

Rank	Countries	1991	2000	10-Year Average	Average Growth Rate (%)	Average 10-Year Market Share (%)
1	Italy	1,195,090	1,467,530	1,425,129	3.74	26.98
2	France	1,217,770	1,482,510	1,319,465	2.54	24.98
3	Spain	624,622	777,302	785,457	4.65	14.87
4	Germany	248,520	241,437	250,926	0.29	4.75
5	Chile	64,723	402,351	210,091	24.07	3.98
6	USA	103,713	276,943	174,670	11.98	3.31
7	Australia	54,149	310,885	150,630	23.71	2.85
8	Moldova	n/a	99,183	136,670	7.44	2.59
9	Bulgaria	57,206	79,300	125,373	7.61	2.37
10	Hungary	76,798	80,225	97,441	1.91	1.84
	Canada*	792	2,506	1,312	23.08	0.02

traditional place of powerhouses France, Italy, Portugal, and Spain, where domestic consumption has halved and grapevine areas have declined from 5 million hectares in the 1960s to 3 million in 2004.

Table 2.2 (*continued*)

2001–2008

Rank	Countries	2001	2009	10-Year Average	Average Growth Rate (%)	Average 10-Year Market Share (%)
1	Italy	1,537,060	1,733,890	1,635,475	2.24	21.91
2	France	1,551,660	1,345,510	1,448,585	−1.89	19.41
3	Spain	904,986	1,698,170	1,301,578	9.94	17.44
4	Australia	376,154	701,050	538,602	9.86	7.22
5	Chile	486,717	581,685	534,201	4.40	7.16
6	USA	284,356	463,817	374,087	7.89	5.01
7	South Africa	165,129	432,789	298,959	17.04	4.01
8	Germany	237,166	358,090	297,628	6.17	3.99
9	Argentina	92,177	430,305	261,241	26.63	3.50
10	Moldova	136,799	89,869	113,334	0.98	1.52
	Canada*	2,902	8,555	5,729	36.10	0.08

* Canada unranked

Meanwhile, a change in UK licencing laws that permitted the sale of wine in supermarkets, as well as reports on the health benefits of red wine from the 1980s, opened new middle-class markets that were more price sensitive and therefore open to the surge of new products, primarily from Australia (Anderson 2004). There is now, by many industry accounts, a "wine lake" of over production, leading to an interesting crossroads for the global market where some shakeout is bound to occur.

Western Europe remains the most important market, accounting for 47% of volume and 49% of global sales in 2009. On a country basis, by value, the top markets are: France 12%, the US 13%, and China with 8%. However, there is a general decline in consumption of wine in Europe, particularly in France, Spain, and Italy (Euromonitor 2010, 16–18). In the Mediterranean producing countries, wine has moved from being a part of daily diet to an occasional drink, though this is partly offset by an increase in Scandinavia, where there is a shift from spirits and beer to wine (Resnick 2008, 52). From the late 1980s to 2004, the share of wine production traded internationally has doubled, in hand with a surge of foreign investment and multinational takeovers, as well as the development of an international labour force of consultants and experts. Therefore, there is concern now with the possibility of an oversupply of wine, leading possibly to a wave of consolidation in the industry. Indeed, there is growing concern in the North, including the US, about the ability to compete with much cheaper wines from the South as imports have surged from Australia, then South America, and most recently South Africa.

The sensitivity of Old and New World countries to a loss of domestic market share tothe upstarts in South America and South Africa is reflected in the recent efforts to preserve "traditional" labels such as Champagne, sherry, and port for their own products. Unlike other beverage industries, globally, wine remains a very decentralised industry, with the three largest firms in the 1990s controlling just 6% of the global market (vs 35% for beer, 42% for spirits, and 78% for soft drinks). As of 2009, the top ten wine companies accounted for around 14% of total sales (Euromonitor 2010, 38). However, within newly producing countries, wine is heavily concentrated, with one company, Montana, controlling more than two thirds of New Zealand's production, five producers controlling three quarters of production in the US and Australia, and half of the production in Chile and Argentina. Initially, New World wines tend to be on the lower price end than European counterparts, pushing out cheaper European competitors, though prices for us production have increased dramatically in recent years, opening the way for the upstarts to follow their playbook (Anderson 2004). Among Old World wine producers, there remains a strong proportion of small, generally family-based producers. Jenster et al. (2008, 41) note that 28% of vine holdings in France are less than one hectare and only 4.5% greater than thirty hectares. This has led in some cases to the formation of co-operatives, and more generally in France and Italy, to a focus on reduced production and marked improvement in quality and price points.

Another response to market changes has been consolidation. A wave of recent acquisitions has led to strong global multinationals in the wine industry. For example, Australia's Fosters Group bought California's Beringer Wines, France's Pernod Ricard bought Australia's Wyndham Estate, and us-based Constellation Wines owns Australia's BRL Hardy, Canada's Vincorp, and California's Mondavi brands (Aylward 2006, 362). The twenty largest wholesalers control 70% of distribution in the us, and 60–80% of all global sales now occur through supermarkets (Castaldi, Cholette, and Hussain 2006b, 23). The desire for global brands and financing are the main drivers behind this movement towards oligopoly (Coelho and Rastoin 2006).

Despite the recent consolidation, the unique flavours of craft-made wine and appreciation for variation by year and region allow for the continuation of small wineries on the basis of craft expertise. These are reinforced by the built incentives for wine experts and trend setters to make new "findings." Thus, efforts at consolidation in line with other beverage markets have so far been resisted. For instance, Coca-Cola's venture into wine production through Wine Spectrum failed miserably (Hussain, Cholette, and Castaldi 2007, 43).

The big story as noted above has been the outstanding growth of the New World producers, particularly Australia, despite its traditionally small market. Australia accounted for less than 1% of world wine production in the 1990s. Australia's success is tied to a clear government-private sector collaboration aimed at encouraging exports, and centred around "Strategy 2025." The strategy includes low taxes and export-promotional measures. Australia has been particularly adept at building new brands, such as Jacob's Creek and Yellow Tail, designed to capture international markets (Hussain, Cholette, and Castaldi 2007, 36). As seen in table 2.2 above, Chile and Argentina have moved from negligible exports in the 1970s to fifth and ninth place, respectively, by 2008.

Hope for the future of global wine expansion resides in two areas. The first is the expectation that New World and Asia Pacific consumers will slowly increase their relatively low per capita consumption of wine. The second is that these same consumers will continue to increase their knowledge of wine, ratcheting up demand for higher priced, better quality wines (Hussain, Cholette, and Castaldi 2007, 39). A 2007 econometric analysis by Wittwer suggests that the US will be the principal source of demand growth; however, we can speculate that this may have changed as a result of the financial crisis. There are also signs that new consumers are more willing to experiment, partly a reflection of the wider availability of wines in supermarkets, broadening the possibilities for direct consumer choice (Campbell and Guibert 2006, 237). Newer consumers reportedly "prefer rich, full-flavoured wines with some oakiness at reasonable prices," (Labys and Cohen 2006, 528) suggesting that New World wines have captured market share partly by expanding the market, and that this trend is likely to continue.

Demand growth for imports in China and India, the great hope, will be slow. While urban consumers may take up the habit, it is unlikely that foreign brands will make any big splash outside of these pockets any time soon (Bernetti, Casini, and Marinelli 2006, 307). In fact, as in other sectors, Chinese producers are actively seeking technology transfer, including employment of Australian experts, for domestic upgrading (Smith 2007, 135). Banks and Overton (2010, 66) put it bluntly: "China increased its area under grapes three-fold in the twenty years prior to 2004 and now has a larger area under grapes than USA, Australia, or Argentina and Chile combined. Even Indian vineyards have expanded rapidly and there is now more than double the area under grapes there than there is in New Zealand." Part of the problem is that Chinese blenders can label wine as their own with just 10% of the wine coming from China (Wittwer 2007, 6–7). Chinese domestic production has been solid, increasing significantly during the past decade. Chinese investors have bought up wine properties in Bordeaux, and leading company ChangYu was tenth in terms of global wine sales in 2007 (Mitry, Smith, and Jenster 2009, 22–3). Indian companies have also purchased established wine companies, notably two purchases by Indage in Australia, as part of a strategy to source wine from ten different countries for the domestic market (Banks and Overton 2010, 70).

A key question is whether the New World producers will be able to move up the value chain – a feat that so far Chile, South Africa, and Argentina have struggled with. This would require strong regional differentiation and brand/type recognition and will take years. A study by Schamel (2006) indicated that with the exception of high quality Napa brands, there are fewer mainstays in the high price range for New World producers. The average price for wines from California is $33.48 ($44.69 for Napa); in France, from Burgundy $52.02, Bordeaux $46.65, and Rhone $40.17; in Italy from Piedmont $37.60 and Tuscany $38.49. In the middle range, wines from Germany average $26.89, from Spain $26.11, from Australia $23.84, and from New Zealand $19.13. At the lower end are Chile $16.65, Portugal $16.85, Argentina $17.45, and South Africa, $17.77 (Schamel 2006, 368). If we are talking about new consumers, the importance of terroir is less important and may spell long-term problems for the basis of built-in comparative advantage for the Old World.

CONCLUSION: CHALLENGES FOR THE WINE INDUSTRY

The age-old challenges of climate, pests, fungi, mildew, and changes in markets all continue the need for state policies and lead to continual technological innovations. For example, there is continued concern with another outbreak of phylloxera, perhaps of mutated form (Johnson 1989, 411). The general knowledge of wine consumers is increasing globally, along with overall supplies, leading to competitive pressures in both price and quality, as reflected in consolidation in the industry. Pressures for product differentiation are leading to continued efforts to extend appellation, such as restricting the term "Napa," and even sub-regions of Napa, such as "Stag's Head" (Brosnan 2007, 32–3). The concern for quality, production, and reliability all have led to continual efforts in agronomy, and the new frontier, genetic mapping, to improve harvests. There is concern with the growing consolidation of greater vulnerability to the mentioned threats, which is leading to further attempts to preserve diversification of stock, such as those by the University of California Davis research center in California (Brosnan 2007, 34).

Quality and product upgrading are the key features that will distinguish the survivors of the continuing market glut. As Jenster et al. (2008, 189) state, "Worldwide consumption is expected to increase at about the same rate through 2010, and then only modestly in the future ... Producers who cannot or will not upgrade to the premium category will be competing for a dwindling number of low-priced consumers."

Beyond these general challenges, we have noted the most important economic/business challenge, namely the relative gains of New World producers at the expense of Old World ones. Therein lies the central mystery to be solved. We do not really know if the source of this change is simply a matter of comparative advantage coming to fruition in terms of the evolution of supply and demand markets, Schumpeterian innovations through entrepreneurship (with New World firms more willing to innovate as the "new men"), differences in the public sector strategies, differences in cluster governance, or some combination of the above. We also have to try to answer the other side of the coin, namely, why potential producers, such as Bulgaria, Uruguay, Peru, and Brazil, have not been able to enter into global markets. For example, Uruguay has a wine industry reportedly comparable in size to New Zealand, but scarcely makes a dent in global markets (Carrau 1997). In the next section we review some of the existing literature's preliminary answers to this central question, which we address more fully in the rest of the chapters.

Trends in Ratings

We can also examine the progress of New World wines by looking at the overall ratings that they receive. We have accomplished this for our case studies and comparable cases by examining *Wine Spectator* ratings for each of them. *Wine Spectator* is the premier source of wine ratings in the industry. We include the first regular entry, showing the relative newness of the New World wineries as well as Australia's head start. We also calculate the number and proportion of wines that are rated 90 (outstanding) or greater. We see that Australia clearly has a higher proportion of highly ranked wines (almost one fifth), even greater than Old World power Spain, with Chile being the laggard. We also see signs of progress across the board in terms of the different New World locations' abilities to produce outstanding wines and thus create a reputation for quality, with Australia, Canada, and Africa showing remarkable improvement, albeit the latter two from a smaller number of wines rated. Italy, of course, is an Old World wine producer and so in a different category. It is interesting to note that Italy produces a stable proportion of wines rated above 90, despite the fact that it produces several times the number of wines as the others.

In short, we see that part of the answer clearly lies in the rapid improvement in the quality of wines by New World and emerging producers. In the next section, we trace out the emerging literature that has examined clusters in the wine industry, as a source of explanation for this development.

Clusters and Value Chains in the Wine Industry

There is a growing body of evidence in the literature that suggests that institutional arrangements may play a key role in explaining the competitiveness of the New vs Old World producers. Giuliani, Morrison, and Rabellotti's study (2011, 205) puts it bluntly: "Networks of private and public actors are key to learning and innovation." France and Germany have lost the greatest market share while Spain has held on.

Table 2.3
Comparing *Wine Spectator* ratings

Country	1st Entry Year	Total Entries	# > 90	Proportion	1990 Total	1990 # >90	1990 Proportion	2007 total	2007 # >90	2007 Proportion
Australia	1955	11,664	2,547	21.8%	161	13	8.1%	506	139	27.5%
Argentina	1977	3,746	467	12.5%	18	0	0.0%	505	84	16.6%
Canada	1989	424	51	12.0%	3	0	0.0%	25	8	32.0%
Chile	1979	5,487	343	6.3%	88	0	0.0%	434	42	9.7%
South Africa	1975	4,262	612	14.4%	41	0	0.0%	315	71	22.5%
Spain	1879	9,119	1,173	12.9%	134	9	6.7%	421	49	11.6%
Italy	1941	37,349	8,055	21.6%	850	168	19.8%	2050	451	22.0%

Source: Author calculations from *Wine Spectator* ratings database, accessed June 2010 and February 2011 (for Italy).

Castaldi, Cholette, and Hussain (2006b, 16) suggest that domestic markets there are saturated, that costs of production related to land and labour are higher, and that the lack of economies of scale are all factors based on economic differences. However, they also suggest that complex labelling and an inability to develop new production and marketing techniques and attract interest in terms of foreign investment are factors as well. While the AOC system (specifying regional terroirs with detailed techniques to be followed in order to claim such on a label) helps to boost the small producers who are thus able to control supply in France, it also constrains the ability to adjust and evolve wines in response to changes in the market. Furthermore, they suggest that there are too many AOC classifications that are confusing and have little effect on market power, that designations are often confusing, and that the regulatory maze governing techniques adds considerably to costs. By contrast, New World producers have a strong will to win export markets by paying close attention to consumer demands and setting clear objectives. Furthermore, their bid to succeed is aided by a consolidated industry structure that allows for resource-based advantages in finance and know-how as well as geographic and value and brand diversification, and a strong effort at public infrastructure, such as state promotion of marketing efforts (Gambel and Taddei 2007, 131–2, 135–6).

Innovation Institutions as Sources of Competitive Advantage

There is evidence that New World producers have paid more attention to innovation, which might explain their growth. Gwynne (2008) describes Chilean wine as follows (24): "The traditional style of Chilean winemaking was common as recently as the eighties. A chronic lack of investment together with an insular mentality meant that winemaking for many Chileans was a crude and haphazard business. Pressing was quick and brutal, fermentations were hot and short, maceration times were kept to a minimum for fear of bacterial spoilage and filtering was conducted as early and comprehensively as possible."

By contrast, in a survey of Brazilian wineries, 60% said that technology was below world standards, that wine was inadequately promoted and lacked quality reputation at the international level, and that government support is weak (Fensterseifer 2007). An analysis of Bulgarian winemaking suggests a lack of property rights, state support, and investment capital are all responsible for poor performance (Noev 2006).

The New World's growth has been reflected in increases in scientific publications on wine (Cusmano, Morrison, and Rabellotti 2009, 23). New World wines have created major industry innovations, such as using oak chips instead of oak barrels to impart deep flavour; using vacuum concentrators on the ripest grapes to enhance flavour and sugars; modifying acidity levels by adding tartaric or citric acid; and using powdered tannin to increase the body of red wines (Labys and Cohen 2006, 529). Aylward (2003, 25) is among those who suggest that innovation under capable institutions is a major factor in explaining the shift to New World wines. He points to the following examples:

- In California, the Californian Association of Winegrape Growers, the American Vineyard Foundation, the American Vintners Association (now Wine America) and UC Davis are all key institutions pushing for research and development and exports. Analysts suggest that California led the way in providing the first full-fledged scientific approach to viticulture (Cusmano, Morrison, and Rabellotti 2009, 22).
- In South Africa, a parallel role is played by the Nietvoobij Institute for Viticulture and Oenology, with 230 people, and linked to the University of Stellenbosch, the Elsenburg Agricultural College, the South African Wine Industry Trust (including government and business), the South African Wine Industry Information and Systems, and the South African Wine Institute.
- In Australia, R&D is coordinated by the Grape and Wine Research and Development Centre (GWRDC), the Australian Wine Research Institute, the Commonwealth Scientific and Industrial Research Centre, the Australian Wine and Brandy Corporation, the Co-operative Research Centre for Viticulture, state agricultural departments, and a host of universities. Research and development are collectively funded through a levy on grapes per ton (Marsh and Shaw 2000, 53).
- In New Zealand, the Wine Institute of New Zealand and the New Zealand Grape Growers council merged in 2002 to form New Zealand Winegrowers for both R&D and export.

Australia has by far been the most rapidly increasing exporter, far outpacing Chile (Wittwer 2007, 10–12), and thus is a particularly interesting case for understanding competitiveness. There is evidence that Australia's success is based on more successful institutionalisation. Australia's "Plan 2025" also pioneered the idea of a national strategy for success in wine markets, and helped to bring domestic players together (Marsh and Shaw 2000, 51). Aylward (2004, 438) suggests that the research of the GWRDC and the conscious development and orientation of the cluster towards exports are instrumental to Australia's success. As he states, operating within a cluster is itself an innovation, and success in innovation brings about a culture of innovation. In a comparison of France and Australia, Jordan, Zidda, and Lockshin (2007, 28) conclude that the French wine industry is "complex and divided," while Australia's more simple and permissive environment allows producers to be more "innovative and proactive." Collaboration in Australia is more extensive, reflecting consensus around a common "strategic orientation." Thus, industry support plays a "fundamental role in explaining success."

Wine Clusters Research

As we saw in chapter 1, cluster research emphasises the importance of an entrepreneurial core, tacit knowledge, and collective goods, as well as locational assets, in explaining the rise of clusters. The literature on wine clusters pushes the emphasis on institutions as sources of competitiveness even further. Those institutions are instrumental for innovation and upgrading. For example, an Inter-American Development Bank econometric study (Cerdán-Infantes, Maffioli, and Ubfal 2008) finds concrete and clear evidence that government agricultural extension services in Mendoza, Argentina, led to gains in both yields and quality, though the gains were unevenly distributed. As McDermott (2007b, 90) notes about the rapid improvement in Argentine wines' quality and export production:

This (Argentine) shift demanded new capabilities in coordinating multiple, continuous process and product experiments across a variety of organizations and microclimates. Increased wine value begins not simply with the adoption of new hard technology and fertilizers or with market and distribution but namely with transforming the middle and upstream segments of the value chain: state-of-the-art quality control and product development running from vine planting to careful vineyard maintenance to flawless harvests to vinification and blending. Enologists work closely with agronomists and growers to introduce and experiment with new modes of growing, pruning, sanitizing, and watering new and old varietals and clones of grapes. They then test, for instance, different types of indigenous yeasts and enzymes as well as methods of refrigeration, processing and storage to optimally ferment the wine and elicit the grape's flavors and aromas. Similar to codesign and co-benchmarking processes used in complex manufacturing, these actors develop new systems to carefully document practices and products, share the information, and evaluate the results over time and space. Because of the variation in climates, soils, varietals and clones, experimentation is contextualized, knowledge is often tacit, and dissemination is necessarily social and interactive, often demanding a complex network of vertical and horizontal ties among firms. Moreover, upgrading is highly time-consuming – any new vine takes 2–3 years to yield testable results and any quality and taste modification to grape growing can take 18–24 months.

In short, an innovation system in wine is in part geographically bound, as it must adapt to the tacit nature of knowledge oriented towards the particularities and changes of the wine terroir in question. McDermott builds upon the social networks literature to explain Argentine success in the wine industry. Echoing Burt, he underlines the importance of institutions as a source of "social and knowledge bridges across previously isolated producer communities" (McDermott, Corredoira, and Kruse, 2009, abstract). McDermott sees the importance of the public sector role as well. He states that "governments can reshape the structure and composition of organizational fields, and in turn, knowledge flows, by instigating the creation of new public-private institutions that recombine existing social and knowledge resources in new ways and at different levels of society" (McDermott, Corredoira, and Kruse, 2009, 1271). His case study comparisons of Mendoza and San Juan provinces attempt to show the social capital embedded in institutions and led by the public sector (government-supported institutions) explains their differential success. Such institutions lead to collective goods, including the development of tailored research and development leading to quality and production upgrading. McDermott states: "This shift in Argentina (towards exports and dramatic improvements in quality) came not simply from new technology or market access but mainly from firms' acquiring new capabilities in coordinating multiple, continuous process and product experiments across a variety of organizations and microclimates" (McDermott 2007, 110). Ultimately, his message is one of underscoring the importance of public-private partnerships.

Giuliani and Arza's 2009 comparison of university-industry linkages in Chile and Italy reaches some surprising conclusions. They find that university-industry links are much stronger in Chile. They also suggest that well-established firms and universities are effective, while relationships where either the partner is weak or the exchange ambiguous, are less effective (916–7). Giuliani, Morrison, and Rabellotti (2011, 204–6) note in their study of innovation in the sector that learning seems to occur when there are both formal and informal networks across both domestic and foreign producers, with New World producers engaging in tech transfer through a variety of methods, including international consultants, investments, and marketing systems.

However, the wine cluster research cautions us against any idealised view of a horizontal fluid matrix of entrepreneurial firms. Rather it notes a great deal of unevenness in substance and process. Giuliani's 2005 study of the Colchagua Valley of Chile revealed a high degree of variation in terms of the intensity of learning within a cluster (see also Olavarria et al. 2009). Most of the firms are export-oriented (162) and relationships with viticultural research centres based at the Catholic University, the University of Talca, and wine business associations all played key roles in technology transfer efforts (168–9). In her comparison (2007) of Italy and Chile, she further states that "firms with stronger KBS [knowledge bases] are indeed more likely to exchange innovation-related knowledge with other firms in the cluster...In contrast, when a cluster is populated almost exclusively by firms with particularly weak KBS, which have poor capabilities to both transfer and absorb knowledge, it seems plausible that the intra-cluster KN (knowledge network) will be poorly connected" (163). Thus, she establishes the importance of relative symmetry and reciprocity in terms of the overall healthy functionality of a cluster. She also suggests the importance of leading firms who act as "technological gatekeepers" (Giuliani and Bell 2005). These observations echo Gwynne's (2008, 21) note that in Chile 40% of exports (in value) are under the control of three firms: Concha y Toro, San Pedro, and Santa Rita.

Other studies cast doubt on whether success is really based on networks or simply a reflection of individual firms. Visser's 2004 report on Chilean wine concludes that collective activity of the cluster is incipient and that there are not high levels of social capital or trust (49). In a 2006 study of Chile, Moguillansky, Salas, and Cares suggest that the relations between the wineries and universities, and the public technological and innovation centres is weak, and that upgrading tends to be imitative of existing world technology (29). Visser and de Langen (2006) write in their study of Chile, "In sum, leader firm behaviour is not at all apparent in the Chilean wine industry, due to trust problems in co-operation efforts and individualistic attitudes in private-public interactions (192) ... Lack of intra-cluster co-operation did not hinder Chilean winemakers from joining global chains. Chilean winemakers started to export on the basis of their basic advantages and individual upgrading attempts, and only later through collectivized upgrading strategies" (195). These observations are backed up by Agosin and Bravo-Ortega's 2009 study of Chile that suggests 1–2 firms led the technological upgrading and other firms followed in imitative fashion, and that the key innovation events happened before the cluster institutions became active. A study of the Ontario wine cluster points to the leadership of a key firm, Inniskillin, and the personal ties between it and followers, in creating the recent success of icewines (Roberts and Sterling 2009).

Our brief survey of the wine industry emphasises a key theme, namely the wave of new producers who have successfully captured global market share primarily over the last two decades, and the parallel drop off of the dominant Old World producers. The premise of our study, that governance underlies competitiveness, is backed up by our review of key events in the evolution of global wine markets and the existing literature on wine competitiveness. In the following chapters, we examine in depth the ways in which governance affects the level of competitiveness of specific wine industries.

REFERENCES

Agosin, Manuel R. and Claudio Bravo-Ortega. 2009. "The Emergence of New Successful Export Activities in Latin America: The Case of Chile." Research Network Working Paper #R–552 (Feb). Washington, DC: Inter-American Development Bank.

Anderson, Kym. 2004. "Introduction." In *The World's Wine Markets: Globalization at Work,* edited by Kym Anderson, 3–13. Northampton, MA: Edward Elgar.

Aylward, David. 2006. "Innovation Lock-in: Unlocking Research and Development Path Dependency in the Australian Wine Industry." *Strategic Change* 15: 361–72.

– 2004. "Working Together: Innovation and Export Links Within Highly Developed and Embryonic Wine Clusters." *Strategic Change* 13: 429–39.

– 2003. "A Documentary of Innovation Support Among New World Wine Industries." *Journal of Wine Research* 14 (1): 31–43.

Banks, Glenn and John Overton. "2010. Old World, New World, Third World? Reconceptualising the Worlds of Wine." *Journal of Wine Research* 2010, 21(1): 57–75.

Bernetti, Iacopo, Leonardo Casini, and Nicola Marinelli. 2006. "Wine and Globalisation: Changes in the International Market Structure and the Position of Italy." *British Food Journal* 108 (4): 306–15.

Brosnan, Kathleen A. 2007. "'Vin d'Etat': Consumers, Land, and the State in California's Napa Valley." In *Wine, Society, and Globalization: Multidisciplinary Perspectives on the Wine Industry,* edited by Gwyn Campbell and Nathalie Guibert, 17–42. New York: Palgrave Macmillan.

Campbell, Gwyn and Nathalie Guibert. 2007. "Introduction: the History and Culture of Wine." In *Wine, Society, and Globalization: Multidisciplinary Perspectives on the Wine Industry,* edited by Gwyn Campbell and Nathalie Guibert, 1–16. New York: Palgrave Macmillan.

– 2006. "Introduction: Old World Strategies against New World Competition in a Globalising Wine Industry." *British Food Journal* 108 (4): 233–42.

Carrau, Francisco M. 1997. "The Emergence of a New Uruguayan Wine Industry." *Journal of Wine Research* Dec. 8 (3): 179–93.

Castaldi, Richard, Susan Cholette, and Mahmood Hussain. 2006b. "A Country-Level Analysis of Competitive Advantage in the Wine Industry." May. DEIAgra Working Papers WP-06–002. Dipartimento Di Economia e Ingegneria Agrarie: Universita di Bologna.

Cerdán-Infantes, Pedro, Alessandro Maffioli, and Diego Ubfal. 2008. "The

Impact of Agricultural Extension Services: The Case of Grape Production in Argentina." Office of Evaluation and Oversight Working Paper 0508. Washington, DC: Inter-American Development Bank.

Coelho, Alfredo Manuel and Jean-Louis Rastoin. 2006. "Financial Strategies of Multinational Firms in the World Wine Industry: An Assessment." *Agribusiness* 22 (3): 417–29.

Crowley, William K. 2000. "Chile's Wine Industry: Historical Character and Changing Geography." *Yearbook, Conference of Latin Americanist Geographers* 26: 87–101.

Cusmano, Lucia, Andrea Morrison, and Roberta Rabellotti. 2009. "Catching-up Trajectories in the Wine Sector: A Comparative Study of Chile, Italy and South Africa." *American Association of Wine Economists* Working Paper No. 34, www.wine-economics.org.

Duncan, Alan, and David Greenaway. 2008. "The Economics of Wine – Introduction." *The Economic Journal* 118 (June): 137–41.

Euromonitor International. 2010. *Global Wine: Challenges and Opportunities Facing the Wine Industry.* May. London: Euromonitor.

– 2008. *Country Watch: Exports a Key Growth Strategy for Latin American Wine Producers.* June 16. London: Euromonitor.

FAO. Agricultural Statistics. http://faostat.fao.org

Fensterseifer, Jaime Evaldo. 2007. "The Emerging Brazilian Wine Industry: Challenges and Prospects for the Serra Gaúcha Wine Cluster." *International Journal of Wine Business Research* 19 (3): 187–206.

Gamble, Paul R. and Jean-Claude Taddei. 2007. "Restructuring the French Wine Industry: The Case of the Loire." *Journal of Wine Research* 18 (3): 125–45.

Giuliani, Elisa. 2007a. "The Selective Nature of Knowledge Networks in Clusters: Evidence from the Wine Industry." *Journal of Economic Geography* 7: 139–68.

– 2007b. "The Wine Industry: Persistence of Tacit Knowledge." *International Journal of Technology and Globalisation* 3 (2–3): 138–54.

– 2005. "Technological Learning in a Chilean Wine Cluster and its Linkages with the National System of Innovation." In *Clusters Facing Competition: The Importance of External Linkages,* edited by Elisa Giuliani, Roberta Rabellotti and Meie Pieter van Dijk, 155–76. Burlington, VT: Ashgate.

Giuliani, Elisa and Valeria Arza. 2009. "What Drives the Formation of 'Valuable' University-Industry Linkages? Insights from the Wine Industry." *Research Policy* 38: 906–21.

Giuliani, Elisa and Martin Bell. 2005. "The Micro-determinants of Meso-level Learning and Innovation: Evidence From a Chilean Wine Cluster." *Research Policy* 34: 47–68.

Giuliani, Elisa, Andrea Morrison, and Roberta Rabellotti, eds. 2011. *Innovation and Technological Catch-up: The Changing Geography of Wine Production.* Northampton, MA: Edward Elgar.

Gwynne, Robert N. 2008. "Firm Creation, Firm Evolution and Clusters in Chile's Dynamic Wine Sector: Evidence from the Colchagua and Casablanca Regions." American Association of Wine Economists Working Paper 20 (Aug): AAWE.

Heien, D. and E.N. Sims. 2000. "The Impact of the Canada-United States Free Trade Agreement on U.S. Wine Exports." *American Journal of Agricultural Economics* 82 (1): 173–82.

Hussain, Mahmood, Susan Cholette, and Richard M. Castaldi. 2007. "An Analysis of Globalization Forces in the Wine Industry: Implications and Recommendations for Wineries." *Journal of Global Marketing* 21: 33–47.

Jenster, Per V., David E. Smith, Darryl J. Mitry, and Lars V. Jenster. 2008. *The Business of Wine: A Global Perspective.* Copenhagen: Copenhagen Business School Press.

Johnson, Hugh. 1989. *Vintage: The Story of Wine.* Toronto: Simon and Schuster.

Jordan, Rohan, Pietro Zidda, and Larry Lockshin. 2007. "Behind the Australian Wine Industry's Success: Does Environment Matter?" *International Journal of Wine Business Research* 19 (1): 14–32.

Labys, Walter C. and Bruce C. Cohen. 2006. "Trends Versus Cycles in Global Wine Export Shares." *The Australian Journal of Agricultural and Resource Economics* 50 (52): 7–37.

Marsh, Ian and Brendan Shaw. 2000. "Australia's Wine Industry: Collaboration and Learning as Causes of Competitive Success." May. Working paper.

McDermott, Gerald A. 2007. "The Politics of Institutional Renovation and Economic Upgrading: Recombining the Vines the Bind in Argentina." *Politics and Society* 35 (1): 103–43.

– 2007b. "The Politics of Institutional Renovation and Economic Upgrading: Lessons from the Argentinian Wine Industry." In *Can Latin American Firms Compete?*, edited by Robert Grosse and Luiz F. Mesquita, 81–124. New York: Oxford University Press.

McDermott, Gerald A., Rafael A. Corredoira, and Gregory Kruse. 2009. "Public-Private Institutions as Catalysts of Upgrading in Emerging Market Societies." *Academy of Management Journal* 52 (6):127–96.

Mitry, Darryl J., David E. Smith, and Per V. Jenster. 2009. "China's Role in Global Competition in the Wine Industry: A New Contestant And Future Trends." *International Journal of Wine Research* 1: 19–25.

Moguillansky, Graciela, Juan Carlos Salas, and Gabriela Cares. 2006. *Capacidad de Inovación en Industrias Exportadoras de Chile: la Industria del Vino y la Agroindustria Hortofrutícola*. Serie Comercio Internacional no. 79. Santiago, Chile: CEPAL.

Noev, Nivelin. 2006. "The Bulgarian Wine Sector: Policy Issues and Implications after 15 Years of Transition." *Journal of Wine Research* 17 (2): 73–93.

Olavarría, Jaime A., Mauricio García, Christian Felzenstein, Cristian Monsalvez, and Yerko Moreno. 2009. "Innovative Performance and Networking in Wine Clusters in Central South Chile." Conference paper, FIRB–RISC Research and Entrepreneurship in the Knowledge-Based Economy Conference, Sept 7–8, 2009, Bocconi University, Milan, Italy.

Paul, Harry W. 1991. *Science, Vine, and Wine in Modern France*. New York: Cambridge University Press.

Phillips, Roderick. 2001. *A Short History of Wine*. New York: Ecco.

Porter, Michael E. and Gregory C. Bond. 2004. *The California Wine Cluster*. Harvard Business School case no. 9–799–124. March 17.

Resnick, Evelyne. 2008. *Wine Brands: Success Strategies for New Markets, New Consumers and New Trends*. New York: Palgrave Macmillan.

Roberts, Peter W. and Adina D. Sterling. "Network Progeny? Pre-founding Social Ties and New Entrant Success in Emerging Regions." Preliminary draft paper, Oct. 2009.

Schamel, Günter. 2006. "Geography Versus Brands in a Global Wine Market." *Agribusiness* 22 (3): 363–74.

Smith, Keith. 2007. "Technological and Economic Dynamics of the World Wine Industry: an Introduction." *International Journal of Technology and Globalisation* 3 (2/3): 127–37.

Stein, Steve. 2007. "Grape Wars: Quality in the History of Argentine Wine." In *Wine, Society, and Globalization: Multidisciplinary Perspectives on the Wine Industry*, edited by Gwyn Campbell and Nathalie Guibert, 99–118. New York: Palgrave Macmillan.

Vergara, Sebastián. 2001. "El Mercado Vitivinícola Mundial y el Flujo de Inversion Extranjera a Chile." Serie Desarrollo Productivo 102. Santiago: CEPAL.

Vine, Richard P. 1981. *Commercial Winemaking: Processing and Controls*. Westport: AVI.

Visser, Evert-Jan. 2004. "A Chilean Wine Cluster? Governance and Upgrading in the Phase of Internationalization." Serie Desarrollo Productivo no. 156. Santiago: CEPAL.

Visser, Evert-Jan and Peter de Langen. 2006. "The Importance and Quality of Governance in the Chilean Wine Industry." *GeoJournal* 65:177–97.

Weaver, Robert J. 1976. *Grape Growing.* New York: John Wiley and Sons.

Wikipedia. 2009. "History of Wine." Accessed November 20, 2009, www.wikipedia.org.

Wittwer, Glyn. 2007. "The Global Wine Market in the Decade to 2015 with a Focus on Australia and Chile." Centre of Policy Studies and the Impact Project. General Working Paper No. G–166. July. Clayton, Victoria: Monash University.

3

The Wine Industry in British Columbia:
A Closed Wine But Showing Potential

ANIL HIRA AND ALEXIS BWENGE

INTRODUCTION

This chapter is based on a 2009–10 study of the competitiveness of the British Columbia, Canada (BC) wine industry. Though the BC industry has recently had remarkable success, we focus on issues on the horizon that threaten the possibilities for growth and stability in the industry. The analysis is based on the application of industrial cluster theory focusing on the four factors laid out in chapter 1: firm adaptability to market evolution, policy interventions, social networks, and coordination of local and global supply chains. The analysis relies upon original data gathered by Anil Hira via fifty-three interviews and surveys with winemakers and suppliers in the Okanagan during the spring and summer of 2010. These were supplemented by the creation of a database on wineries in the region, as well as input from experts in the industry.

Our suggestion in chapter 1 – that industry competitiveness depends on policies that guide and aid firm adaptation to markets, institutions, networks, and supply chains – is borne out by the case of BC. We focus on the area with the greatest concentration of wineries in BC, the Okanagan Valley (OKV). Our approach focuses on the potential role of public and collective support institutions to promote industry competitiveness in clusters. Our analysis reveals the validity of an evolutionary view of the role of such institutions, reflecting recent work that concludes that a successful public-private partnership requires continual adaptation to changes in markets (Hira, Wixted, and Arechavala 2012. We can reject the false dichotomy that prevails that either markets (private companies) or states (governments) determine economic success. Productive public-private interactions are fundamental to successful industries. The nature of public-private partnerships is also important – they need to be responsive, flexible, and proactive.

THE RECENT CREATION OF THE OKV WINE INDUSTRY: POLICY RESPONSES TO MARKET EVOLUTION[1]

The preconditions for viticulture exist in BC, however, conditions alone are unable to explain the development of the BC industry. We demonstrate in this section that policy responses ultimately guided the industry to its present level of success.

Early Winemaking in BC: Limited in Quantity and Quality

Lake Okanagan and the presence of a suitable range of mesoclimates make the south central Okanagan Valley (OKV) an attractive location for viticulture. The OKV stretches far, about 155 km from north to south, but is only about 9–16 km in width. In addition, a grape-growing region in the south from east to west, from Osoyoos to Princeton, principally the Similkameen Valley, spans an additional 100 km. Over 90% of BC's tree fruit acreage and 95% of its grapes are grown in the OKV. The Cowichan Valley on Vancouver Island, and the Fraser Valley just east of Vancouver, the other main areas for wine production, have about 50 hectares of vines as opposed to over 9,000 in the OKV. The BC Wine Institute's "2009 BC Crop Survey" indicates that 96.35% of all BC wine is produced in the OKV.

Early wine was reportedly made from loganberries grown at Saanich on Vancouver Island and in the Fraser Valley. Early varieties of grapes in BC, as in the rest of Canada, were native (primarily Labrusca), rather than European ones, because of a perceived need for frost-hardiness. In the 1920s, J.W. Hughes, an immigrant from Iowa, began growing commercial grapes and started Pioneer Vineyard. His fruit operations were to evolve into the giant Sun-Rype Products (Nichol 1983, 129). Fruit growers began to produce wine as a side business in the 1930s, including importing vinifera grapes from the US for blending with Labruscas. The taste of the early wine was considered poor, so much of the early wine was fortified into port or sherry for drinkability (Schreiner 2000, 8). By 1960, the total planted area for grapes in BC was just 572 acres (Select Standing Committee 1978, 44–5).

Policy Efforts Create A Local Industry

Policy initiatives by the provincial government from the early 1960s focused on developing the local grape industry as a key supplier, as part of a new ambition to create a BC wine industry. Given his roots in the industry, it is not surprising that W.A.C. Bennett, then premier of the province, pushed for local sourcing of grapes, a seeming quid pro quo for the government's role in distributing wineries' products (Ross 1995, 33). As a result, the British Columbia Liquor Control and Licensing Board (BCLCB) sought to increase the local use of grapes in the wine industry, increasing the required quota from 25% to 50% in 1962, and up to 65% in 1965. The results were impressive, with grape acreage increasing by 400% in BC by 1967, and the average local grape content of wine increasing to 81%, finally settling at 80% in 1969 (known as the 80/20 rule). The end result was greater vertical integration between wineries and local suppliers and movement towards long-term contracts. At the same time, it increased pressure for improved quality of grapes, as wineries had to shift from their previous dependence on higher-quality American grapes (Adams 1992, 28; Kingsbury 2004, 3).

While these initial policies were successful in establishing the industry, the general orientation of both the BC and Ontario vineyards was towards mass production of low cost, high-alcohol-content wines to serve local markets, called "jug" or "plonk" wine. In both places, a highly regulated oligopoly of a few large firms characterized industry structure (Hickton and Padmore 2005, 86–7; Select Standing Committee 1978, 16–17). BC grape supply was grown exclusively in the OKV; the 1978 Standing Committee report estimates that 43% of the total provincial acreage of 3,000 acres was in and around the OKV. Regulatory protection that had existed de facto since World War II, in the sense that few imported table wines were listed in BC liquor stores, began to dissipate in 1974 as the listing of imported wines grew (Schreiner 2000, 8). Furthermore, a crisis of overproduction of grapes in the late 1970s led to more active provincial and industry efforts to improve grape varieties in order to expand a viable wine industry in line with changing tastes (Select Standing Committee 1978, xix). At the same time, consumer attitudes towards wine were beginning to change, with a new generation demanding more but higher quality wine with less emphasis on alcohol content (Select Standing Committee 1978, xxviii). These wines were known as "mod" or "pop" wines in that they had low alcohol and carbonation (similar to what we call wine coolers now) (Miles 1981, 1). This led to a rise in import shares from 15% in 1970 to 31% by 1977 (Select Standing Committee 1978, 31), pushing the government and industry to adjust.

Typical of infant industries, early improvement focused more on cosmetic upgrades than more challenging forms of upgrading. Early responses to the new market demand included packaging improvements, such as changing labeling and moving to European style bottling and corks (Select Standing Committee 1978, 33). Such efforts coincided with the growth of capacity to produce quality wine based in good part on a limited series of agricultural projects from the late 1960s and 1970s, including the planting of Johannisberg Riesling. The industry in BC transitioned at this time towards the production of Baby Duck champagne, in response to changes in the local market towards less sweet and lower alcohol content wine (Schreiner 2000, 8; Hickton 2005, 7).

Policy Struggles To Support Upgrading from the 1970s

Recognising the success of the early industry, policy began to respond with longer-term initiatives towards upgrading. The roots for long-term change lay in 1974 when the Canadian federal government purchased 4000 vinifera vines[2] and conducted an agro-experiment at eighteen different sites across BC (BC Wine Institute 2010). In 1975, George Heiss Sr, the owner of Gray Monk, began working with Helmut Becker, a legendary director of wine research in Germany's Geisenheim Institute, to test the ability to adapt vinifera to the OKV, testing close to fifty varieties (Riesling, Gewurztraminer, Pinot Blanc, and a Rotberger that led to a true Rosé). According to some informants, this came on the heels of an earlier experiment with Inkameep. The experiment lasted over eight years in two spots (in north and south Okangan) and developed the varieties that "have become the industry's backbone" (Schreiner 2000, 9; Hickton 2005, 74).

The lack of coordination between vineyards and growers led to overproduction of grapes, an inability to improve quality, reduced usage of European varieties, and poor locations. This created some consternation about the role of the BC Grape Marketing Board. The Marketing Board derived from the rapid increase in grape cultivation and production, from 1,100 tons in 1958 to 10,000 in 1972, as tree fruit planters switched over, partly in response to growing demand by wineries. The BC Grape Growers Association had interlinked members with the BC Tree Fruit Marketing Board, so they knew from experience that such boards could regulate the industry. Therefore they set up a marketing board with the permission of the government in 1970. The Marketing Board created standard prices per ton by variety of grape each year. However, in an odd twist, growers registered with the Board prior to 1977 received Class A licenses for existing acreage, meaning wineries were obliged to buy their grapes first, even if they were of the Labrusca variety. The Marketing Board created fierce resistance among wineries who lost their ability to individually negotiate with growers, and thus, they claimed, to establish long-term relationships aimed at improving quality. These issues reflected an overall conclusion that grape and labour costs would price BC wines above imports without drastic change (Ross 1995, 32).

In 1976, import agents formed a forty-two-member lobbying association to deal with the provincially run Liquor Distribution Board. This led the wineries to utilize the BC Wine Council (est. 1974) to promote their product, begin to generate statistics about the industry, develop better relationships with the grape growers, and lobby the government (Select Standing Committee 1978, 37, 69). By 1980, the wine industry was in full crisis, with none of the wineries reporting a profit that year (Miles 1981, 2). From 1970–80, imported wine sales increased over 500%, and by 1988 imported wine sales accounted for 53% of all wine sales in BC. At the same time, sales increases were preponderantly in white wines, leading to a surplus of red grapes (Adams 1992, 20). The BC wineries won the day, and key changes were made to market regulations that further spurred the industry, including (Senate Standing Committee 1978, 38–9):

• reducing the mark-up on BC wines containing under 14% alcohol from 66 to 46% while lowering the mark-up on imported wines from 117% to 100%; .

- banning new imports that retailed under $2.75;
- creating minimum volumes and standard sizes in order to be permitted to sell;
- creating shelf space for local products;
- allowing more frequent ads;
- permitting for the first time retail sales at the winery; and
- preventing sales at grocery stores (which might lead to a downgrading of product or less shelf space for local producers who were smaller).

The changes followed from a 1978 provincial law that allowed for the establishment of small-scale wineries. Liquor Board mark-ups for them were set at 15% for sales in Liquor Board stores and 0% for direct sales to customers and licensees. The idea was to build estate wineries around the prescribed guidelines, a precursor to the VQA system we discuss below (Miles 1981, 6–9). These steps were closely tied to an idea of an agri-tourism basis for the industry. The already existing bounty of skiing, hiking, golf, and beaches provided the conditions to make the OKV a world-class tourism spot. The original idea, then, was that the wineries would combine forces with the fruit stands, including pick your own, country markets, etc., to provide a bucolic experience for urban tourists (Hackett 1998, 57–8).

In short, the industry and the government consciously worked to lay out the pre-conditions for the transformation of a low-value, low quality production structure to one that could improve considerably and charge higher prices through a combination of upgrading and protection, with emphasis on estate wineries that could improve quality. As can be seen from the above events, there was no "road map" for these efforts, rather policies were experimental at first, then responded to market events in evolutionary fashion.

The result of successful experimentation was the foundation, between 1977 and 1982, of now-leading Canadian estate wineries Sumac Ridge, Cedar Creek (formerly Uniake), Mission Hill, and Gray Monk, as well as Claremont Estate Winery, Vinitera (reorganised in 1984 as Okanagan Vineyards), and Divino. Moreover, 1979 saw the introduction of French vinifera varieties. Despite these significant advances the OKV wine cluster remained a relative backwater, with a mere thirteen wineries of inconsequential size. In 1988, the estate wineries produced 627,536 L, accounting for 2% of wine sales in BC.

Nonetheless, these same wineries laid the foundation for future success and demonstrated the efficacy of public-private partnership in the incipient stages of wine industry development (Hickton 2005, 74; Adams 1992, 13–14).

Industry Transformation through Policy
Spurred by Free Trade Agreements in the 1990s

Though the usefulness of public-private networking is notable at this stage it did not constitute evidence of a conscious effort to establish an industrial cluster until after the ratification of the Canada–US Free Trade Agreement (cusfta), the precursor for the North American Free Trade Agreement in 1989. In fact, the precursor of the transformation to free trade occurred in 1987, when a gatt panel supported the European Community's suggestion that provincial liquor boards were unfairly marking up wines (Kingsbury 2004, 3). The decision marked the start of a new era, one that would require more direct competition with imports. The view for the bc industry was quite pessimistic at the time, with one analyst stating that the ruling and agreement "have left the bc wine industry vulnerable and unable to compete" (Adams 1992, 2, 6).

The immediate result of the movement towards free trade was a shake-up in the relationships between wineries and grape growers. Many of the wineries cancelled their contracts with grape growers, invoking a *force majeure* clause in light of the loss of 50% of the preferential mark-up – fourteen months after cusfta went into effect (Kingsbury 2004, 38). Commercial wineries were freed from the 80/20 rule and allowed unlimited access to US grapes, while the rules for estate wineries stayed the same. Market share for bc wines fell from 60% in 1988 to 48% in 1991 (Adams 1992, 75, 78).

The signing of cusfta resulted in increased market pressure to raise quality standards and there was a broad concern in the Canadian viticulture industry that wine from the Napa Valley could come to dominate the domestic market. Of foremost concern was the phase-out of a price advantage for bc wines. Previously, bc wines had a 50% mark-up before sale vs 110% for imported wines; cusfta meant a phase out of this price advantage, gradually over ten years (Hickton 2005, 10).

The crisis brought bc wineries, grape growers, and the government together for extensive consultations on what to do. On September 21,

1989, the BC Cabinet established the Premium Wine Industry Strategy
to rigorously raise quality standards in an effort to save the industry
(Adams 1992, 79–80). The strategy was consummated in the British
Columbia Wine Act (Bill 58–1990), which laid out the regulatory
groundwork for the transformation of the industry. This bill set up
the guidelines for the BC Wine Institute (BCWI), appellation standards,
and the Vintner's Quality Alliance (VQA), which the BC provincial
government adopted to ensure that all wines labeled as BC wines were
made from grapes grown in the province and had passed a critical or
sensory standard to ensure quality. The creation of a standards system
was augmented by a $28 million grant from the Canadian federal
government, called the Grape and Wine Sector Adjustment Assistance Program (GWSAAP), to provide $8,100 per acre to growers who
removed the old Labrusca varieties in favour of European vinifera
varieties. In fact, $27 million went to pay grape growers to uproot
their vines and exit the business. As a result, the number of growers
dropped from 225 to 90, and 2,308 acres of hybrid and Labrusca
grapes were removed (BC Wine Institute 2010; Kingsbury 2004, 38–9).

The VQA (Vintner's Quality Alliance) was the first conscious effort
to establish a standards system and unite the OKV wine industry under
one brand. In the 1990s, the new developments attracted a large
number of new small wineries who could take advantage of the VQA
label and the realisation that climate did not prevent the production
of high quality wines (Hickton and Padmore 2005, 87). A number of
the smaller grape growers transformed themselves into farm wineries,
with estate wineries aiding in terms of providing supplies in smaller
quantities than commercially available (Kingsbury 2004, 39). A rush
of investment from eastern Canadian and international companies
from the late 1990s sent land prices soaring (Hickton 2005, 12). A
1994 economic study of the industry reported a remarkable transformation – with revenues and profits increasing significantly from
1988, and with estate wineries growing by 66% in revenues over the
same period (Ross 1995, 61).

The GWSAAP program also gave $1 million to help establish and
finance the BC Wine Institute for five years, from 1990 to 1995. The
original head of the BCWI was also the founding Chairman of the
BCEWA. The BCWI was launched in 1990 by nineteen founding members and the Ministry of Agriculture, Food, and Fisheries (MAFF)
(Adams 1992, 80). The 1990 Act gave multiple roles and responsibili-

ties to the BCWI, including setting standards for testing, labeling, and advertising; the ability to raise levies upon membership; promotion and marketing; and R&D and the development of a database of information. At this time, all wineries considered it a legal obligation to join the BCWI (Kingsbury 2004, 54). The early impression of the BCWI's VQA and marketing efforts seems uniformly positive, as information about quality spread throughout the BC market (Kingsbury 2004, 61–3).

EMERGING SUPPORT INSTITUTIONS   While there are the beginnings of a set of support institutions for the emerging cluster, they are still in the nascent stage.

REGULATORY BODIES   The main regulatory bodies for the wine industry in BC are the Liquor Control and Licensing Branch, that controls where and how alcohol is consumed; the Liquor Distribution Branch, that controls the supply; and the new BC Wine Authority. The regulatory system has a strong element of protection for local industry. The BC Wine Authority was set up in 2005 to take over the wine standards and tasting part of the VQA program from the BC Wine Institute (which still controls the marketing side). It has a three-member board and a chair that are independent and that conduct taste tests and ensure that regulatory standards in the production of BC VQA wine are met. Following is a description of the key support institutions.

PACIFIC AGRI-FOOD RESEARCH CENTRE (PARC)   PARC is a federal agency located in Summerland and conducts research on tree fruits and grapes. Wine research topics at PARC include fruit and wine quality, pest and disease management, environmental physiology (which they state includes nutrients, water relations, and response to climate), and biochemistry of fruit and wine. PARC has received support from the BC Wine Grape Council and the BC Wine Institute in the past for research.

BC WINE INSTITUTE   The Institute was established in 1990 by an act of the BC legislature, reflecting a desire for the public and private sectors to collaborate towards developing a competitive wine industry. The aforementioned project of replacing existing grapes with vinifera varieties started the work. The current functions are marketing and research, with a focus on VQA wines. BCWI also appoints members of the VQA stores. Members pay a levy so that they have a direct input into activities and the research agenda. Other services are provided on a fee per service basis. Members gain access for their products to nineteen VQA stores, marketing efforts, and learning opportunities.

OKANAGAN WINE FESTIVAL SOCIETY (OKWS)   This group grew in the 1980s to promote the wine industry. In 1994, a spring wine festival was started, and in 2002 a summer festival. The OKWS has helped to promote quality improvements in the industry by bringing in international judges to their festival competitions.

BC WINE GRAPE COUNCIL   The BC Wine Grape Council was formed as a research body to replace the BCWI Research and Development Committee, which no longer had funds to continue. The Council was set up through an industry-wide referendum (Collings 2011). Funds come entirely from members who pay in equal amounts, with a budget of less than $5,000 in 2004. The Council traditionally met at PARC or one of its members (Kingsbury 2004, 114–15). The Council has a research and development committee and now hosts its own annual conference.

MINISTRY OF AGRICULTURE, FOOD AND FISHERIES (MAFF)   There is currently only one employee from MAFF involved in the industry, and he covers both grape and fruits. He spends most of his time on R&D and other industry boards.

UNIVERSITY OF BRITISH COLUMBIA (UBC)   UBC has a wine research centre devoted to grape and wine research in Vancouver, including scientific studies of both grape growing and winemaking. There is a second campus, UBC Okanagan, located in Kelowna, where research also takes place, and which offers technical training courses.

OKANAGAN COLLEGE   Okanagan College, with its primary campus in Penticton, offers wine-assistant and related courses for training.

OTHERS   There are numerous groups in the OKV that seem to have informal lives (and occasional deaths) of their own. Notable are the smaller sub-regional ones discussed below.

CURRENT MARKET CHALLENGES:
FIRM AND POLICY RESPONSES

As described above, market changes and policy responses precipitated the growth and evolution of the okv winemaking industry. While comparative advantage allows for the making of wine, changes were necessary in the policy environment to create an industry. The first key set of policies were government protection of local grape growing and wine industries. The second set of policies, precipitated by market changes as well as the Canadian government entering into a free trade agreement with the us, was focused on upgrading. Policies in this case included a downgraded but still important element of protection, massive investment in creating estate wineries of high quality, and tourism promotion. One scientist interviewed also suggested that climate change allowed for the cultivation of vinifera grapes in several areas previously deemed too cold. The fruits of these efforts are remarkable success in both the proliferation and revenues of the industry, and the okv has the makings of a quiet gold rush.

A large expansion of the industry took place as industrial giants (such as Vincor) and institutional investors noted the growth and bought up properties. In addition, a large number of interviewees highlighted the wide scale conversion of fruit farmers into grape growers and grape growers starting their own wineries (with some fruit growers bypassing the intermediate step). There are also strikingly large numbers of winery owners who come to the business with no background in the industry, not necessarily to strike it rich but out of a passion for wine. Many interviewees described the dedication that has led them to invest their life savings in the idyllic dream of running a winery and vineyard.

In 2011, there were rumours of many (up to 30) wineries being put up for sale, including one long-time family business with several wineries declaring bankruptcy. And there is certainly a gradual recognition by entrants about the arduous and tempestuous nature of the business. Several interviewees remarked that it is really more like farming than winemaking, and subject to all the volatilities (weather, pests, disease, etc.) of that occupation. One interviewee, coming from the financial sector, remarked, "I've never worked so hard in my life. I

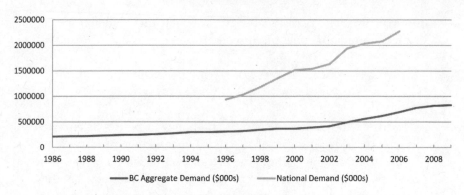

Figure 3.1   Growth in BC and national demand
Source: *Annual Survey of Manufacturers* by Statistics Canada

had no idea it was going to be this labour-intensive." This has led several of the smaller wineries, as well as a growing proportion of absentee investors, to hire consultants to run their wineries.

Demand and Supply Trends

The long-term growth of the Canadian wine industry, as a national marketplace, is clearly established by figure 3.1.

Annual Survey of Manufacturers by Statistics Canada

Evidently, the average consumption of wine increased substantially over time, with an increase in the national average consumption between 1983–95 of 3.36 litres per adult, according to Hope-Ross (2006). The boost can be attributed to changing consumer trends influenced by an increased quality of wines resulting from greater availability of US wines as a result of CUSFTA.

BC supply has followed the positive trajectory of demand as demonstrated in figure 3.2.

The BC Wine Institute puts the value of the 2009 grape crop at C$40,205,170. The growth in annual VQA wine sales between 1992 and 2010, from $6.8 million to $182.1 million, indicates the increased importance of the provincial and domestic market for BC wines (Schreiner 1992; BWI 2010). The VQA system's ability to improve quality likely helped to push overall gains in sales. By 2007 BC VQA wines represented

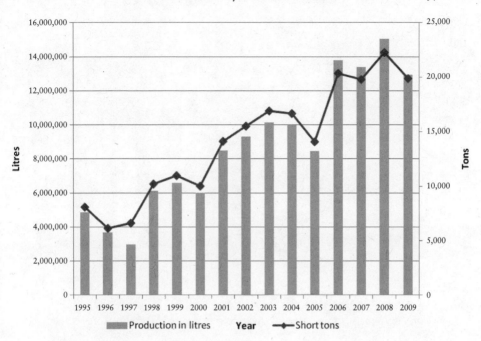

Figure 3.2   BC upward supply trends
Source: B.C. Wine Institute: http://www.winebc.com/quickfacts.php. Accessed
Jan. 25, 2011; short ton=2,000 lbs.

19.9% of total BC wine sales and Canadian wines as a whole represented
42.4% of total BC wine sales (BC Wine Institute 2007). The increasing success of the industry is corroborated by increases in acreage of vinifera
grapes, tonnage yields, and value of the yields. Notable is the increase
over a short period of time and the extent of the growth primarily occurring in the OKV, regardless of the size of the winery.

Market Saturation

Undoubtedly, phenomenal growth in demand has fuelled the BC wine
industry's remarkable expansion in the last two decades.
     Figure 3.4 below, based on our constructed database of information
about Okanagan wineries, demonstrates the acceleration in the creation of new wineries, especially after the post-CUSFTA adjustment program in the OKV itself.

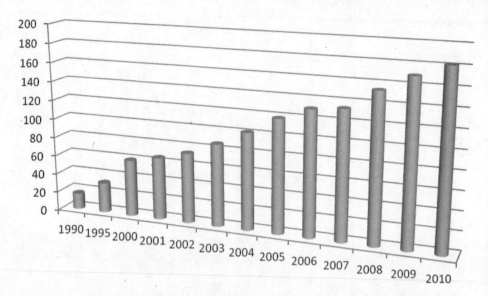

Figure 3.3   Number of wineries in BC, 1990–2010
Source: BC Wine Institute: http://www.winebc.com/quickfacts.php. Accessed Jan.
25, 2011.

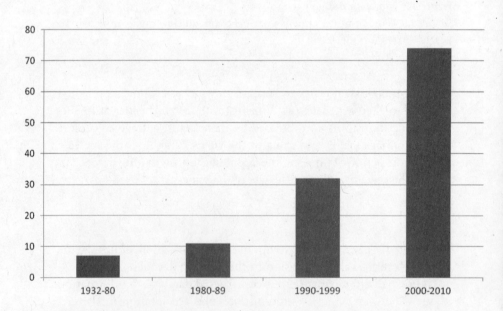

Figure 3.4   Increasing number of wineries founded in the Okanagan
Notes: Author calculations from own database; total datapoints = 125; updated
as of June 2010

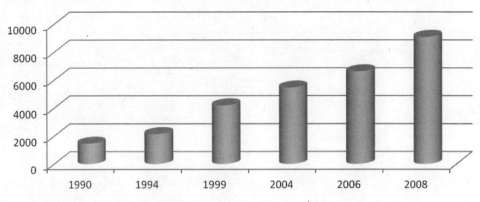

Figure 3.5   BC grape acreage, 1990–2008
Source: BC Wine Institute: http://www.winebc.com/quickfacts.php. Accessed Jan. 25, 2011.

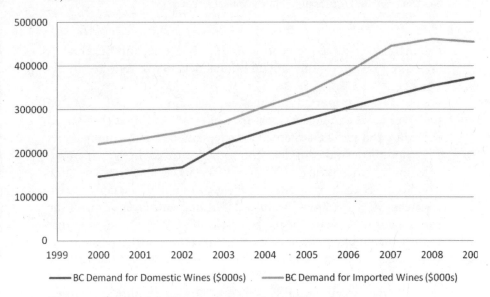

Figure 3.6   Demand for imports outpaces demand for BC wines
Source: BC Liquor Distribution Branch Annual Reports.

These trends are matched by phenomenal increases in grape acreage in the province, as demonstrated by figure 3.5.

It is important to note, furthermore, that increases in demand have been spread through both domestic and imported supply, with imported wines experiencing a higher rate of increase.

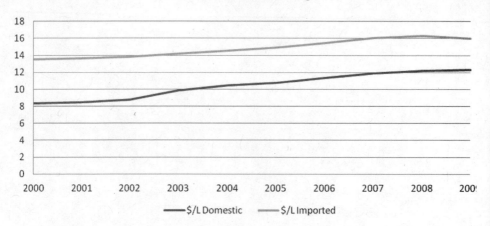

Figure 3.7   Imported wines fetch a premium vs BC wines
Source: BC Liquor Distribution Branch Annual Reports.

If increases in price and quality continue to evolve, imported brands are more likely to capture this additional demand, as reflected in figure 3.7.

Interviewees reported positive recent results – 52% reported increases in revenues over 2009–10, while 21% said that they stayed the same, and just 12% claimed a decrease. While some interviewees were optimistic and confident about the future of the BC wine market, most were sceptical that it can continue its current pace. The question becomes, then, at what point the growth will decelerate or reach a plateau. Since the Lower Mainland (Greater Vancouver) remains the sole anchor of demand for the BC wine industry, any changes in that market, including a likely economic slowdown in the near future, must affect the positive trajectory of growth, and with it the fortunes of the myriad new wineries. Obviously, demand growth has natural limits by the overall size of the Vancouver market; a number of interviewees opine that supply is already beginning to surpass demand. The result will be ramped up competition. While the attractive result for consumers will be lower prices and improved quality, the large number of entrants in the "boutique category," catering towards small market niches of customers willing to pay higher prices, suggests that some shakeout is likely to occur. A large number of interviewees agreed with this general premise, though they each thought that their own products could distinguish themselves enough to thrive.

Increasing Costs of Land and Inputs

A particular challenge within the industry, related to demand slow-down or demand plateau, is that business plans for the new wave of wineries are based on the present revenue stream. In fact, the cost of land has risen astronomically in the okv, meaning that the capital burden of most of the wineries in the okv, established over the last decade, has risen accordingly.

One industry source states, "The growers of the day sold their properties after taking the $8,100/acre subsidy and bailed out. Good vineyard properties sold in the early 1990s for as low as $2,000/acre. By 1993/94 the price had increased to just over $4,000/acre for raw vineyard land. In 2002 the price in the south okv had increased to about $40,000/acre (planted). It peaked in 2008 at about $120,000/acre (planted) but has settled back now to an estimated $80,000–$90,000/acre (planted)." A real estate agent in the Valley states that winery and vineyard prices rose constantly from 1992–2004, then dropped from 2005–07. An influx of Albertan money "willing to purchase at any price" was responsible for the rapid inflation. However, there are signs that the bubble is bursting. Oliver and Naramata land prices are now half ($90,000 and $100,000/acre respectively) of what they were at their peak in 2004. According to this source, those who bought property in the 1990s are generally "ok," having had time to establish brands when the market was expanding. New entrants to the market (from 2006) are "in trouble," however.

Most wineries in the Okanagan are quite small, making cost reduction challenging; 45% of our sample owned less than 20 acres. Yet, surprisingly few interviewees complain about a lack of access to finance. This may reflect the thus far propitious conditions both in terms of market forces and growing conditions over the last decade. Indeed, the 7–8 year preparation time of the vineyard, and the likely even longer lead time to establishing a brand reputation, along with the quite low volumes of production of the majority of the wineries in the okv, and the reliance on outside management teams and consultants, bring into question how many can thrive or even survive over the long run. The logical response to market saturation would be to improve quality and to seek out new markets. In the rest of the paper, we discuss why such an adjustment will be extremely challenging without changes to the industry and to government policy. The end

Table 3.1
Increasing geographic spread of wineries in the OKV

Year	Lake Country	Kelowna	Summerland	Penticton	Ok Falls	Oliver	Osoyoos	Cawston	Total
1932–80	1	2	2		1	1			7
1980–89		3	2	1	2	2		1	11
1990–99		6	2	10	2	11		1	32
2000–10	3	11	8	23	4	12	4	9	74
									124

Notes: Based on author database, 125 datapoints, as of June 2010; Kelowna includes West Kelowna and West Bank; Summerland includes Peachland; Penticton includes Naramata; Ok Falls = Okanagan Falls, including Kaleden; Cawston includes Keremeos.

result of the skyrocketing of real estate prices in the okv, as well as the demonstration effect of success, is the growing spread of wineries to the far flung corners of the Valley. Table 3.1 gives our calculations on the geographic spread of the okv wineries over time.

This table demonstrates that as the price of land around Kelowna has increased, the number of wineries has spread out as well. During the 1990s, the spread was concentrated in the southern okv. In the last decade, these areas have continued to grow at a hot pace, but there is also growth at the geographic margins of the province. Several wine-makers and other experts with long-term experience in the industry pointed out that the high cost of land is leading to a higher risk profile as more marginal lands are being brought into play, with potential quality and environmental problems resulting. And all wineries will be subject to this factor – 24% of our sample said that they purchased 21–50% of grapes off estate, and another 42% said they bought 51–100%.

Heavy Reliance on Tourism

Tourism is the lifeblood of the okv wine industry, and so presents the same challenge as reliance on bc restaurant sales for estate and boutique wineries. In our survey, there was virtual unanimity that tourism was "extremely important" to wineries. Many of the wineries, especially the smaller and small estate ones, do not have the same sense of urgency about exports outside of bc because tourism is by far their most important source of income, and has been a reliable source of revenues thus far. Their investments go primarily into facilities to attract more tourists and to get them to spend more, thus their policy priority would be to put more money and effort into that area. Thus, tourists are their primary source of information and feedback for new products.

Dependence on Regulatory Protection

Protectionism revolves around the fact that the bc Liquor Distribution Branch (LDB) has a monopoly position over the supply of all alcohol in the province. After national counterparts, Ontario's LCBO and Québec's Societé des alcools du Québec, it is the third largest buying consortium for alcohol in the world (Wilson 2010). No other agent can import or sell alcohol in BC without the express permission of the LDB. The LDB sells the vast majority of alcohol in the province through its BC Liquor Stores, including not only individuals but also pubs, restaurants, and clubs who purchase from them. According to the LDB, there are 1,360 retail liquor stores in BC, 200 of which are government-run, and 700 of which are retail stores operating under license from the Liquor Control and Licensing Branch. Effectively, then, the LDB is able to set the prices for all alcohol with a high mark-up price, which provides the provincial government with a huge revenue stream.

Just as important are the ways that the LDB controls supply. First, the LDB controls shelf space in its stores. It uses this power to show preference to BC wines (Todd 2009). Secondly, all imports go through an arduous process whereby an import agent must fill out reams of paperwork asking the LDB to order the wine on their behalf from the winery. The wine must be shipped to a bonded warehouse and can only be processed when LDB receives a valid order for the wine from a customer (private store, restaurant, or government store). This generally means considerable delay, possibly months, before the product can be placed on shelves. VQA wine is also exempt from BC LDB mark ups. The end result of this system, as columnist Anthony Gismondi (2006) writes, is that "Despite what you read about our burgeoning local industry and the rise in quality wine production, the best [BC] bottles are seldom seen in government stores because local producers have the freedom to sell direct and avoid the massive tax levied on wine sold in government stores and private wine shops." He refers to direct sales to restaurants, on-line, and at retail winery shops, which are exempt from price mark-ups and taxes.

Canadian customs regulations prevent day trippers from bringing back any wine without paying heavy duties at the border. This has led to complaints by US producers and government officials. Canadians must be out of the country for at least 48 hours before they can bring just two bottles of wine back duty free. The LDB sets the prices for all items, at a high mark-up including processing fees, which is estimated to be over 100% of the retail price in other areas. A successful GATT complaint by the European Union led to the abolition of the favourable mark-up treatment for BC wines by the LDB. However, even BC wine that is sold in government stores receives a portion of the mark-up back as a rebate through the VQA Support Program or Quality Enhancement Program (Hicken 2010).

These regulatory conditions demonstrate amply the precarious nature of the BC wine industry in its reliance on provincial regulatory protectionism. Complaints about wine have been brought up in various international fora, such as a 1991 World Trade Organisation (WTO) complaint by the US about protectionism in beer, in which Australia complained about wine in its comments, and a 1998 Trade Policy Review of the WTO, in which Spain, the EU, Chile, and Australia all raised questions about provincial treatment of wine, particularly how listing decisions were made. The EU and Canada reached an updated agreement in regard to wine and beer in 2008. In both the EU and the CUSFTA, the principle of national treatment is embraced. This could be the basis for future challenges.

Industry participants seem to take the status quo for granted, however. The principal complaint/suggestion by the wineries interviewed in regard to public policy was, not surprisingly, that taxes should be lowered and the government should "stay out" of the industry. Several said that the sole role of government was to "gouge" industry, as one put it.

The controversy around the "cellared in Canada" label whereby several large wineries import bulk wine and then bottle it here is the best example of the distortions of protectionism. In fact, the BC Wine Institute states on its website that "cellared in Canada" wines are the best selling category of wines, ahead of VQA sales (Wine BC 2011). The label is considered by critics to be disingenuous, and the BC LDB has responded by separating out such wines from its BC shelf space into a separate space for wines bottled and/or blended in Canada. The wines are apparently good revenue producers, and they avoid the morass of import hassles described above, so they are likely to continue. One insider from a company that produces such wines states "cellared in Canada wines are a big part of our portfolio and provide high paying jobs to numerous BC residents. The province could not support the agricultural base required to supply such wines and it allows us to compete with low cost bottle imports." One interpretation is that producers of such wines see them as competing in a different category than BC estate wines. Perhaps that distinction needs to be made clearer to clear up the controversy. On the other hand, Mark Hicken's (2010) important blog on wine law in Canada, www.winelaw.ca, suggests that the issue will not die down, and may be challenged on the basis that federal law requires a listing of countries of origin. Howev-

er, since blend mixes change according to price movements, businesses will resist this.

The BC wine industry is hardly a cluster in the sense of creating shared
goods that benefit multiple firms. The sheer spread of the OKV – it
takes two hours to drive from the northern to the southern vineyards
– impedes the development of a strong informal culture. The lack of
interaction also reflects the nature of the market. As one winemaker
interviewed puts it, "Okanagan is unique from other regions because
of its domestic focus. So there is direct competition and people are
careful of information sharing." Hickton (2005, 16) notes that despite
the influx of outside investment, the OKV on the whole has a culture
of social relationships revolving around kinship ties, reflecting the
family ownership behind the origins of many of the wineries. Much
of the training is therefore tacit, now being passed on to a second generation (Hickton 2005, 16). A number of winemakers interviewed
suggest Oregon and California as touchstones of best practices, rather
than any local firm.

To analyze the level of social organisation, part of our survey asked
for the level and strength of ties that wineries had with other wineries. Unfortunately, our sample size, about thirty-three wineries was
small but highly varied. Thus we could not calculate standard network measures, since what we noted was that several different networks existed, depending on timing of entry, location, and size of the
winery, as discussed below. In keeping with this finding, we created
social network maps anonymizing the responses using the following
coding ID:

• location (Kelowna, Oliver, Okanagan Falls, Summerland, and Lake
  Country);
• size (small = less than 20 acres; medium = 21–50; large = 51–100;
  extra-large = more than 100 acres); and
• year started selling wine or year of founding (early = before 1998;
  recent = 1998–2005; and new = 2006–present).

We use these maps to illustrate our points from the interviews.

The level of social organisation depends greatly on the size of the
winery and its location in the OKV. In Kelowna, the key city where the

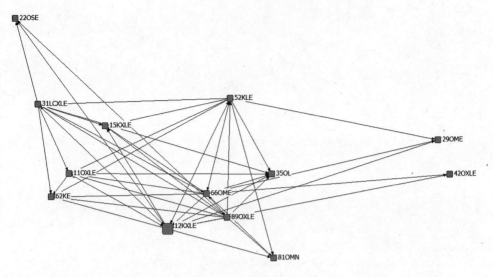

Figure 3.8   Social networks of early extra large Kelowna winery

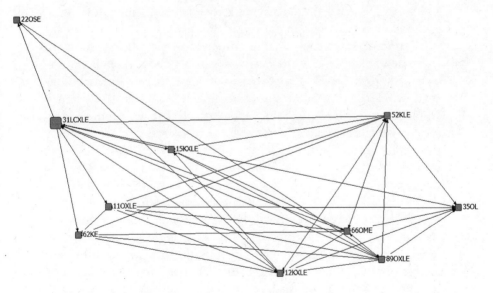

Figure 3.9   Social networks of early extra large Lake Country winery

early wineries started, there is a domination of the industry by large
and estate wineries, with a handful of family wineries, none of which
are geographically concentrated. The large early wineries in Kelowna

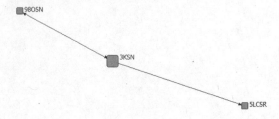

Figure 3.10   Social networks of new small Kelowna winery

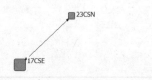

Figure 3.11   Social networks of established winery in Cawston

and Lake Country seem to have ties across the OKV. Though the latter group has less ties, they are not geographically bound.

By contrast, in general, small and medium-sized wineries have far fewer ties. Small wineries in Cawston, a valley about an hour southwest of Kelowna, and in Kelowna itself, are relatively isolated. One small winemaker in Kelowna said he/she felt "surrounded" by larger wineries. One winemaker said, "I sometimes chat with some of the local winemakers at the local pub when I run across them," indicating the haphazard nature of social interactions in the industry. Several indicated that only once in a blue moon did they even interact with neighbours, such as to borrow equipment. Many of these are "isolates" or nearly so, with few regular ties to other wineries in the area.

So, there really are few cross-valley ties. Instead, our field research indicates smaller subcultures of informal networks among similar wineries that are within about a twenty-minute drive of each other, i.e. almost directly contiguous. These are reflected in the current move towards sub-appellations, such as Golden Mile, Black Sage, and Naramata Bench, where a handful of firms are moving towards both informal ties and co-operation in marketing. The Naramata Bench near Penticton, made up of some twenty-five long-standing estate wineries clustered together geographically, is the best organised group, and is cited by several of the small and smaller estate wineries as an example to follow. The only exception in this area is Red Rooster, which was

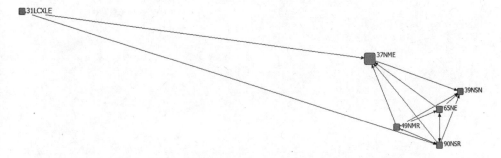

Figure 3.12   Social networks of early medium-sized Naramata wineries

bought in recent years by Andrew Peller Estates (formerly Andrés). Naramata is working towards joint marketing and meets on a regular basis, informally. These efforts are reflected in a high level of local social capital.

The conditions are not good for either extending the Naramata Bench organisation or re-creating it elsewhere. To the north of Penticton (a town forty-five minutes south of Kelowna) comes Summerland, with just a handful of estate and family wineries. South of Penticton is Okanagan Falls, with just a handful of wineries, followed by Oliver, with a mix of family, estate, and large wineries (including Vincor's Jackson-Triggs), and Osoyoos, which is even more spread out and contains estate, large, and native wineries (Nk'mip), and large grape-growing tracts for wineries in the north Okanagan. The wineries around Oliver and Osoyoos have created the South Okanagan Wineries Association. Within this area, there is movement towards sub-appellation in the Golden Mile and Black Sage (Oliver) areas. These large wineries seem to have a stronger level of social capital, though it is generally concentrated with local large wineries as seen in figures 3.13 and 3.14.

Being a smaller winery in Naramata or Oliver does seem to lead to greater ties with other local wineries, though even in these regions there are isolates.

WHY SUB-APPELLATIONS ARE INSUFFICIENT

What can be done to improve social capital in the okv? Throughout our field research, sub-appellations were a major source of hope, particularly for estate wineries falling into certain areas. In fact, there are

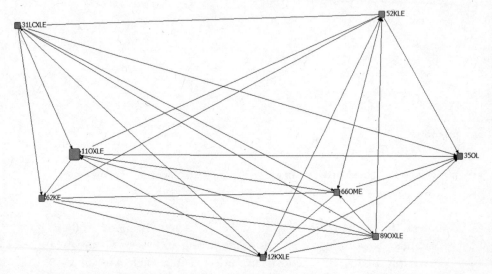

Figure 3.13   Social networks of large early Oliver wineries – example 1

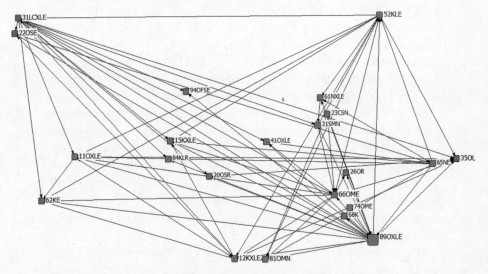

Figure 3.14   Social networks of large early Oliver wineries – example 2

several networks beginning to develop in each micro-cluster despite the obstacles. The South Okanagan Winery Association meets monthly. The Bottleneck Drive group in Summerland began meeting in 2009 and developed common signage to guide tourists in their area.

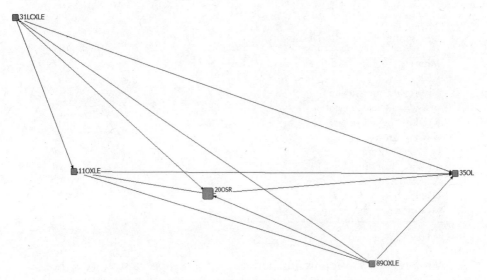

Figure 3.15 Social networks of recent small Oliver winery

The Golden Mile area, like Naramata, is seeking new regulations to create its own sub-appellation. Several have also discussed joint marketing efforts.

Ontario decided in 2005 to create and regulate sub-appellations that can appear on VQA labels, and this was the catalyst for a number of these regional associations to begin to come together. Interviewees were anxious to push sub-appellations as a way of distinguishing the locality of origin and the terroir it represents, however, they also related concerns held by those on the margins about who would be included. They are pushing the BCWA to create regulations that allow sub-appellation, to avoid a parallel of the "cellared in Canada" controversy. This could help them to differentiate their product and reflects supply saturation of the BC market. But none of these associations have anywhere near the critical mass to develop the collective institutions and policy needed to address the vulnerabilities of the industry. Moreover, one can be sceptical that such efforts will pan out into significant market differences given successful sub-appellations.

The Problem with OKV Institutions

The weakness and fragmentation of BC wine institutions underscores the lack of social capital in the OKV. We asked respondents to rate the

Table 3.2
Low rating of institutional support

Ministry of Agric, Food, & Fisheries	1.9
PARC	2.8
Okanagan University-UBC	1.9
UBC Wine Research Centre	1.8
BC Wine Grape Council	2.2
BC Grapegrowers Association	2.9
BC Wine Institute	3.5
BC Wine Authority	2.2
Association of BC winegrowers	2.2
Okanagan Wine Festival Society	3.4
Okanagan College	1.4

importance of support institutions using a 5-point scale (1 = not important; 2 = slightly important; 3 = neutral; 4 = somewhat important; and 5 = extremely important), with the average scores shown in table 3.2.

The table points to the Wine Festival Society and the Wine Institute as the only institutions that are of neutral importance. The problem of fragmentation and lack of institutional support is even deeper. Kingsbury relates in a detailed analysis the slow unravelling of the BCWI as the key to understanding the fragmentation of the emerging cluster. He highlights foremost problems with the governance of the institution. The government appointed the eight members of the eight-person Board of Directors, however, it took input from various sectors. The BCEWA gave two candidates, and the MAFF representative had one slot. Financing came primarily from the provincial and federal governments (88%); the rest was from a levy on membership by ton produced and wines bottled, with an additional $.05 per litre levy being added in 1993 for VQA marketing. In 1993, the BCWI started a number of new committees to make recommendations to the Board, which by 1995 included: Domestic Marketing, Export, Finance, Policy, Technical, and Strategic Plan. The committees were filled by volunteers from the wineries (Kingsbury 2004, 41–7). There was concern within BCWI that the BC market could become saturated, and that international recognition of quality was needed in turn for full acceptance within Canada of the quality of BC wines. Therefore, in 1993 the BCWI began a long-term export program. It began with a strong effort in the UK to promote BC wines. In 1995, the BCWI partnered with the Ontario VQA to create a Canada VQA appellation. However, the program fell apart as only a few firms had the capacity to export in volumes large enough for international markets (Kingsbury 2004, 63–5). The fallout from the decline of the BCWIlikely led to the development of the BC Wine Authority taking over important parts of its turf.

These new BCWI programs occurred at the same time as government funding was diminishing, leading to an increase in levies to $90/ton, and in the costs of taste tests for VQA from $25 to $50. The changing in funding also led to cutbacks in promotional programs and growing concerns about financial management issues. While medium-sized firms paid the most in levies, the aggregate amount from small wineries was increasing as their numbers increased over time. The shift in constituency as well as the above-mentioned issues led to a loss of faith in the BCWI by the smaller wineries, which began to withhold their levies. The smaller wineries felt disenfranchised from the Board and the committees. The situation worsened when the first elections for the Board took place in 1999, which included a proviso that any Board decisions could be re-voted on a second time based on votes weighted by dues paid (Kingsbury 2004, 70–85). The unraveling of the organisation led to a reduction of the overall levy as well as a flexible levy system. Each winery's levy was reduced to $5/ton, with additional fees for marketing promotion domestically and for exporting. The shortfall in resources led to the closure of the Vancouver offices (Kingsbury 2004, 105–8).

The new BC Wine Authority (BCWA) seeks to address some of the problems with BCWI by offering a more neutral body to taste for VQA. The BCWI suffered from the perceived conflict of interest that it only represented some of the larger wineries and that it also had to market and promote the same wines (Mitham 2008). Under the new statutes, all wineries seeking VQA labeling must be members of the authority. It is difficult to say what role the new BCWA will play at this point, though initial indications are that it will be limited to tasting, and several interviewees suggested it was reluctant to sort out the basic labeling issues described above.

POOR COORDINATION OF SUPPLY CHAINS
AND WEAK GLOBAL INTEGRATION

Lack of Alternative Markets

While the market growth of BC wine is impressive, it may be built upon faulty premises. Of our sample 76% said they sold 90–100% of their wines in BC. Therefore, lack of diverse markets is clearly a huge challenge for BC wines that led a number of interviewees to express their concern about the future of the industry. Most farm/small family wineries cited tourism as their main source of revenue. Estate wineries generally said that the ability to sell directly to restaurants was their key market. It is interesting to note that there are a few new wineries in the OKV who sell only online, such as Pentage and Soaring Eagle. We suspect that this reflects the heavy reliance of many boutique and estate wineries on direct restaurant sales. There are a few other new ones who do not seem to be open to tourists, such as Intrigue Wines and Pacific Breeze. Some of these new entrants have mailing addresses in Vancouver, suggesting that they may not even own land in the OKV. Indeed, several interviewees noted that restaurants had already cut back on purchases overall and that their attempts to move much beyond the principal price point of $20 were halting or failing at best, as Vancouver buyers tighten their belts due to the economic downturn. In addition, British Columbia introduced tougher drinking and driving laws in September 2010. Many restaurants have reported a decline in wine and liquor sales since the new laws took effect.

Almost universally, interviewees mentioned the difficulties of interprovincial shipping and sales (often called "exports" by industry participants) as a major obstacle to expansion of wine markets. However, an inside source, commenting on industry lobbying for liberalisation of interprovincial shipping, stated that any changes in this regard, according to WTO and "national treatment" provisions, would have to allow all foreign wines (or their agents) the same privileges as well. On the other hand, the industry is split among large, medium, and smaller wineries, with the latter two citing quite limited ability to export (particularly internationally), thus they do not support any major policy or industry initiatives in this area. The shipping issue is based on the 1928 Importation of Intoxicating Liquor Act, passed at the federal level, that prevents interprovincial sales unless it is to government agencies, i.e. the provincial distribution monopolies. The

Act was passed in the context of the Prohibition era when provinces adopted varying levels of bans on alcohol. While that is no longer a valid reason, clearly the revenues enjoyed by the monopoly government distribution boards are, with BC's LDB providing around $800 million in annual revenue. BC wineries who had shipped to customers in Alberta, Ontario, and Manitoba, have received warning letters from the provincial governments there (Hicken 2008).

Difficulties in Learning How to Export

Exporting would seem the logical solution. However, there are major problems with recognition of BC wines in global markets. A review of 424 wines rated in *Wine Spectator* between 1989–2008 revealed the limited reach of Canadian wines into global markets. Wine Spectator is the premier source of international ratings for the industry. About two thirds of the wines reviewed were from Ontario, and the other one third from the Okanagan. A third of all Canadian wines rated are icewines, including 41% of the Ontario wines vs just 14% for BC, showing the greater range of varietals of the latter. This suggests that Canada is known principally for icewines, and these are more likely to be rated. We see that the average score of Canadian wines reviewed is in the "good" range, 80–90. The average price of Ontario wines is considerably higher than BC wines, at $37 vs $24, likely reflecting again the premium afforded to icewines.[3]

Exporting globally is even more problematic, as a number of interviewees suggest that few BC companies are able to produce adequate volumes for export markets and that they were not competitive at international price points with producers who "exploited cheap labour," such as Chile. Only one winery expressed that they did any systematic research on prospective markets and trends. Canadian wines lack any clear reputation or branding at this point (Hickton 2005, 41). Interviews with a couple of winemakers who were producing wines for export markets revealed a perceived lack of policy support for such efforts, especially stark if one compares it to the high level of export promotional efforts of other winemaking clusters. One logical solution would be to brand OKV wines around a clear varietal, such as Argentine Malbecs and Willamette Valley (Oregon) Pinot Noirs, to establish a high end global niche. However, interviewees universally reported that there is almost no likelihood that a regional specialisation around a varietal will take hold given the variety of mesoclimates in the Okanagan and the changing sources of grape supplies. Almost universally, winemakers cited their interest in organic growing and sustainability, something that could be taken up by support institutions, but it is unclear as to whether an exporting market niche upon such a basis could be established. Several winemakers interviewed expressed that they had been approached by Asian buyers for China and Japan, but that the prices were so low and the channels so unclear as to make it not worthwhile.

Janet Dorozynski of the federal Dept. of Foreign Affairs and International Trade (DFAIT) contacted the author and pointed to the National Export Strategy Working Group for wine that she is a part of. The group also includes Agriculture and Agri-food Canada, the Canadian Vintner's Association (CVA), the BC Wine Institute, and several large Canadian wineries and corporations. In May 2009, DFAIT announced that it was spending US$81,000 during the first year of a 3–5 year campaign to promote Canadian wine exports. The goal is to double exports from their 2007 volume of 3 million litres and US$20.1 million values. CVA President Dan Paszkowski stated: "We looked at Australia, New Zealand, and other countries that aren't that far ahead of us in terms of export growth but have national strategies that really helped their wineries move in tandem into exports" (Wine Business Monthly 2009). The strategy focuses on getting Canadian wines into trade fairs and competitions, and targeting several identified key markets in large international cities. The strategy appears to be based on a consultant's report by Susan O'Dell and Associates (DFAIT 2009). The report (13–16) reinforces the following governance issues:

- export initiatives continue to be sporadic and one-offs, not contributing to sustained sale;
- allocated funding (by the federal government) is not fully spent;
- Ontario and BC are "separate silos" diluting export effectiveness;
- potential partners are confused about how to help industry; and
- the strategy may not be "actively embraced" and implemented by the regional and national associations.

WEAK COORDINATION OF SUPPLY CHAINS AND LOW LOCAL VALUE-ADDED

Power in the value chain has changed over time as the OKV industry has transformed. As noted, previous to CUSFTA, a grape reference price existed, set by the BC Grape Marketing Board. Though the grape marketing board continues to exist, after the reference price was eliminated in 1995, it has had little influence on supply since grape prices are freely negotiated between wineries and grape growers (Hickton 2005, 11). An interviewee suggested the board ended in 1997 based on a referendum. As of 1998, there were 235 grape growers in the OKV, of which 119 were supplying wineries. The average vineyard size was 12–14 acres (Hackett 1998, 61). In 2001, Quail's Gate started a trend by changing the nature of its contracts to grape growers, so that it paid set amounts for grapes of high quality, rather than by the ton (Schreiner 2003, 98). There are long-standing trends that reflect the desire of grape growers to enter into the winery business, such as Desert Hills. This seems to be a growing trend (Schreiner 2003, 105). However, interviews with the winemakers in the OKV reveal a haphazard patchwork of ever changing contracts that lack the long-term stability or consistency to lead to quality improvement. The possibility that estate wineries could be expanded (with wineries simply growing more of their own grapes) was rejected as implausible by interviewees owing to the prohibitively high price of land. This leads to the inability to focus on certain varietals as a strategy, as almost all decent-sized wineries have to outsource their grape supply, which comes from a variety of terroirs and mesoclimates around the Valley. Rising costs and a shortage of labour have led to increasing use of temporary migrant workers, many from Mexico, and accompanying concerns about labour practices in the industry. Workers are not unionized, but activist efforts have led to some notice about their conditions.

It is also fuelling the expansion in the number of wineries as grape growers feel that they are not getting a fair share of the final profits, and so decide to move into winemaking themselves. All of this will change if either the demand or supply of grapes changes, as is inevitable at some point, bringing up the question of whether the anarchic structure of winery-grower relations can adapt. Most importantly, the uncertainty around these arrangements means that it is difficult to improve quality among the grape growers, as investments by the wineries could lead to defection (sales to other wineries) and the feeling among grape growers that such investments are not worthwhile when demand for their product is so high.

The OKV lacks local equipment suppliers. Most equipment, including corks, bottles, labels, chemicals, and other inputs are imported

(Hickton and Padmore 2005, 97, 107). In Oliver, Okanagan Barrel Works operates as the only cooper in the region, using wood imported from elsewhere. Interviewees note a bias against local products; for example, many said that many local wineries insist that the wood used must be imported from France. Many interviewees cited local suppliers when they really meant local agents for imported equipment. Local suppliers face problems similar to the wine industry as a whole – with inadequate demand, they are unable to reach economies of scale, and so find it difficult to compete with the behemoths of the industry, especially with Canadian skilled wages being relatively high. Their comparative advantage is that they are able to tailor products and services to particular needs, and to provide local service. Suppliers interviewed suggested that their quality was improving in line with the demands of the wineries. Suppliers interviewed universally suggested entrance from a non-winemaking background and almost all noted that they were self-trained.

LACK OF TRAINING OPPORTUNITIES
AND RESEARCH DISSEMINATION FOR INNOVATION

Training opportunities for BC wine personnel are quite limited. A surprising number of wine personnel, including winemakers, come from another background and have had limited formal training. There is assuredly a refreshing quality about this, with abounding blue sky enthusiasm coming through in interviews. One supplier interviewed (himself not formally trained) observed that the ability to take risks and to learn on the job were more important than formal training, and that he had seen a number of "PhD types" fail for lack of such attributes. Nonetheless, he and other wine suppliers as well as the winemakers themselves universally noted that the industry's push to increase sophistication was hitting major obstacles given the lack of educational and outreach support.

Given the lack of formal training opportunities, in the late 1990s, the provincial Ministry of Agriculture, Forestry and Fisheries (MAFF) operated a business planning program, that both examined grape production and taught basics on viticulture investment and financial planning (Hackett 1998, 125). However, the one employee dedicated to grape growing retired and was never replaced. A number of interviewees pointed out that the lack of expertise and "grounding" in the industry generally is what left them sceptical that the government could play any helpful proactive role.

In terms of support institutions, there is little coordination between PARC and UBC's Wine Research Centre. PARC is spread far too thin, covering a wide variety of crops from tree fruits to wine grapes with just a handful of experts (PARC disagrees). UBC sees its role as international in scope, and focused on the discovery of scientific processes and products that would be valuable to the worldwide market, as seems appropriate for the nature of its genomics-based research. The idea of having a middleman from the BC wine industry has occurred to them, however Director Hennie J.J. Van Vuuren states that while it would be good to have an ex-winemaker play this (bridging) role, "it is important to me to have personal relationships with the winemakers themselves." Thus the interactions of the research centre seem to be focused on a handful of leading large wineries in the OKV. One can see this as a situation where these leading wineries would become first adopters and then other wineries would imitate their lead, however, the nature and speed of that dissemination given the lack of collective institutions or middlemen is bound to be slow and haphazard at best.

Reinforcing this observation is that fact that there is neither a university-level training institute similar to those in the US, Europe, or Australia, nor even a BA equivalent such as that offered by Brock University in Ontario. The UBC Okanagan campus offers three programs for training at the BA level, that have operated since 1997: Viticulture, Winery Assistant, and Wine Sales. Each program has a common course on grapes and grape growing, and then three specialised courses for the particular program, as well as a practicum course to allow for hands on learning. As several interviewees noted, this is hardly sufficient for those working above the retail level. It is worth noting that two courses on Oenology were being offered at UBC Okanagan in 2011 in biochemistry, with enrolments of fifty and seventeen students, respectively. Previously, wine chemistry courses had been offered every two years by a chemistry professor, with unknown enrolment numbers. Okanagan College has offered three certificate programs since 1999: Viticulture, Wine Sales, and Winery Assistant. Enrolments have varied between twelve (1999) and forty-four (2008–09), with thirty total students in 2009–10.

Some of the smaller wineries suggested that formal training was either unnecessary or that it was inaccessible. One suggested a need

Table 3.3
Few training opportunities

How Training is Provided	
In-house training	87.88%
External provision of training	42.42%
via UBC Okanagan	6.06%
Consultants	42.42%
via Okanagan College	12.12%
Other, please specify	6.06%

for more distance education offerings. The lack of recognition of the potential value of industry research was revealed early on in the project, with the lack of response or even hostility to requests to respond to surveys and interviews, including requests made to the support institutions. To complete the project required six months of active personal entreaties and networking through multiple channels.

As with the other issues, the needs of the industry are filled only through a patchwork of make-do solutions. Almost all respondents said that suppliers (such as Cellar Tek) and independent consultants were the most important sources of innovation, and self-teaching seems to be the predominant *modus vivendi*. A few interviewees said that there was nothing new in winemaking, so there was no need for innovation knowledge. While some of the larger wineries have their marketing personnel who research market trends, most wineries make do or guess. One interviewee stated that he/she just follows the general lead. Most interviewees at the medium- and larger-sized wineries indicated that the lack of training opportunities was clearly an impediment in comparison with other wine-growing regions.

The research by the UBC Wine Research Centre was praised highly by a few of the larger wineries in the OKV, but most of the interviewees did not seem to have any knowledge of it or what it did. The UBC Okanagan campus's activities seem to have an even lower profile. Several interviewees suggested that the Wine Research Centre should relocate to Kelowna, but the real problem seems to be a lack of a middleman to translate the value and meaning of cutting edge research in grape growing and winemaking to the average winery. Table 3.3 summarizes the findings about education and training.

Table 3.4
Few sources of local innovation or dissemination

Internal Company Sources	4.5
Suppliers of equipment, materials, components or software	3.7
Clients or customers	2.9
Joint research with Other BC Wineries – Marketing	2.3
Wineries outside of BC	2.3
Consultants	3.4
Conferences, trade fairs, exhibitions	3.5
Trade magazines or journals	3.7
Internet	3.8

Clearly, there is a major institutional gap in terms of training opportunities in the Okanagan Valley. Of our sample, an average of just 30% of employees at these wineries have any formal training, and this is probably an overstatement as we included those who might have completed just one course. While the employees of wealthier wineries are sending their children abroad, this does not provide the rich environment needed for employees at lower levels or for the creation of an atmosphere of local learning and exchange. Particularly in the case of agriculture, training and research should be oriented towards and tailored for the local environment.

These findings underscore what we found out about institutions. While 55% said that their production processes had improved "a lot" over the past two years, almost no respondents identified any institutions as being above a score of 1 in terms of help with innovation. The industry relies heavily on easy access sources for ideas for innovation as illustrated in average scores in table 3.4 (1–5 scale).

In terms of possible areas where innovation had occurred, we found the results shown in table 3.5. Clearly, there is great interest in soil adaptation and fermentation processes, as well as further training. This demonstrates a major gap between the support institutions and the winemakers, that should be filled by support institutions. The limited nature of innovation dissemination reflects that a number of interviewees mention the lack of any agricultural extension agency for the industry. In 1994, a major breakthrough for BC wineries took place, as Mission Hill won a top trophy at a London wine competition for its Chardonnay. The winery had hired John Simes, a top winemaker at a New Zealand winery, in 1992 (Schreiner 2003, 96), and thus started a

Table 3.5
Innovation of interest despite lack of support

Retail sales	51.52%
Marketing	66.67%
Finance	30.30%
Plant Breeding	9.09%
Use of Genetics	3.03%
Soil Adaptation	54.55%
Fermentation	63.64%
Information Systems	45.45%
Education/Training	60.61%

trend of hiring Australians or New Zealanders, and to a lesser extent Canadians trained there, that appears to be accelerating today. There was also universal chagrin at the lack of agricultural extension support. While PARC was mentioned positively by some medium-sized wineries, most of the smaller and larger wineries stated that it was unimportant to them. One interviewee said that PARC was "helpful in terms of viticulture, and AgCanada [Agriculture Canada] in terms of pesticides and some related areas of agriculture, but really offered nothing in terms of winemaking advice, or practical knowledge." This still brings up the issue, if PARC does not do extension, and the province does not, who fills this crucial role in BC? At present, the answer is no one, a crucial gap and detriment to the industry's fortunes. PARC and BCWI's responses reflect the defensiveness pervasive throughout the BC industry and the ubiquitous inability of almost anyone to see the bigger picture industry issues reflected throughout this report.

CONCLUSIONS

The BC Wine industry, centred in the Okanagan, has undergone an amazing transformation from "plonk" wine manufacturer to a viable industry, with some firms beginning to meet world class standards of quality. However, the industry is more of a proto-cluster, with key issues stemming from a lack of organisation, coordination, and policy foresight. Policy changes are constrained by the use of liquor sales and accompanying protectionism as a cash cow through the provincial monopoly, which has created the conditions for the growth of the sector. The BC case is not a good fit for lessons about how to engender clusters generally, given these idiosyncrasies. However, it does support many of the key concepts behind cluster theory: that geography matters crucially in some industries and explains their locational concentration, that a proactive policy can help to catalyze an industry, and that social networks and collective action are essential to clusters' long-term success.

While lauding the present success, we are likely entering into a new phase for the maturing of the sector, one in which growing pains will start to become evident unless there are major adjustments. Adjustments cannot occur in the absence of a long-term view of the industry as a whole, or the growth of the policy and collective networks of the industry. Interviewees from all areas of the private sector universally decried the lack of co-operation and organisation of the sector. Without major efforts to create a cluster policy, the vulnerabilities noted above could lead to major problems in the industry. As one interviewee put it rather nicely, "We don't need consensus (à la the BCWI early experiment) to move forward. But we do need a push towards a culture of co-operation, and organizations to improve our collective efforts and policy."

The bottom line is that no one in BC has a strategic long-term vision for the industry. In general, the policy literature tells us that major policy change does not occur unless there is a crisis. This seems to hold true for the BC wine industry.

ACKNOWLEDGMENTS

The research for this chapter was generously funded through a grant by Genome BC, Genome Canada, and co-funded by Simon Fraser University. Field research was carried out by Anil Hira in spring and summer 2010, when thirty-three one-hour surveys and interviews were conducted with winemakers and winery owners, with a response rate of 30%. A solid cross-section of small, medium, and large wineries are represented here. In addition, over twenty interviews with suppliers and consultants were carried out. To allow for freer discussion, an ethics agreement was signed promising anonymity for all participants. The assistance of the BC Wine Grape Council was crucial, particularly allowing the author to participate in the 2010 annual oenology and viticulture conference. Research assistance, partly funded by

BC's Work Study Program, was carried out by Justin Domareski, Stewart Wilkinson, Alexis Bwenge, Gavin Cheung, and Neil Boehm from 2009–11; all made important contributions. Bwenge is responsible for some parts of the supply and demand trends analysis. Janet Dorzynski, Ingo Grady, Lynn and John Bremmer, Karen Ayers, Jim Wyse, Art Cobham, and Kirk Seggie made helpful comments. John Schreiner, foremost historian of the industry, and Bill Collings, former director of the BC Grape Marketing Board, BC Grape Growers Association, and BC Wine Institute, made extensive helpful comments and provided needed encouragement. Patty Hira helped with crucial research and editing in the final round. The Scientific Advisory Board of this project provided helpful feedback. David Aylward, Peter Phillips, and Camille Ryan provided crucial advice, particularly on survey design and social networking analysis. We would like to thank all those noted above for their support, as well as the generosity that participants showed me in granting the interviews, and my partners at UBC and Genome BC for their continual encouragement and feedback throughout the challenge-filled process.

NOTES

1 A comprehensive discussion of the BC wine industry is found in Hira's 2011 paper, "The Wine Industry in British Columbia: Issues and Potential," published by the American Association of Wine Economists on their website.
2 Vines from the European varieties are considered more palatable than the native labrusca variety.
3 Further quantitative analysis is available upon request.

REFERENCES

Adams, Derek. 1992. "The Estimation of the Degree of Pricing Competition in the British Columbia Wine Industry (1957–1986)." MSc Thesis, Dept. of Agricultural Economics, UBC.
BC Ministry of Agriculture, Food and Fisheries. 2004. *An Overview of the British Columbia Grape Industry*. Dec.
BC Wine Institute. 2010. "Annual Report for 2010." Accessed Feb. 2011, http://www.winebc.com/library/reports/2010_Annual_Report.pdf

- 2010. "The British Columbia Wine Grape Crop Survey 2009." Accessed Feb. 7, 2011, http://www.winebc.com/library/reports/2009%20BC%20Crop%20Survey%20web.pdf.
- "History." Accessed Feb. 2010, http://www.winebc.com/history.php.
- "2007 BC Wine Grape Acreage Report." Accessed Feb. 2010, http://www.winebc.com/library/reports/2007VintageReport.pdf.
- 2006. "BC Wine Basics: The Okanagan Valley." Accessed Feb. 2010, http://www.winebc.com/wineregions-okvalley.php.
Collings, Bill. 2011. Correspondence with author.
DFAIT (Dept. of Foreign Affairs and International Trade). 2009. "A National Export Strategy for Canadian Wines." Report prepared by Susan O'Dell & Associates. http://www.international.gc.ca/commerce/assets/pdfs/Wine_Strategy_English.pdf.
Gismondi, Anthony. 2006. "Best of BC Release." *Vancouver Sun*. Nov. 11. http://www.gismondionwine.com/articlelist.php?grp=5
Hackett, Nancy C. 1998. "Vines, Wines, and Visitors: A Case Study of Agricultural Diversification into Winery Tourism." Unpublished research project, report No. 214, School of Resource and Environmental Management, Simon Fraser University.
Hicken, Mark. 2010. BC Wine and Trade Agreement Trouble, Feb. 16. www.winelaw.ca.
- 2008. "Brief History of BC Wine and Liquor Laws." Mar. 18. www.winelaw.ca.
Hickton, Caroline. 2005. "Transformations in the Okanagan Wine Industry and Reflections on Communication, Diffusion of Innovation and Social Capital in the case of the Okanagan Wine Cluster." Extended essays, MA in Communications, Simon Fraser University.
Hickton, Caroline and Tim Padmore. 2005. "The Okanagan Wine Making Cluster." In *Global Networks and Local Linkages: the Paradox of Cluster Development in an Open Economy*, 83-154, edited by David A. Wolfe and Matthew Lucas. Montreal: McGill-Queen's University Press.
Hira, Anil, Brian Wixted, and Ricardo Arechavala-Vargas. 2012. Explaining Sectoral Leapfrogging in Countries: Comparative Studies of the Wireless Sector. *International Journal of Technology and Globalisation* 6 (1/2): 3-26.
Hope-Ross, Penny. 2006. *From the Vine to the Glass: Canada's Grape and Wine Industry*. Ottawa: Statistics Canada.
Kingsbury, Aaron. 2004. "Cooperative Fermentation: Formal Cooperation, Business Interest Associations, and the Okanagan Wine Industry." MA Thesis, Dept. of Geography, Simon Fraser University.

Miles, Christopher Allan. 1981. "The Feasibility of Establishing an Investor Owned Estate Winery in British Columbia." Research Project, MBA, Simon Fraser University. Aug.

Mitham, Peter. 2008. "BC Wine Authority Up and Running." *Wines and Vines.* Oct. 10. www.winesandvines.com

Nichol, Alexander E. 1983. *Wines and Vines of British Columbia.* Vancouver: Bottesini Press.

Ross, Kimberly J. 1995. "An Analysis of the Effect of the Free Trade Agreement on Profitability in the British Columbia Wine Industry." MSc thesis. Department of Agricultural Economics, University of British Columbia.

Rowe, Percy. 1970. *The Wines of Canada.* Toronto: McGraw-Hill.

Schreiner, John. 2003. *British Columbia Wine Country.* North Vancouver: Whitecap.

– 2000. "History of the British Columbia Wine Industry." In *BC Wine Country: The Book,* 8–9. Kelowna: Blue Moose Publications.

The Select Standing Committee on Agriculture, BC Legislature. 1978. *The Grape and Wine Industries of British Columbia: A Commodity Report.* Aug. Phase III Research Report. Victoria: BC Govt.

Todd, Robert. 2009. "Labelling Wars Heat Up." Oct. 19. www.lawtimes news.com.

Van Vuuren, Hennie. 2011. Personal interview with author.

Wilson, Tony. 2010. "Why BC's Liquor Board Gets Away with Complacency." Mar. 12, wwww.lawyersweekly.ca

Wine BC. 2011. http://www.winebc.com/quickfacts.php Accessed Jan 11, 2011.

Wine Business Monthly. 2009. "Canadian Government Helps Domestic Wineries Step onto the World Stage." *Wine Business Monthly* May 15. http://www.winebusiness.com/wbm/?go=getArticle&dataId=66045.

4

Competitiveness of the Wine Industry in Extremadura, Spain

FRANCISCO J. MESÍAS, FRANCISCO PULIDO,
AND ANGEL F. PULIDO

Translation by Elisa Ferreira and Anil Hira

INTRODUCTION

This chapter is based on a 2010 study of thirty wineries in Extremadura, Spain. It analyses the competitiveness of the Extremaduran wine industry, focusing on the advantages and disadvantages that have affected the development of this sector. We examine the role of private and public regulatory bodies in creating competitiveness. We apply the framework developed by Hira, Howlett, and Giest in chapter 1. Their approach focuses on the potential role of public and collective support institutions to promote competitiveness.

Our analysis reveals that the lack of public-private and private-private interactions is a key factor for explaining the partly unsuccessful and incomplete expansion of the Extremaduran wine sector in international markets. Even though the sector enjoys advantages in climate, soil, and the price of grapes, these have not been translated into a fully competitive wine sector.

Extremadura is one of the main Spanish wine regions, with 88,000 hectares of vineyards and an average production of around 3 million hectoliters. It is located in south-western Spain. It is a zone of low population density, with just over 1.1 million inhabitants spread through 41,600 km². The climate is continental Mediterranean, and the annual average temperatures vary between 16 and 17°C. The summers are long, hot, and dry; the average temperature in July is usually over 26°C, with the maximum often surpassing 40°C. The winters are normally mild with an average temperature of 7.5°C. Rainfall is irregularly distributed and varies between 300 and 800mm annually, with large variations between years.

Extremadura has traditionally been a supplier of non-bottled wines, bound for other regions that place greater emphasis on the sale of bottled wine. While commercial channels have evolved with the increased sales of bottled wines directly from processing industries to hotels, restaurants, consumers, and retailers, sales of non-bottled wine still compose the majority of total sales in Extremadura.

Among the problems faced by the productive sector is the use of a quality label (Designation of Origin Ribera del Guadiana) in which just over 20% of the wineries in the region currently participate. In addition, structural problems have resulted from an inadequate selection of grape varieties, with great weight on the production of white wine in relation to market demands.

One of the most striking aspects is the commercial behaviour of wine companies, which show fairly homogeneous groups, both in terms of size and legal form. Medium-to-large companies stand out, with great importance given to co-operatives and relatively limited attention to non-bottled sales. Small wineries base their business on selling bottled wine, utilising different channels of commerce. The limited commercial development of the larger wineries, along with a weak relationship between companies that could generate synergies, are the major bottlenecks of the Extremaduran wine industry.

THE EXTREMADURAN WINE SECTOR

The wine sector is particularly important in Extremadura, with an average turnover of 50 million euros (2008–09), representing 5% of crop production in the region. It is also quite important on social grounds, because of the large amounts of manual work it requires and the consequent employment opportunities it offers. The surface area of vineyards in Extremadura, 88,000 ha in 2008, accounts for 8% of Spanish vineyards, up from 6.1% in the 1990s. With regard to wine production, Extremadura has an average output of 3 million hl (8.3%

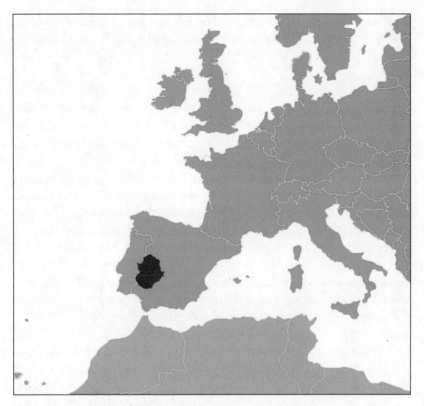

Figure 4.1   Location of Extremadura

of the Spanish total) but with large fluctuations due to the uneven distribution of rainfall. In 2007, the harvest was 2.65 million hl, in 2008 it was 3.4 million hl, and in 2009 the area harvested produced 2.2 million hl.

Extremaduran production is based mainly on native varieties of white grapes including Pardina, White Cayetana, Chelva, and Beba. Currently, these varieties account for more than 60% of the wine-growing area of Extremadura, down from over 80% in the 1990s. These data reflect the profound transformation that has occurred in terms of an increase in red grape production as a result of the adjustments to new varieties (mainly red) that have been undertaken in the last ten to fifteen years.

The most common red grape varieties are Tempranillo, Garnacha, Cabernet Sauvignon, Merlot, and Shirah (Mesías and Barrera 2004).

Historical Background

The earliest wine-related archaeological remains in Extremadura date back to the seventh to fifth centuries BCE, which provides an idea of the profound historical significance of this crop. Yet, it was the Roman occupation of the Iberian Peninsula that spread and generalised the crop, following its inclusion in the diets of armies and other citizens (Falcó 2000; Díaz 2010). Numerous legacies have been preserved from this period, both artistic (mosaics on the production and consumption of wine) and productive (the remains of the largest Roman wine cellar known to exist in the Iberian Peninsula is located in Extremadura). The cultivation has continued, with fluctuations, until the present. The wines of Guadalcanal (a famous type of Extremaduran wine that halted production after the phylloxera attacks) were among the first to be brought to America.

In the late eighteenth century, and especially during the nineteenth century, the wine sector developed dramatically in Extremadura, encouraged by the increased consumption of wine that resulted from the industrial revolution and colonial processes. The appearance of phylloxera in the region in 1897 was a major setback for the crop as the pest razed much of the Spanish and European vineyards. However, unlike other areas where the crop was not able to recover due to the significant costs of re-planting a vineyard, the Extremadura area recovered quickly and even expanded. This was due to the increasing demand for wines by the many vineyard areas that were not able to be, or had not yet been, replanted.

Phylloxera also brought about a change of grape variety in the region, including the practical monoculture of the Pardina native variety that is well adapted to the agro-climatic conditions of Extremadura. The Pardina variety is resistant to diseases and is a highly productive rain-fed crop (between 5,000 and 10,000 kg /ha). This variety was also well suited for a new use of Extremaduran wines intended to produce alcohol, highly demanded by the sherry industry (that requires adding alcohol to its wine to increase alcohol content). The characteristics of production and suitable market conditions allowed vineyard acreage to continue its expansion in the region, reaching its peak, 116,000 hectares, by the late 1970s and making Extremadura the second largest producer of the region, only behind La Mancha.

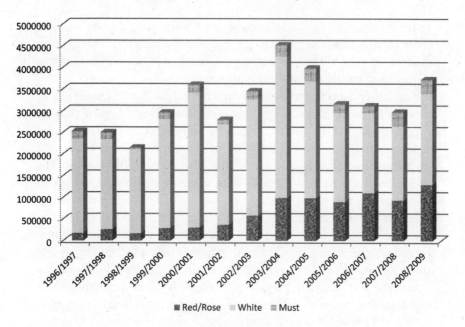

Figure 4.2   Evolution of wine and must production

This boom also led to the rise of vineyards in other parts of Spain, and the country reached overproduction. As of the 1960s the market was faced with structural surpluses and these lasted until Spain joined the European Union. These surpluses were fought with compulsory use of a percentage of the wine for alcohol production and with a ban on new plantations, although they had limited success due to the scarcity of resources devoted by the Spanish government. In fact, until the mid 1990s, the commercial destination of the majority of Extremaduran wine was distillation, with little more than 20–30% of production sold as wine.

Evolution of Vineyard Acreage and Wine Production: The Effects of EU Policies

First, figure 4.2 shows the data on the evolution of wine and must production in Extremadura during the period 1996/97–2008/09, distinguishing between red/rosé wines, white wines, and wine must.

It is important to take into account the inconsistency of production due to the irregularity of rainfall distribution between harvests and limited irrigation in the region, at least until recent years. Despite these fluctuations, the trend is clearly upward with a total average production of 3.19 million hl, swinging from 2 million hl in 1998/99 to a harvest of nearly 4.5 million hl in 2003.

Two other aspects are also clearly reflected in figure 4.2. To begin, there is significant (although variable) production of must that on average accounts for about 200,000 hectoliters annually. The second aspect is the increasing production of red wine in Extremadura. As mentioned previously, the traditional production of wine in the region used mostly white grapes, with some production of red in certain zones. In the 1990s, growers and wineries that were more market-oriented began to switch from white grape varieties to red, which was the beginning of later significant quantities of red and rosé wines. Farmers began to receive significantly higher prices for red grapes and thus continued to increase their production of them. Already in the 2000s, the restructuring programs financed by the EU enhanced this trend, leading red wine production in recent seasons to reach between 35% and 38% of total wine production.

Regarding the production of quality wines (QWpsr, Quality wines produced in specified regions, according to the EU's nomenclature), figure 4.3 shows the trend in the percentage of red/rosé and white QWpsr with respect to the total production of red/rosé and white wines. Although QWpsr rates show a clear downward trend in the red varieties and a stable trend for the white, it is important to note that the production of red wines in the region has increased substantially in recent decades. Thus, in absolute terms, the amount of quality red and rosé wines has followed a clear upward trend, while the quantity of white wines produced has remained constant.

In Spain, as in EU, QWpsr must be produced under the scheme of a Designation of Origin (DO). The only DO in Extremadura is DO Ribera del Guadiana, which started its works in 1996. It has more than 3,000 growers and twenty-four wineries registered, of which only 40% sell bottled wine. The other wineries are dedicated to the sale of bulk wine.

The vineyard area covered under this DO was 27,200 hectares in 2009, having witnessed a sharp increase starting in the year 2000, mostly due to the above mentioned restructuring plans financed by the EU (which forced farmers to register the new vineyards in a DO if they were going to ask for subsidies).

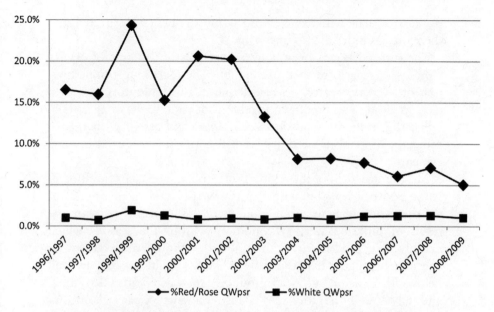

Figure 4.3   Percentage of quality wines with respect to the total production of red/rosé and white wines in Extremadura

The amount of quality wine produced (that can be labeled as qwpsr) has in recent seasons been between 9 and 10 million litres, yet the distribution by type of wine has been changing. While in the 1990s the distribution appeared to be 50% white and 50% red, currently around 80% of quality wine is red. The volume of marketed bottled wines (sold as qwpsr) is between 1.7–1.8 million litres (García, Del Moral, and Galera 2010). The difference between both figures is the result of bulk sales. In these cases, however, the wine is not usually differentiated commercially from those that are not do labelled. Despite its fifteen years of existence, the Designation of Origin Ribera del Guadiana has not been able to become a key player within the wine sector. Although the use of do branding in wines is a widespread strategy in the eu, where it is seen as a marketing tool that helps the companies to differentiate their products (Martín 2009; García, Del Moral, and Galera 2010) this is not the case in Extremadura. The vineyard surface registered under the do has been kept at less than 30% of the total vineyard surface, the number of wineries has decreased over the years, and the amount of qwpsr is just around 3% of the total wine production. The wineries are not finding the benefits expected, and therefore, consider the DO unworthy.

The sector has not been able to increase the amount of quality wines with regards to total production. The increasing competitiveness of the wine sector, where external quality indicators provide a clear method of differentiation and introduction to the market, highlights the limitations (Osorio 2006; Seisdedos 2008). With this in mind, the limitations faced by Extremaduran wine producers become evident.

The average yield of the region is of 41 hl/ha, with significant oscillation between years but with a clear upward trend. As mentioned in the discussion of wine production, these variations in yields are the result of differing weather conditions within the seasons which notably affect productivity of the vineyard. Although these returns are considerably higher than the Spanish average (30 hl/ha), they are well below other major European producers such as France (58.9 hl/ha) and Italy (56.5 hl/ha) (OIV 2007). This represents a clear lack of competitiveness of Extremaduran wines, at least in regard to costs.

Industrial Structure

There are no recent studies on the industrial structure of the wine sector in Extremadura. In recent decades this sector has undergone an intense transformation, due mainly to the implementation of co-operative enterprises – which currently produce over 50% of the wine in the region – that have led many small family-owned wineries to join co-operatives as a way to cut costs (Mesías and Pulido 1996). Thus, Extremadura has gone from having 535 wineries in 1980, to 123 in 2010, considerably increasing the average capacity and profitability of the facilities. These mergers have made room for investment in technological advancements and have opened markets that were not feasible for small wineries to be part of beforehand. Storage capacity has shifted, reducing the number of stone warehouses and increasing those made of steel. In recent years, the use of stainless steel has risen as well, in line with the mass-introduced technological improvements in the sector.

A few wineries, in very small numbers and mainly from the main vineyard area, Tierra de Barros, are also engaged in the production of sparkling wine (cava). The co-operative wineries, which produce

more than half of the wines in Extremadura, have the most superior
technology and the greatest capacity due to their higher likelihood of
receiving financial assistance, and given the fact that they are relatively new (in most cases they were created in the 1980s). The privately
owned wineries are usually smaller in terms of capacity than the co-
operatives and tend to have less advanced technology at their dispos-
al. However, they have a more developed marketing structure, with
higher percentages of sales of bottled wine.

An analysis developed by Mesías et al. (1998) identified the main
deficiencies in the marketing structure of Extremaduran wineries
(sales of bulk wine, scarcity of bottled wines, and productions not
adapted to the markets), particularly in the case of larger wineries and
co-operatives. Although these types of companies have considerable
social and economic importance in the sector, the leading companies
are small businesses that are not able to compensate for the deficits
previously described. Some of these constraints still remain, such as
the high percentage of wine sold in bulk, with the loss of added value
for the producers and wineries of the region, and the lack of clear
marketing strategies. Most wineries lack marketing departments –
even the big co-operatives – and usually the only strategy is to "follow
the leader" with the limitations and difficulties of such a strategy.

THE DEVELOPMENT OF THE WINE INDUSTRY
IN EXTREMADURA

As discussed in previous sections, the origin and early development of
the wine industry in Extremadura was encouraged after the phylloxera incident in Spain and was closely linked to the production of alcohol for Sherry wines. These beginnings led to two distinct types of
businesses. On the one hand, there were the majority of small wineries
ies usually linked to growers, producing 1,000–3,000 hl in volume. On
the other, there was a small group of large companies that largely
acquired the wines from smaller wineries, dedicating themselves to
producing the alcohol demanded by their ultimate customers, the
Sherry wineries. This structure was maintained until the 1970s, when
co-operatives began to emerge mainly due to the crisis of the traditional system of production. The structural surplus of wine in Spain
was resolved through the distillation process. The offer of wine alcohol increased substantially and prices declined, as did the profits of

Table 4.1
Distribution of Extremaduran wineries by wine-growing area

Wine Areas in Extremadura	Total	%
Tierra de Barros	23	76.67
Cañamero	2	6.67
Matanegra	2	6.67
Ribera Baja del Guadiana	2	6.67
Ribera Alta del Guadiana	1	3.33

Extremaduran wineries. With this, numerous family-owned wineries disappeared, and many wine producers joined co-operatives as a way to secure the sale of their productions and thus be able to stay in the wine sector.

From its peak in the mid 1970s with more than 800 wineries in the region, the numbers began to decline. In 1980 there were 535 wineries and 307 in 1995. In 2010, only 123 wineries remained. Table 4.1 gives the distribution of the wineries included in this study by wine-growing areas.

Figure 4.4 discloses the information provided by the wineries that were surveyed in relation to the date they were founded and when they began selling wines. The previous trend becomes apparent as the percentage of wineries that survived the first half of the twentieth century and earlier is minimal considering the number of companies that were said to exist.

The large number of wineries created in the 1980s is linked to the rise of co-operatives discussed earlier. A large portion of these companies was created due to a policy that promoted co-operative enterprises, launched by the Ministry of Agriculture. Essentially, technical and human resources were provided to farmers via the Ministry. This included especially the Agricultural Engineers of the Agricultural Extension Service, who provided information and drafted technical projects, reducing the burden of the initial steps of setting up a company. In addition, it provided low-interest preferential financing through various administrative agencies to facilitate the implementation of the Ministry's strategies.

This policy of promoting large co-operatives that could have added to the sector of large and competitive modern businesses failed as a

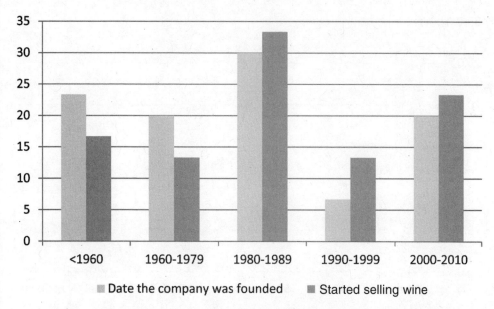

Figure 4.4   Percentage of wineries by founding year and starting year of wine sales

result of the Ministry's limited intervention in planning and management. The Law for Cooperatives that was enforced at the time, as well as subsequent laws, enshrined the principle of democratic management of these businesses. The highest body of management at these co-operatives was thus formed by farmers, with little to no knowledge of business, who for the most part depended on the manager of the company to assist them with decision making.

The effects of this policy continue to be felt today, with periodic cases of co-operatives facing financial difficulties as a result of inadequate financing and production policies. The Ministry of Agriculture has not been able to successfully address the fundamental problems faced regarding the lack of clear and qualified leadership for co-operatives. Meanwhile, both the regional and the Spanish Ministries of Agriculture continue promoting the co-operatives as the solution to all of the problems of the agro-industrial sector.

The high percentage of generally medium-sized enterprises founded in the last decade for the production of quality wines bottled for sale to mainly international markets, is also remarkable. In many cases, they are subsidiaries of national companies in the wine sector that

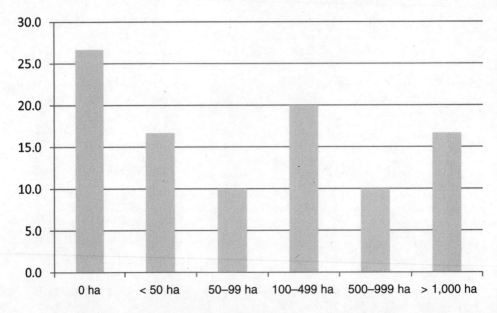

Figure 4.5   Percentage of Extremaduran wineries according to the surface area of their vineyards

invest in this region, acquire vineyards, and directly purchase the produce of local farmers. These companies usually have their own distribution networks and by producing in Extremadura they get a wine with a very high quality/price ratio, as grape production costs in the region are among the lowest in Spain.

While a considerable number of wineries do not have vineyards and purchase their supplies of grapes from wine growers, most use their own vines. This is particularly the case for wineries with the largest vineyards, which are usually co-operatives that are supplied by the vineyards of their partners. These companies can bring together hundreds of growers, thus making the total area held by their businesses quite high. The small size of many of the wineries can be seen not only in the small area of the vineyards, but also in the number of workers. Hence, two thirds of the sample has fewer than ten employees and only 16% have over thirty employees, results that accord with those obtained in other studies (García, Del Moral, and Galera 2010). Eighty-three percent (83%) of the wineries have indicated that they are not part of "global companies." This can be explained by the fact

Table 4.2
Origin of the grapes purchased by Extremaduran wineries

	Nº of wineries	%
Do not purchase	5	16.7
Region	25	83.3
Spain	0	0
International	0	0

that 60% of the sample is composed of family businesses. They generally have been linked to the area since their inception.

As we will see, these characteristics will appear repeatedly, and they determine the behaviour and development of the region's wine industry – small industries, with strong family structure, and primarily regional implementation. Due to their size, they have difficulty hiring specialised human resources to develop R&D or marketing activities, which ultimately results in little national or international deployment.

MARKET BEHAVIOUR OF EXTREMADURAN WINERIES

Supply and Sales Policies

As table 4.2 indicates, although a small group of wineries are supplied exclusively by their own grapes, the vast majority buy grapes in the region to supplement the grapes from their vineyards in variety or quantity.

There are no wineries that purchase their supply from other regions in Spain or other countries, because, as stated previously, Extremadura is one of the major grape-growing regions of Spain, with a great tradition. Moreover, the restructuring of vineyards subsidised by the EU and discussed in previous sections has not reduced the total regional production, although this was one of its objectives. Vine growers used the subsidies to uproot unproductive, old vineyards, and new varieties with more demand in the market were planted. But they also introduced modern growing techniques (irrigation, trellises, etc.), which have kept overall grape production at its previous levels. Therefore, there is a large grape market in the region that traditionally caters not

Table 4.3
Destinations of Extremaduran wine sales, 2007–2010

Percentage of wine sales / Destination	0–25%	25–50%	50–75%	>75%
Extremadura	33.3	26.7	16.7	6.7
Spain	43.3	33.3	3.3	–
Export	43.3	13.3	16.7	6.7

only to the wineries of the area but also to those in other regions. Here they obtain good quality grapes for relatively low prices.

Regional, national, and international sales for Extremaduran wineries are shown in table 4.3. Given the small size of the domestic market (population of 1,100,000), most wineries sell significant amounts outside the region but only a few are dedicated specifically to export. Generally, all wineries participate in the three markets (regional, national, and export), with a clear tendency towards foreign markets, especially that of the European Union, due to the ease of moving goods in an area without borders, and a single currency. The American market and Asian markets are also destinations that some wineries seek to enter. However, only the largest wineries can afford to do so because of the amount of resources needed for such a venture.

Extremaduran wineries appear to be counteracted by their historical tradition, that link them to the sale of bulk wine to areas of Spain such as Jerez or Rioja for distillation or blending with other wines; this was particularly so for the wines made from traditional white varieties such as Pardina and Cayetana. Despite the intense varietal restructuring, the rate of production of these white wines is still important, given that it consists of a large portion of the wineries' sales, especially in the case of co-operatives.

The wine co-operatives in Extremadura are the largest wine-making companies with adequate facilities and technology, and they also have an elevated economic capacity, yet in some cases, these companies also reveal high levels of indebtedness as a result of such investments in infrastructure. It is important to note, however, that these companies do not have the capacity to reject the products of their partners or even guide the farmers toward new varieties. All of the factors discussed above, combined with the requirement of democratic gover-

Table 4.4
Income variation in Extremaduran wineries, 2009–2010

Income variation	% wineries	% income variation	% wineries
Decreased	31.0	< 10%	6.9
		10-20%	10.3
		>20%	13.8
Increased	48.3	< 10%	31
		10-20%	6.9
		>20%	10.4
Maintained	20.7		20.7
Total	100.0		100.0

nance of the partners, lead these companies to exhibit only minor adaptations to the new trends in the market, and more risk aversion, than wineries owned by individuals or companies.

Despite the crisis that has been hitting the Spanish wine sector, 97% of the surveyed wineries indicated they are not producing wine in excess of their demand. This, in our understanding, must be interpreted in the sense that wineries adapt their supply to demand *a posteriori* (i.e. multiannual cycles). After excessively abundant seasons, or where demand is reduced more than expected, wineries respond by reducing the production of the following seasons, thus avoiding structural surpluses that, in the long run, could not be borne. Due to the scarce connectivity between wineries and grape growers, this adjustment to changing market conditions is carried out at the expense of the latter, who have to absorb drastic declines in the price of grapes when the wineries are not demanding the whole harvest.

Trends in Prices and Income

Table 4.4 shows the variation of income produced in the period 2009–10 in the wineries surveyed. These data have to be analysed taking into account that, in the last three harvests alone (SMERAF 2011), the average price paid to farmers for their grapes has dropped 30%, while the wine selling price has not increased in the recent years (Martín 2006; OIV 2007). The result is a comparative advantage for the industry to the

Table 4.5
Wine sales variation in Extremaduran wineries, 2009–2010

Wine sales variation	% wineries	% income variation	% wineries
Decreased	27.6	< 10%	13.8
		10-20%	10.4
		>20%	3.4
Increased	58.6	< 10%	38.0
		10-20%	10.3
		>20%	10.3
Maintained	13.8		13.8
Total	100.0		100.0

detriment of grape growers. Thus, 48% of wineries have declared increasing incomes, and only 31% of wineries have experienced reductions in the last year. Regardless, increases in income have been slight.

The absence of a guiding or price fixing policy is not exclusive to the wine industry, but affects the entire Spanish agricultural sector. This leads to heightened tension amongst the growers, who experience decreases in income while final consumer prices increase every year. Among Extremadura's grape producers the effect of this price tendency is especially grave, since average grape prices are considerably lower than in other Spanish regions, as a consequence of the region's specialisation in bulk wine and distillation. The continuing fall in prices, along with the advanced age of many farmers has led to the abandonment of numerous hectares of arable land.

Finally, table 4.5 shows the changes in wine sales over the period 2009-10. Sales tend to increase more clearly than income, which seems to indicate a decrease in prices on a global scale, according to previous findings (Bardají 2004). Even so, the levels of increase in sales are similar to those in income, and are usually minor.

SOURCES OF COMPETITIVE ADVANTAGE: HEAVY RELIANCE ON PRICE AND EXPORTS

The wineries were asked about their reliance on different sources of competitive advantage. The results are indicated in table 4.6.

Table 4.6
Extremaduran wineries' dependency on competitive advantages (scale of 1–5;
1 = not important, 5 = very important)

Competitive advantages	Average score
Exports	4.23
Position in market regarding appropriate price levels (price competitiveness)	4.03
Continuous improvement in production procedures	3.87
Product differentiation	3.80
Distribution Channels	3.70
Brand development	3.60
Access to the most recent information in wine and grape production	3.57
Marketing	3.57
Employee training	3.57
Agents	3.53
New product development	3.23

Their position relative to the aforementioned external markets clearly demonstrates that status as an "export" is the competitive advantage that is given the most importance, along with the other main element of competitiveness of Extremadura's wine, price. The importance of price is a clear adaptation to the tendencies prevailing in some of the main markets for the Extremaduran wines, such as Germany (Alonso 2008). It is striking that, although some of the important components for survival in a market so saturated and mature get only average scores – such as "differentiation" and "improvements in production procedures" – others such as "employee training" and "new product development" receive even lower scores.

Extremadura's wine companies thus hope to be competitive by appealing to external markets with their very low prices relative to the quality of the wine. This strategy, that could be useful at any given time for a particular company, is fundamentally wrong for an entire business sector, as Extremaduran wineries become followers of companies from other wine regions who think further into the future and spend on research, development, and innovation. The focus on price, as well as the lack of R&D and product differentiation, are causes for the lack of association amongst the different wineries, which (as will be discussed in other sections) can hardly be said to form a cluster.

A justification for this behaviour may lie in the already mentioned structure of the wineries (small and family-type), with a lack of both economic resources and R&D. In this context, the role of the Government to establish ties among industries and research organisations (and also between industries) is essential, although to date, it has had little significance

The Spanish and regional governments' policies to support the export of wines have barely contributed to the objective of promoting the unity of companies, as they have traditionally consisted of grants to attend fairs and/or participate in trade missions, where each company aims to defend its own interests and achieve its own goals. The only entity that organises joint marketing activities is the Designation of Origin Ribera del Guadiana. However, it only deals with propagating the image of the quality of wine, leaving the wineries to carry out their individual policies for exports.

NETWORK TIES BETWEEN WINERIES
AND WITH SUPPORT INSTITUTIONS

Institutions That Support the Wine Industry in Extremadura

There are numerous institutions that provide, to a greater or lesser extent, assistance to the wine sector. However, only government agencies concerned with the regulation of markets within the EU's Common Agricultural Policy (CAP) have an impact on the entire sector. The other institutions listed, due to the poor relationship between companies and the voluntary nature of their operations, have a limited impact on the sector.

EXTREMADURAN MINISTRY OF AGRICULTURE AND ENVIRONMENT (EMAE) In Spain, individual regions have complete authority over issues of agriculture, and therefore the EMAE in Extremadura holds more influence than the Spanish Ministry of Environment, Rural Affairs, and Fisheries. EMAE manages all policies related to subsidies from the EU and the control of market surpluses. In the wine sector this translates into direct premiums to farmers and to the wineries so they can continue to dedicate part of their produce to distillation, especially in "difficult" years (e.g. with high surpluses). Although this measure is being dismantled by the European Commission, distillation has been for years, as already noted, a major commercial destination for wines from Extremadura.

EMAE also has an agricultural research centre, La Orden–Valdesequera, where research on viticulture is conducted, with projects on issues such as clone selection, strategies for irrigation, and mechanised cultivation and harvest. However, despite the large number of hectares of vineyards in the region, the research centre has devoted few resources to research. As such, there have been no results of interest that have moved into the production sector and that have resulted in technological or productive improvements.

SPANISH MINISTRY OF ENVIRONMENT, RURAL AFFAIRS AND FISHERIES (SMERAF)   As previously mentioned, SMERAF has limited powers in terms of agriculture in general, so its role in the wine sector is minimal. It is important to note that contact between the EU and the regions in questions regarding CAP issues related is made through SMERAF. The Ministry is also the recipient of EU funds and is responsible for distributing said funds among the regions.

UNIVERSITY OF EXTREMADURA (UEX)   The University of Extremadura offers an Oenology program, with several research groups engaged, although not exclusively, in working in viticulture and oenology. The lack of interest in R&D b y companies in the sector has resulted in few relationships between UEX and the wine sector, as well as a lack of funding for research projects.

REGULATORY COUNCIL OF THE DESIGNATION OF ORIGIN (RCDO)   The main features of the Designation of Origin have already been discussed in previous sections. The Regulatory Council is the governing body thereof, in which grape growers and winemakers are represented. It could be considered the basic body of a cluster as it deals not only with the control and the promotion of quality, but also with the marketing and promotion activities abroad. However, the wineries' strategy mentioned earlier leads most of them to not be interested in this type of movement, to the extent that the Designation of Origin covers only 20% or less of the wineries and vineyards in the region, greatly limiting their abilities and influence.

ALMENDRALEJO WINE INSTITUTE (AWI)   Almendralejo is the main city of Tierra de Barros, the largest wine area in Extremadura. The Almendralejo Wine Institute was created in 1915 as part of a national network of Wine Institutes and since then it has been devoted mainly to the analysis of wines (chemical and microbiological), but also to the development of research and the spread of new technologies for wines and vines. In this context, it has helped the Extremaduran wineries, but mainly as a body for quality control.

AGRI-FOOD RESEARCH INSTITUTE (INTAEX)   INTAEX was created to meet the needs of the agri-food industries in Extremadura with the goal of providing technology services of high added value, by conducting research, technological development, and technology transfer projects, and by offering technical assistance. It tries to improve the competitiveness of the food and farming sectors through the promotion of innovation and technological development in small and medium enterprises (SMES), improving thus the quality of their products. It provides the following services:

- creation of research projects and technological development in the area of food innovation;
- development of technical support activities conducted by researchers and/or agri-business technologists, aimed at improving and optimizing products and processes;
- analysis of performance of chemical and microbiological agents;
- organisation and delivery of training activities in the agro-food sector, both within the Institute, and in collaboration with other entities, aimed at the specialisation of professionals; and
- compilation of information for clients and the general public on the activities undertaken at the Centre and the results of research, offered in person and through various forms of media.

ASSOCIATION OF EXTREMADURAN WINE PRODUCERS (ASEVEX)   This Association, which initially grouped only wine bottling companies (it was then called Wine Bottlers Association of Extremadura (APAEVEX), and it is often known by this name), now encompasses fifty-eight companies related to the production and bottling of wine and grape derivatives in Extremadura. It conducts training activities for its members on issues of corporate management, international trade, occupational hazards, and quality management. It also represents the sector in many consulting and regulatory agencies, both regional and national.

Interaction with Institutions

The wineries surveyed were asked to indicate the degree of interaction they had with the institutions described above, classifying these relations in terms of their importance, their frequency, and whether they were formal or informal. Table 4.7 summarises the acquired results. The lowest level of importance has been given to the interactions with UEX and INTAEX. Both institutions are basically publicly funded, and their relationship with companies in the sector is not necessarily determined by the needs of wineries, but by particular interests of research groups or by specific political decisions. In this sense, the dependence of the Spanish research system on public funding to develop research activities could be considered one of its main failures. Universities and other research bodies get their funds for research mainly in public calls, and do not need to carry out applied research that could be of interest for private companies.

However, more valued institutions such as AWI and RCDO provide continuous and practical services to wineries, as does ASEVEX, which is also reflected in the increased frequency of interactions. In particular, AWI is widely used for its ability to certify the quality of wine in the transactions; RCDO facilitates business contacts, attendance at trade fairs, and, in the case of sales, provides the appropriate labels, so its wineries must contact it frequently. Finally, ASEVEX helps member companies in the reports to be filed before the regulatory authorities (SMERAF in the case of reports related to the EU's subsidies, and the Spanish Ministry of Economy for tax reports, as alcohol is highly taxed in the European Union). The affiliations with EMAE are similar to the description in the preceding paragraph, because, as mentioned, this entity manages European subsidies and thus receives the respective statements from the wineries.

ASEVEX and RCDO could play an important role in forming a powerful wine cluster in Extremadura, as both have close relations with companies and experience in advising them on important issues such as management, exports, and marketing. However, the voluntary aspect and the cost mean that not all wineries are integrated. In fact, as

Table 4.7
Interaction with entities that provide support to the wine industry (scale of 1–5; 1= not important, 5 = very important)

Importance and Frequency of Interactions	Average Importance (1–5)	Frequency				Relation		Yes, it helps with Innovation
		Annual	Semester	Monthly	Weekly	Formal	Informal	
Extremaduran Agricultural Council	2.52	65.4	19.2	7.7	7.7	89.3	10.7	51.7
Ministry of Environment, Rural Affairs and Fisheries	2.13	87.5	8.3	0.0	4.2	93.1	6.9	35.7
University of Extremadura	1.63	96.6	0.0	3.4	0.0	89.3	10.7	10.7
Regulatory Council of the Designation of Origin	2.53	44.4	33.3	14.8	7.4	75.9	24.1	55.2
Almendralejo Wine Institute	2.55	50.0	15.4	26.9	7.7	76.7	23.3	44.8
Agro-food Research Institute (INTAEX)	1.83	87.0	4.3	4.3	4.3	93.1	6.9	21.4
ASEVEX (Extremaduran Wine Producers Association)	2.17	63.6	4.5	27.3	4.5	89.7	10.3	32.1
APAEVEX (Extremaduran Wine Bottlers Association)	1.69	87.0	0.0	13.0	0.0	96.0	4.0	11.5

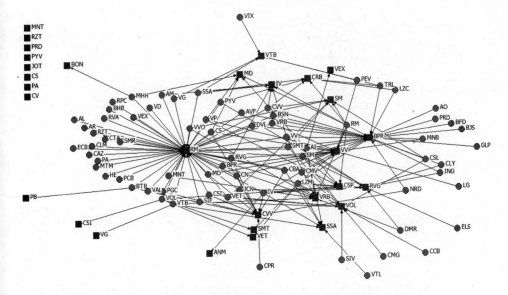

Figure 4.6   Ties that Extremaduran wineries have with other wineries

already mentioned, RCDO represents only a small group of wineries, and the most active and innovative groups in the area are not members. In this sense, SMERAF and EMAE could contribute to the structuring of this cluster, with ASEVEX or RCDO acting as binders. The subsidies granted for export, attendance at fairs, corporate image development, etc., could be linked to cluster membership, which in turn should come with not only advisory powers but also executive powers. This political decision has not been taken as both Spanish and Extremaduran governments are reluctant to impose a certain organization on an industrial sector, preferring that the companies organize themselves.

Level and Strength of Ties among Wineries

Figure 4.6 shows the general ties that Extremaduran wineries have with each other. Boxes represent the surveyed wineries, and circles represent the whole group of wineries in the region, although the wineries that have not shown any ties have been deleted.

As can be seen, a couple of wineries (RM and BPR, both in Tierra de Barros wine region) show a great number of ties, while a high number of companies have ties with just one other winery. These two wineries are family-owned and although they produce their own wine (RM even

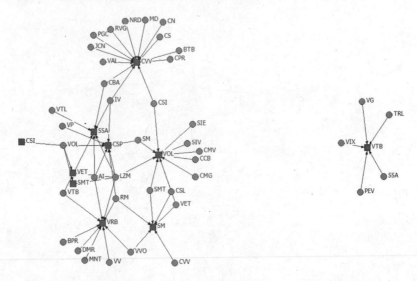

Figure 4.7   Ties that Extremaduran co-operative wineries have with other wineries

sells significant amounts of bottled wine), their main business comes from buying bulk wine from other companies and selling it later to big wineries in other regions or countries.

The relationships have been analysed considering the main types of companies – co-operatives and non-co-operatives. The ties of co-operative wineries are shown in figure 4.7.

VOL is a remarkable case, as it is a co-operative whose members are other wine co-operatives. Due to its nature VOL markets the wine produced by the various member co-operatives, and thus shows a large number of ties with other co-operatives. Moreover, most co-operatives revealed few relationships with other companies, except in the case of CVV, and to a lesser extent, VRB. These relationships are mainly as providers of bulk wines for other non-co-operative wineries, such as those which showed the highest activity in figure 4.6, BPR, RM, and VV. Although the leading co-operatives in the region produce both bulk wines and bottled wines, the importance of bulk wines is still too high when compared with other regions or types of wineries. Co-operatives are often the larger companies and therefore have the capacity to move towards export markets, and therefore they do not need to a great extent the relationships with other wineries in the

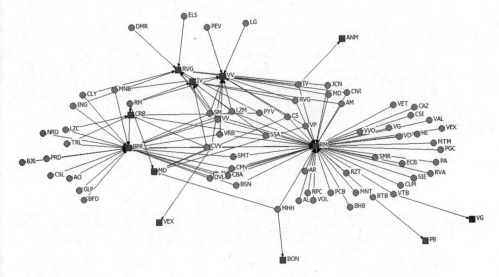

Figure 4.8   Ties that Extremaduran non-co-operative wineries have with other wineries

region. In addition, Spanish law limits the ability of co-operatives to acquire, process, and sell products that do not come from their partners, thus reducing their chances of forming relationships with external companies.

Figure 4.8 reflects the relationships shown by non-co-operative wineries with other wineries. As displayed above, unlike co-operatives, many of the non-co-operative wineries surveyed list several relationships with other wineries. Clearly highlighted are RM and BPR, and to a lesser extent, a few wineries with a lower level of relationships, like vv or iv. These family-owned wineries sell considerably more wine than is produced in their vineyards (RM for example has no vineyards in its property, but sold about 10 million litres of wine), and in fact are the most active companies in the region. It is also interesting to note that in the case of non-co-operative wineries, there are more companies with few or no relationships with other companies. This is due to the increased presence of new wineries in this group. These companies, since their inception, have been focused on the production and sale of quality wines in markets outside the region, usually for export. Therefore, their relationships with other companies in Extremadura is scarce or nonexistent.

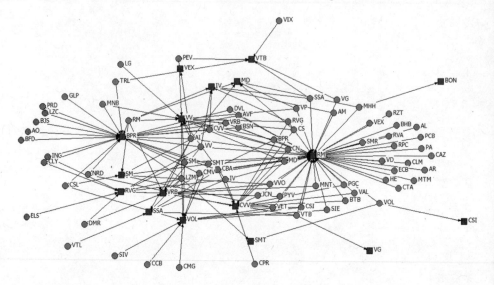

Figure 4.9   Ties that Tierra de Barros wineries have with other wineries

Ties among Wineries by Wine Areas

We performed a similar analysis of the relationship between the wineries according to the wine region to which they belong. The results appear in the figures below, although two of the wine areas of the region are not displayed, either because no wineries were sampled there (Montánchez area), or because the wineries surveyed in the area indicated no relationships with other wineries. First, we show the results for the main wine region, Tierra de Barros, where the largest number of wineries is located (figure 4.9).

The large wineries that have already appeared in the previous analysis are shown here again, since it is in the area of Tierra de Barros where most of Extremadura's wineries and vineyards are found. It is logical, therefore, that ties are more developed in this area. However, in the commercial sector, Tierra de Barros' wineries are not the most developed, serving as a supplier of bulk wine to other companies that later age and/or bottle wine to sell it in domestic and international markets through their own brands. In this sense both RM and BPR operate similarly, because, although they bottle wine under their own brands (RM recently also started producing Cava), most of their rev-

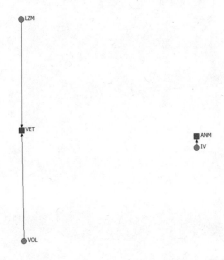

Figure 4.10   Ties that Matanegra wineries have with other wineries

enue comes from bulk wine sales, primarily to companies in other wine regions of Spain and other countries.

Figure 4.10 shows the results for Matanegra wine country. VET is a co-operative that has ties only with VOL, the co-operative that sells part of its production, and with LZM, one of the most important wineries in the marketing of table wines in Extremadura. The other company, ANM, is a medium-sized, family-run winery, selling most of its production in bottles. IV, the only company having ties with ANM, is also a family-run winery, but they sell both bulk wine and bottled wine.

Lastly in the analysis of wine regions, figure 4.11 demonstrates the ties between the wineries in Ribera Baja and Ribera Alta del Guadiana. In this case, both areas were included due to their relative homogeneity, allowing the same figure to display more companies.

In the figure above it is important to highlight the fact that wineries with ties to firms in Ribera Alta/Baja are essentially from Tierra de Barros, which makes sense if one considers them to be the key drivers of the sector. By marketing products from other wineries and/or providing bulk wine, Tierra de Barros's wineries are fundamental to the relationships of any winery in the region. Shown in figure 4.11 are some wineries such as RM, LZM, and VOL, whose importance in the sector has been previously stated.

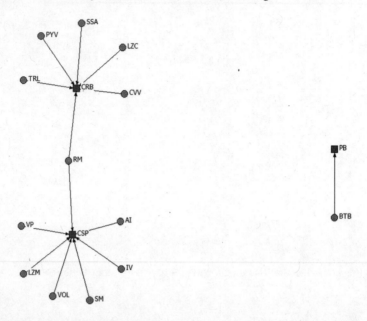

Figure 4.11   Ties that Ribera Baja and Ribera Alta wineries have with other wineries

The previous figures show the different scenarios in which the Extremaduran wine industry is developing. The business area of greatest density, Tierra de Barros, is obviously where the highest level of interaction between the wineries is found, and where companies are more competitive. A clear relationship between both factors can therefore be assumed. Nevertheless, it cannot be forgotten that in other wine areas we also find growing wineries with good market deployment.

It can be concluded, therefore, that if a wine cluster is to be developed in Extremadura, the origin must be clearly in Tierra de Barros wine country. As noted above, it is in this area that the largest number of wineries is concentrated, and therefore where we can currently find the highest level of interaction. In addition, the wineries belonging to the other wine countries also have strong ties with wineries in Tierra de Barros, which could greatly facilitate further business developments.

To complete the analysis of interactions among wineries, the surveyed wineries were asked to indicate the importance granted to their

Table 4.8
Importance granted to geographical proximity to other firms or industries

	Nº of Wineries	%
Important	18	60
Marginally important	5	16.7
No impact	5	16.7
A disadvantage	2	6.6

geographical proximity to other wineries or industry bodies. The results are presented in table 4.8.

As revealed in table 4.8, most companies consider the proximity to other companies advantageous, although there is a certain group of companies that consider proximity to be irrelevant or even a disadvantage. Co-operatives, which rely on other wineries to sell their wines, mainly have considered proximity as "important," while some medium-sized family owned wineries (well-established companies with recognised brands) view other wineries as their "competitors." However, despite this consideration, and as shown in the previous figures, a good number of wineries do not develop the potential of this proximity at all, perceiving other companies as competitors and not as a potential source of competitive advantages.

THE ROLE OF INNOVATION AND TRAINING

A General Lack of Innovation

With regard to innovation, wineries were initially questioned on the development of new products (brands or lines) and on improvements in products and processes. In the previous two years, 33% of wineries have not developed any new products; 41% developed one or two products; and the remaining 26% of wineries developed three or more products. VOL has developed ten new products or brands, however, this is a special case because it began marketing activities for bottled wine only recently.

The vast majority of wineries (86%), note significant improvement in the products during this period, although 25% said that during this period their production process "has not improved much," compared

Table 4.9
Areas of innovation in Extremaduran wineries in the previous three years

	% of affirmative answers
Retailing	30.0
Marketing	66.7
Finances	26.7
Plant breeding	40.0
Breeding	23.3
Soil adaptation	33.3
Fermentation	73.3
Information System	63.3
Education/Training	60.0

to 56% that indicated "a little" improvement, and 21% "a lot." With growing competitiveness in global wine markets, companies have to enhance their relative positions, and a way to do that is through product improvement.

When asked about the companies that they considered leaders in innovation, most (89%) responded "none." The other companies mentioned two firms from Tierra de Barros, VOL and RM. The former, as already mentioned, is a co-operative integrated by other wine co-operatives of the region, and created to advance and develop the processes of marketing wine; the latter is a family business with twenty years of existence that has managed to grow and diversify itself during this period. These results reveal not only limited innovation among companies in the sector, but also the lack of ties between them which leads them to not recognise or not want to recognise their competitors' innovations, as it highlights their own weaknesses.

Regarding the areas of the companies where innovation had occurred over the previous years, the results for the sample of Extremaduran wineries are shown in table 4.9. Clearly, the focus on innovation in these companies has rested on technology (fermentation) and on marketing-related issues such as new forms/formats for sales, new channels, internet presence, etc. Important issues regarding the quality of wines such as breeding, plants, and soil are outside the scope of business, requiring costly investment projects for which the results take many years to be perceived, if at some point they are successful.

Table 4.10
Importance of different actors in innovation processes developed by companies
(scale of 1–5; 1 = not important, 5 = very important)

	Average score
Companies' internal resources	3.8
Suppliers of equipment, materials, components or software	2.8
Clients or consumers	3.6
Joint research with other regional wineries	1.7
Wineries outside of the region	1.5
Consultants	1.8
Conferences, trade shows, exhibits	2.9
Trade magazines or newspapers	2.4
Internet	3.0

An adequate policy of R&D between EMAE (through its research centre) and the companies could lead to substantial improvements in the
sector, such as identification and distribution of clone varieties adapted to the soil and climate characteristics of Extremadura, preparation
techniques, and disinfection of soils, etc. However, agri-food R&D in
Extremadura lacks an adequate policy to define the objectives and
lines of research (addressing the demands of companies and producers in different sectors), which results, as noted in previous sections, in
weak interfaces between companies and research organisations.

It is also relevant to note the lack of innovation in retailing, an area
where we have seen a revolution in the agri-food sector in recent
years, with the implementation of online sales and the development
of logistics and distribution networks. This fact reflects, to a large
extent, the low involvement of Extremaduran wineries with the final
consumer.

Table 4.10 shows the importance given by the companies to the different actors involved in the innovation processes undertaken by
Extremaduran wineries in the previous three years. Since the major
areas of innovation were those related to marketing and production
processes, one can say that clients or customers, equipment suppliers,
and trade shows or exhibitions play an important role in innovation.
The importance given to internal company resources comes as a surprise, especially when one considers that many companies are of small

Table 4.11
Importance of sources of financing for innovation
(scale of 1–5; 1 = not important, 5 = very important)

	Average Score
Personal Finances	3.2
Banks, Rural Banks, Savings Banks	2.9
Venture Capital Investors	1.2
Spanish Government	2.1
Regional Government	3.0
Local Government	1.7

or medium size, and that, considering the whole, very few wineries have an R&D department. As in previous sections, the lowest score is for other companies, both in the region and elsewhere. These data serve to reinforce the finding of weak ties with other companies.

Funding is a key element in innovation, either as a constraint (companies without the adequate funding cannot carry out the desired and needed innovation) or as an opportunity to develop the innovation that can increase the competitiveness of a company. In this context, the wineries were asked about the importance of the different sources of funding that had been used to develop innovations. Results appear in table 4.11.

To finance innovation, wineries rely more heavily on their own resources and on those generated by the regional government than on the resources provided by the financial system. This makes sense when one considers that many companies are co-operatives that prefer to obtain funding directly from their partners, thereby avoiding paying interest. Another important group is formed by family businesses that rely on their own (although often scarce) resources.

Of the various administrations that could support the wineries to develop innovation, the regional government is the one with the most specific options for financing agribusiness, with capital grants and/or interest grants. This is the reason for the high importance given by the respondents to the regional government in financing innovation. Although the regional administration has defined priority areas of investment, these relate to agri-food sectors to which aid will be granted (that were previously defined by the EU regulations, often co-financier of these grants).

Table 4.12
Reasons why Extremaduran wineries have not developed innovation

	% of affirmative answers
Not necessary for the company	42.9
Too expensive	46.4
Lack of Human Resources	25.0
Lack of technological information	21.4
Lack of information on potential markets	21.4
Difficulty in finding cooperative partners	14.3
Lack of an adequate and clear regulatory framework	7.1
Not informed on what is available	7.4

A coherent plan for promoting the competitiveness of the wineries in the region could begin with financing for innovation and, in accordance with business specifications, precise subsidising actions that could benefit many wineries, not just one. This would also help to consolidate this cluster of wineries that increasingly appears as fundamental for the persistence and improvement of the sector's profitability. There is a near absence of foreign investment in the wineries, which is explained by the regional nature and small size of Extremaduran wineries, at least when compared to large industrial groups with a national or European presence that have the capacity to attract risk investment. Finally, table 4.12 presents the reasons why Extremaduran wineries have not developed innovation (only for those that have not carried out further innovation processes).

Not surprisingly, table 4.12 shows that in the current economic environment, the high cost is the most important reason companies cannot carry out processes of innovation. Also noteworthy is the fact that 43% of the wineries suggest that innovation is not necessary for the company. This indicates a lack of initiative and of long-term vision, which hinder the future development of the sector. The third reason is the lack of adequate human resources, related in part to the structure of enterprises; this could be avoided, at least in part, with combined actions by all the wineries.

Finally, wine tourism could be considered an innovation, as it creates new opportunities for the companies, attracts new customers, and diversifies the sources of revenue. To check the importance of wine tourism for Extremaduran wineries, the surveyed companies were

Table 4.13
Methods used by Extremaduran wineries for training

	% of affirmative answers
Training by the company itself	76.7
External training	73.3
University of Extremadura	23.3
Consultants	36.7

asked if wine tourism was an important part of their strategy. Only eight of the surveyed wineries assigned minimal importance to this activity, while six others granted it limited importance, and the remaining seventeen, considerable importance. On a scale from 1 (not important) to 5 (very important), the average score was 3.3. Although the wineries could consider this potential source of diversification of activities and resources as important, Tierra de Barros, where we find most of the wineries, has the least environmental and landscaping interest, as it is devoted almost exclusively to the cultivation of vineyards and olive groves.

Training

Despite the previous statements about the lack of adequate human resources for innovation, when the wineries were asked about the training of their employees, they indicated that, on average, 84% of their workers were trained, and 63% of the wineries indicated that all employees were trained. Obviously, innovation is not seen as relevant to companies, so neither is the training of staff to develop innovation. When the wineries indicate that most of their employees are trained, this refers to training in the more traditional technical areas in the wine business, and not in innovative aspects that could improve the competitive position of the companies. Table 4.13 shows the different methods used by the Extremaduran wineries to provide training for their workers.

In another example of both their independent behaviour and their scarce relationships with other entities in the sector, companies rely mainly on themselves for training, even if it is terribly difficult for a small company to be up-to-date in topics that are changing as fast as technology, communications, and marketing.

CONCLUSION

The wine sector in Extremadura has undergone vast changes over the past thirty years, from being a producer of bulk wines intended primarily for the production of alcohol, to producing quality wines that are exported to many countries. Producers have adapted varieties towards those most in demand by the market, and wineries have introduced technological improvements that have enabled them to achieve high levels of quality with very competitive prices. However, throughout this chapter it has become clear that there are no ties between the industries that would allow one to speak of a cluster in the Extremaduran wine industry, or even that it is in its initial stages, although organisations like the Designation of Origin or the Association of Extremaduran Wine Producers could provide a suitable starting point.

In this sense, the role of the Spanish and regional governments has been detrimental given that, unlike other countries, there has not been a clear policy to promote business integrations here. However, both governments have taken up several initiatives that, with proper planning, could encourage companies to increase their coordination and organisation and the strength of their ties. A key feature of the Extremaduran wine industry is the significant role of co-operatives in the production of bulk wine, although this is not reflected later in the marketing of bottled wines. Here we see the result of an incomplete policy for promotion of social enterprises, which was subsidised in its early stages to facilitate their creation and implementation. The state failed in this aspect by not encouraging or forcing these companies to integrate and improve their management, which has led to the appearance of many co-operatives with little or no relation to each other and with strong managerial deficits.

The pricing policy has been key to the maintenance and development of Extremaduran wineries. The region, as a result of its soil and climatic features, has excellent conditions for grape production, even taking into account the scarcity of rainfall between harvests, which greatly affects production. The result is a raw product of good quality at a price well below that of other Spanish or European regions producing wines of similar quality. This has provided an element of competitiveness to the wineries of Extremadura, at the expense of the grape producers who have spent several years in crisis.

The other key element is the strong tendency for export, caused by the limited domestic market and facilitated greatly by the integration of Spain into the European Union. The EU offers Extremaduran wineries a potential market of 500 million consumers, in which customs barriers do not exist or are very much reduced, and where more than 300 million of these consumers use the same currency. These facts, together with the development of logistics networks, have led companies to turn to foreign markets, where competitive prices allowed them to enter the markets.

However, the lack of business ties between companies and the various advisory and administrative bodies leads to the excessive spending of resources, both human and material, since the advancement and empowerment of the brands, attracting distributors, and market research, in many instances, does not receive adequate funding compared to the amount of resources invested in export. In this sense, an organised structure with management capacity (and not simply advisory powers) would optimise investments in foreign markets and thus complement the benefits of price advantages and generate large competitive advantages for wineries in Extremadura.

Another aspect that stands out in the sector is the lack of innovation, and more pointedly, the lack of interest in innovation, which may also be explained by the "individuality" in the sector. Most companies, because of their family-based characteristics, cannot afford an R&D department. Large companies, such as co-operatives, that could afford one, often focus on the production of bulk wines, where they find it is more important to reduce costs than to innovate. The lack of clear guidance by the regional and Spanish governments further complicate an already bleak picture, in which there is no sign of improvement despite the presence of research centres (INTAEX, AWI, and La Orden-Valdesequera Research Centre) that could actively work with the wineries of Extremadura.

The development of a wine cluster is seen as a possible way to improve the competitiveness of the sector. It could start with the current structure of the Designation of Origin or with that of the Association of Extremaduran Wine Producers. Regardless, it should be encouraged by the Spanish and Extremaduran governments through the compulsory membership of the companies that want to receive any subsidy granted by the EU under the Common Agricultural Policy. However, this would require political decisions to be undertaken by the sector.

REFERENCES

Alonso, Andrés. 2008. "Factores Económicos Clave del Sector Vitivinícola." In *V Foro Mundial del Vino*. Logroño, Spain: Caja de Ahorros de Badajoz.

Bardají, Isabel. 2004. "Tendencias en el Mercado Español del Vino." *Distribución y Consumo*, November-December: 57–68.

Díaz, Marcelino. 2010. "Historia de la Vid y del Vino en Extremadura." In *La Agricultura y la Ganadería Extremeñas en 2009*. Badajoz, Spain: Caja de Ahorros de Badajoz.

Falcó, Carlos. 2000. *Entender de Vino*. Barcelona, Spain: Martínez Roca.

García, María M., Alejandro Del Moral, and Clementina Galera. 2010. "Valoración de la Importancia de la Denominación de Origen desde la Perspectiva de la Empresa. El Caso DO Ribera del Guadiana." *Revista de Estudios Agrosociales y Pesqueros* 227: 99–123.

Martín, Víctor J. 2006. "Consumo de Vinos. Principales Características y Distribución Comercial." *Distribución y Consumo*, Enero-Febrero: 60–101.

– 2009. "Denominaciones de Origen y de Calidad Diferenciada en el Mercado Alimentario Español." *Distribución y Consumo* July-August: 89–102.

Mesías, Francisco J. and Manuel Barrera. 2004. "Ribera del Guadiana: European Growth." *Eurowine* 20: 38–9.

Mesías, Francisco J. and Francisco Pulido. 1996. "Caracterización Tecnológica de las Bodegas Extremeñas." In *La Agricultura y la Ganadería Extremeñas en 1995*. Badajoz, Spain: Caja de Ahorros de Badajoz.

Mesías, Francisco J., Antonio Rodríguez de Ledesma, Miguel Escribano, José M. Coleto, and Francisco Pulido. 1998. "Flujos Comerciales de los Vinos Extremeños." *Viticultura y Enología Profesional* 57: 21–6.

oiv (International Organisation of Vine and Wine). 2007. *Structure of the World Vitivinicultural Industry in 2007*. http://www.oiv.int/oiv/info/enplubicationoiv#situation

Osorio, Juan M. 2006. "Promoción de los Vinos Españoles en el Mundo." In *IV Foro Mundial del Vino*. Logroño, Spain: Gobierno de La Rioja.

Seisdedos, Hermenegildo. 2008. "El Marketing en el Desarrollo Integral de las Regiones Vitivinícolas. El Vino Como Motor del Branding de un Territorio." In *V Foro Mundial del Vino*. Logroño, Spain: Gobierno de La Rioja.

smeraf (Spanish Ministry of Environment, Rural Affairs, and Fisheries). 2011. "Agricultural Prices and Salaries." http://www.marm.es/es/

estadistica/temas/precios-percibidos-pagados-y-salarios-agrarios
/Indicadores_05_tcm7–14513.pdf

– 2010. *Agricultural Statistics Yearbook 2010*. Secretariat-General of the Spanish Ministry of Environment, Rural Affairs and Fisheries, Madrid.

– 2009. *Agricultural Statistics Yearbook 2009*. http://www.marm.es/es/estadistica/temas/anuario-de-estadistica/2009/default.aspx

– 2008. *Agricultural Statistics Yearbook 2008*. http://www.marm.es/es/estadistica/temas/anuario-de-estadistica/2008/default.aspx

– 2007. *Agricultural Statistics Yearbook 2007*. http://www.marm.es/es/estadistica/temas/anuario-de-estadistica/2007/default.aspx

5

Understanding Competitiveness: The Chilean Wine Cluster

CHRISTIAN FELZENSZTEIN

INTRODUCTION

This chapter is based on the results of a 2011 survey related to the competitiveness of the Chilean wine cluster. The main aim of this chapter is to understand the competitiveness of the Chilean wine cluster, specifically:

- What does the Chilean wine cluster case tell us about the challenges to competitiveness in the wine industry?
- How is Chile attempting to be one of the top producers and exporters of wine in the world, and what can be learned from this experience?
- What are the relationships of different actors in this industry and how might they influence competitiveness?

Using an analytical approach, this chapter examines the key characteristics of the wine industry in the emerging economy of Chile; market evolution and trends; policies; institutional and social networking; and global supply-chain issues related to the competitiveness of the industry.

CHILEAN WINE HISTORY

Chile has been highlighted as a global producer of excellent wines and spirits. Flavour, color, and centuries of experience, are some of the features that make Chilean wine popular in world markets. The valleys of Chile have an ideal combination of soil, sunlight, temperature, and humidity, which lead to world-class grapes and wine. Chilean wines are among the most organic. Due to the dry summer season, Chilean vineyards resist infestation, and natural geographic barriers have protected the country from the arrival of phylloxera and other diseases. The absence of these threats allows producers to grow their vineyards with reduced dependence on chemical agents.

Chilean wine history begins with the arrival of Spanish conquerors. In the mid-sixteenth century, missionaries introduced vines to produce wine for Catholic mass rituals. Grapes from the Santiago area were used in the mass production of wine, according to records dating back to 1555. In 1830, Frenchman Claude Gay convinced the Chilean government of the need to create a state agricultural station to be called "Quinta Normal Agriculture." In 1850 the "Quinta Normal" had more than 40,000 vines and seventy different varieties of grapes. With the arrival of Bordeaux varieties, Chilean wine history entered the modern era of winemaking.

In 1851, Don Silvestre Ochagavía Echazarreta brought varieties from France, and most classic winemakers of the period planted their land in Talagante. Ochagavía introduced varieties such as Cabernet Sauvignon, Merlot, Pinot Noir, Sauvignon, Semillon and Riesling. These would be the basis for the beginning of the modern wine industry in Chile. The vines are easily adapted to the climate in Chile and it is believed that the vines are the only existing clones of grapes that existed prior to the phylloxera epidemic that persist in the world. Chile is the only producer of wine on a large scale that has never had an outbreak of phylloxera.

In the 1970s and 1980s there was a decline in domestic demand for Chilean wine, causing a dramatic drop in the price of grapes. About half of Chilean vines were uprooted. The political climate during the General Pinochet dictatorship and the economic recessions in the 1980s were factors that weakened the Chilean wine industry. Upon the return to democracy in 1990, the Chilean wine industry began a slow but steady recovery. Between 1990 and 1993 an additional 10,000 hectares of various strains of wine grapes were planted in conjunction with large investments in new technologies for the production of wine. This was accompanied by a new commercial and marketing focus on the growth of international markets, which seen by entrepreneurs as the most viable route to growth both in market shares and sales volumes.

In 2007, total exports of Chilean wine exceeded $1.256 billion, destined to five continents, and imported chiefly by the UK, US, and Canada. Some of the factors behind this international success include the international vision of some entrepreneurs, like the owners of Concha y Toro wineries, individual companies and the Wines of Chile Trade Association, who aimed to open new international markets and position the Chilean wine industry in the global marketplace.

Foreign investors, among which are Torres Winery and Chateau Lafitte, have significantly influenced the development of the Chilean wine industry. Today, Rothschild, Pernod Ricard, Kendall-Jackson, Francisco State, and Bruno Prat are among those international vintners with substantial investments, international know-how, and technology transfer in the Chilean wine industry. All of them were attracted by the ideal geo-climatic conditions, the promise of premium quality fruits, healthy crop conditions, and a growing demand for Chilean wines around the world.

THE CHILEAN WINE INDUSTRY
IN THE GLOBAL CONTEXT

Chile is the world's seventh largest wine producer, the fifth largest exporter, and the most important producer in Latin America. In 2010, Chile enjoyed a market share of 8% of the volume of the international wine market. More importantly, Chile exports more than 70% of its wine production, making it the world's most export-dependent wine industry. With 150 destination countries and 1.5 billion consumers per year, Chilean wines are positioned as the country's most symbolic international product. The primary export markets in terms of volume are the UK, US, Germany, and Canada, which together represent 50% of the total exports. During the last few years most of the decrease in the share of sales in the internal market has been caused by a diversion toward developing new emerging markets such as China and Brazil, rather than to existing markets. The figure below shows a drop of 15% in the domestic market over the last decade as companies further divert sales from the internal market toward new emerging markets such as China and Brazil. Among the reasons for this shift are the limited internal demand in terms of population and

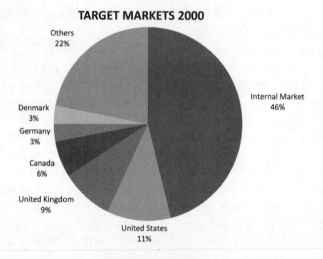

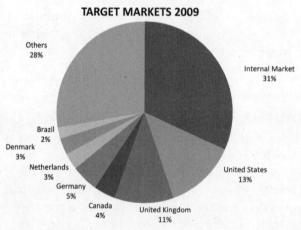

Figure 5.1   Target markets
Source: Prepared based on information from SAG (www.sag.gob.cl) and Wines of Chile

income distribution, and the growing international market demand from the BRIC countries (Brazil, Russia, India and China) as well as other newly developed or emerging economies (like Taiwan).

   Chilean wines face very high levels of competition in different markets from many regions and brands (see table 5.1). One of the main characteristics of Chilean wines in international markets is that its average prices are comparatively lower than those of its competitors.

Table 5.1
Evolution of exports

	France	Bordeaux	Burgundy	Italy	Spain	Australia	Chile	United States	South Africa	New Zealand	Argentina
1989						39	28	83		4	
1990						38	43	110		4	45
1991						54	65	125		6	28
1992						79	74	147		7	23
1993						103	87	132		9	25
1994						125	110	133		8	23
1995					675	114	129	147		8	197
1996					720	130	184	180		11	112
1997					973	154	216	227	110	13	120
1998					1.15	192	231	272	117	15	109
1999					972	216	234	291	128	17	88
2000				1.764	902	285	267	294	141	19	84
2001				1.586	1.054	338	311	304	177	19	88
2002	1.554	220	69	1.579	1.037	418	349	282	217	23	123
2003	1.502	202	64	1.328	1.281	519	395	349	238	27	185
2004	1.425	178	60	1.427	1.469	584	468	461	268	31	155
2005	1.383	172	64	1.609	1.45	670	418	388	281	51	215
2006	1.472	182	70	1.83	1.434	722	474	405	272	58	293
2007	1.515	193	79	1.883	1.558	787	610	455	313	76	360
2008	1.37	179	66	1.751	1.69	715	589	491	412	89	414
2009	1.251	155	56	1.9	1.44	752	694	418	430	113	283
GROWTH RATE											
1990–1999	-3%	-5%		1%	11%	20%	25%	14%	8%	16%	72%
2000–2009	-3%		-2%	1%	5%	14%	12%	5%	13%	22%	16%

Note: for those countries for which there is no available data, the average is calculated based on available years

Source: Wines of Chile, based on information from national generic offices

According to Wines of Chile (2010) the industry's present profitability levels are low, and there is an urgent need to elevate the premium positioning and average prices in international markets to achieve a sustainable return in the long term (Felzensztein and Deans 2013). During 2010, the Chilean wine industry prepared a new international marketing strategy outlining guidelines for a vigorous ten-year programme of international development. Chile aims to be recognised by 2020 as the most successful producer and exporter of wine from an emerging market. To achieve this goal the country and industry leaders are planning to export close to US$3 billion in bottled wine in that year (La Tercera 2010). The goal is ambitious, considering the strong competition coming from other New World wine producing countries such as Argentina, Australia, and New Zealand (Felzensztein 2011).

Chile has thirteen wine regions located within a range of 1,000 km (Knowles and Sharples 2002). The majority of Chile's premium wines are produced in the regions of Maule, Maipo, Aconcagua, Cachapoal, and Colchagua. All of these regions are located close to Santiago, Chile's capital city. The wine industry in Chile is more concentrated than in continental Europe, but less so than in Australia and New Zealand. There have been important tacit knowledge transfers as many foreign firms chose to establish in Chile through joint venture agreements oriented to the production and commercialisation of high price wines, a segment of the market where the Chilean wine industry was weak. These joint ventures controlled 30% of the high price segment. It is important to clarify that most of these joint ventures with Chilean firms are from large international wine-producing companies mainly from France, Italy, and Australia. Some small firms also enjoy strategic alliances with foreign producers from France, Italy, and Australia. The effects included an increase in exports as Chilean wineries with foreign involvement were the first to export to a wide range of premium price market segments. An additional effect of the arrival of foreign firms was the access to distribution channels in the major markets and the improvement of the Chilean wine image (Björk 2005).

Co-operation through alliances or networking with foreign wine companies is very beneficial for Chilean wineries especially for transmitting knowledge related to upgrading production functions like grape growing, wine making, and wine marketing (Kunc 2008).

Another example of co-operation is the link between domestic firms and importers or distributors. Since small- and medium-sized wineries rely on the marketing knowledge and capacity of overseas distributors as well as importers to manage their wine brand(s), lessons learned from foreign firms about successful co-operation between importers and distributors with small- and medium-sized wineries was important in the development of the Chilean wine industry (Kunc 2008).

Economic Importance, Cluster Configuration, and International Marketing

One of the Chilean government's 2011 policies aims to grow Chile into one of the world's top ten exporters of food products over the course of the next ten years. The wine industry is doing its part to achieve this goal, and Chile is now the world's fifth largest wine exporting country. In recent decades Chile's food and agriculture sector has pursued a successful strategy of internationalisation, which has become a pillar of the agro-export basket and of the country's economic development. Chile's fruits and vegetables, wine, seeds, and agricultural and forestry products reach hundreds of countries around the world and provide employment for more than 800,000 people.

Wine exports make up 2.6% of Chile's total exports and 14% of the forestry-agriculture-livestock sector exports (Felzensztein and Deans 2013). The sector consists of more than 260 companies with annual exports greater than US$50,000, of which 21% or fity-two companies export more than 100,000 UF (approximately US$4.2 million) per year. This means that the majority (79%) of Chile's wine exporters are small- and medium-sized companies. Chile produces an average of 887 million litres of wine per year, 70% of which is for export markets, which have grown steadily in value by 11% per year. These exports are sent to 150 countries, with the United States and the United Kingdom being the most important markets.

The wine industry operates in several regions of the country, from the Coquimbo region in the north to the Araucanía region in the south. The Maule and O'Higgins regions have the greatest concentration of area planted to vine (53.4%), although the Metropolitan, Valparaíso, and Biobío regions also have a significant amount. The industry's continuous development and geographic diversification have attracted both domestic and foreign investment to historically less-developed zones such as the Maule region, which had previously been overlooked as an area worthy of investment. This development has also benefited the many agents involved in the value chain, including suppliers of materials, technology and complementary services, and particularly the large number of grape growers, most of whom are small producers. At the same time, the wine industry continues to be a major source of tax revenue for the government through the Alcohol Law (ILA). From 2005 to 2009, the Wine ILA accounted for an average of 0.21% of the country's total tax revenue. In 2009 alone, the Wine ILA generated tax revenues of US$58 million.

The emerging wine tourism industry is a new and under-developed area of business that has great potential, as it offers high quality employment that not only diversifies risks and sources of revenue, but also fosters more comprehensive and sustainable development in the regions and communities in which these services are located.

More than other Chilean products, wine reaches millions of homes and consumers around the world with a well-identified country brand that associates the name "Chile" with quality and diversity. This makes the brand a unique vehicle for positioning the country's image, which is considered one of the nation's strategic assets and also facilitates the introduction of new products and services. In 2009, Chile exported 42 million cases of wine, the equivalent of 510 million bottles. From a conservative perspective, each bottle is seen by at least three people, which means that "Brand Chile" reaches 1.5 billion people each year. Assuming a moderate marketing cost of US$0.852 (which is the average cost per contact on the Internet in the United States), the value of this impact is US$1.275 billion per year.

Developing the "Wine of Chile" category in key international markets will improve and expand Chile's position in the minds of consumers. Positioning Chile as a country that produces high quality wines will reinforce the country's positive attributes such as good agricultural practices, high quality cuisine, attractiveness as a tourist destination, a country with its own identity and traditions, a good quality of life, and a sociable people who know how to enjoy themselves and make the most of special occasions, among other qualities.

Consumers in the United States and United Kingdom have a low affinity with Chile, which is not true of Australia, New Zealand, Italy,

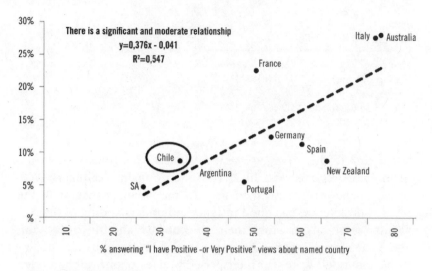

Figure 5.2   Relationships between views about named country and frequency of wine consumption
Source: Vinitrac® US, Dec 07; Base=US regular wine drinkers n=2,015

and France. This is a consistent result in several country image studies that conclude that Chile has a neutral or no image among international consumers at the mass level. This implies that for mass consumers, Chilean wine is a product of unknown origin.

Although higher-income and more-frequent wine consumers from the United States drink Chilean wines, they have a low affinity with the country. The cases of Italy and Australia stand out in that there is coherence between the positive perception of the country and regular consumption of wines from those regions. Figure 5.2 shows these country image trends.

METHODOLOGY

An electronic survey in Spanish was designed and adapted for the Chilean context. We have applied the framework and survey developed by Hira and Ayward (see appendix) for the British Columbia (BC), Canada wine industry. Their approach focuses on the potential role of public and collective support institutions to promote industry competitiveness in clusters. This is part of a wider international research project on wine cluster competitiveness.

Table 5.2
Represented wine valleys

Maule Valley	36%
Cachapoal Valley	33%
Colchagua Valley	31%
Curico and Casablanca Valleys	21%

The link to the survey was sent to all 110 wine companies in the main wine regions of Chile. The questionnaire recipients were owner-operators, general managers, or marketing managers of the firms and therefore had good insights and understanding of the prevailing conditions in which their firms operate and function (Kahn and McDonough, 1997). Over a period of three months, two electronic reminders were sent interspersed by a telephone call reminder. This resulted in a 30% percent response rate.

RESULTS

Sample Characteristics, Location, and Profits

The location of respondents is shown in table 5.2.

Most of the surveyed firms were small- and medium-sized firms (SMEs), the majority having between eleven and fifty employees (45%) or between fifty-one and one hundred employees (26%). Only 13% declared to have between 101 and 250 full-time-equivalent employees. Results are interesting, as it seems that small- and medium-sized firms may be growing in terms of numbers and importance as the Chilean wine industry is becoming more competitive and reaching new, international, developed markets (UK, Canada, and USA) and emerging markets (like Brazil and China). This situation is generally a call for new entrants as new business opportunities emerge. Nevertheless, the importance of large, vertically integrated wine companies remains notable, and these have very professional management teams and are internationally oriented. It is important to remember that large firms produce about 40% of the total volume sold to export markets.

The vast majority of firms (88%) declared themselves to have Chilean capital and private ownership and only 12% are part of a global conglomerate, while about 60% of the firms are family busi-

Table 5.3
Size of firms

Less than 10	8%
11–50	45%
51–100	26%
101–250	13%
More than 250	8%

nesses. National Chilean capitals are local conglomerates with equity in the industry. Some of these large firms are also publically listed in the Santiago stock exchange, like Concha y Toro.

The vast majority of firms (70%) declared that their profits and sales have increased in the last year (2010). As table 5.4 shows, 62% of the companies report an increase in income between 10% and 30%, while 12% of the firms report an increase between 31% and 60%. This increase includes both volume and value; almost 80% of the firms have increased their sales volume, with 58% of firms reporting between 10% and 30% increases in income. These results show an industry whose growth in sales and volume is commensurate with its new international marketing strategy and a stronger presence of large and medium-sized Chilean firms in international markets with sales and marketing offices in the UK, SA, and some parts of Asia. It is expected that this growth will continue in the near future, as in 2011 some Chilean wine companies, like Concha y Toro, were buying wine companies in California, aiming to maintain their strong positioning and internationalisation strategy. This new growth strategy represents the maturity and international learning process of the Chilean industry. It also represents the success of the large firms selling their production in international markets and is part of a growing strategy following very successful international marketing campaigns such as those of Concha y Toro, the official sponsor of the Manchester United football club in the UK.

New mergers and acquisitions and strategic alliances may also be expected as the industry continues growing. This is part of the more mature stage of the industry and its ambition to be positioned as the most important and successful wine-export-oriented country in the world. Chile also aims to take international market share from other New World wine producers, like Australia and New Zealand.

Table 5.4
Percentage of increase in income during the last year

Less than 10	27%
Between 10 and 30%	62%
Between 31 and 60%	12%
Between 61 and 90%	0%
More than 90%	0%

Table 5.5
Percentage of grapes coming out of wine company

Less than 10	41%
Between 10 and 30%	37%
Between 31 and 60%	11%
Between 61 and 90%	11%
More than 90%	0%

Vertical Integration and Sources of Competitive Advantage

As table 5.5 shows, about 41% of the firms answered that less than 10% of their grapes came from their own winery but from the same regional area/wine valley. Most large Chilean wine companies have backwards vertical integration, owning their own grapes and controlling their required quality for their different labels and export markets. Sites for the grapes of large and medium-sized firms can be located in different valleys as part of the strategy to have differentiation in grapes varieties (varieties include Merlot, Carmenere, Cabernet Sauvignon, Syrah, Sauvignon Blanc, and Chardonnay, among others).

It is important to know that red varieties comprise 73% of the varieties produced and 27% are white. Of the red, 63% are those in high demand (Cabernet Sauvignon, Merlot, and Syrah). In white grapes, 66% of the surface area planted corresponds to Sauvignon Blanc and Chardonnay. With respect to exports by varietal, Sauvignon Blanc has both grown in value and volume over the past seven years to reach an average growth rate of 18% and 16%, respectively. Cabernet Sauvignon and Carmenere follow in importance.

Chilean wine firms follow a long-term strategy of quality consistency that has characterised the global positioning of the Chilean wine industry. This strategy can be a positive factor for firms selling

Table 5.6
Percentage of sales in the last three years

	1 to 30%	31 to 60%	Does not apply
Same region	36%	4%	24%
Chile	60%	16%	4%
Export markets	16%	80%	0%

Table 5.7
Key sources of competitive advantage

Export orientation	83%
Price competitiveness	71%
Distribution channels	54%
Production process	46%
Marketing	38%
New Product Development	38%
Branding	33%
Training of employees	33%
Agents	33%
Product differentiation	30%
Access to information	25%

their wine to private labels such as Tesco Value and Tesco selection wine in the UK market.

For the wineries that buy grapes from other firms, most of the firms buy their grapes from firms located in the same wine valley and/or other valleys in Chile, but not abroad. This means that Chilean firms rely more on local and regional suppliers than foreign suppliers. Again this is because of vertical integration of most of the wineries, and quality consistency across the industry value chain, in Chile. It is important to remember that surveyed Chilean firms are export oriented, exporting more than 80% of their production to foreign markets (see table 5.6). Even new small wine firms follow this tendency, focusing on niche-quality production (e.g. organic wine) for premium wine distributors like Odbins retailers in the UK.

As shown in table 5.7, surveyed firms declared that their main competitive advantage came mainly from export orientation (83%), distribution channels (54%), price competitiveness (71%), product differentiation (50%), and new product development (50%). Price competi-

Table 5.8
Key networks in the industry

Ministry of Agriculture	33%
Wines of Chile	29%
Universidad Talca	19%
Universidad Catolica	5%

tiveness can be related to the perception that Chilean wines enjoyed in international markets, that they were "good value for money" (Felzensztein and Dinnie 2005), though average prices of Chilean wines are increasing (there was a 8.6% increase in price between January and June 2011). Product differentiation and development can be related to new grape varieties like Carmenere, a grape that was rediscovered in recent years in Chile and that had been completely lost in Europe many years ago. This grape is gaining a distinctive positioning in international markets and may represent "the Chilean grape" for international marketing strategies in the main export markets.

Network Relations, Interaction, and Sources of Innovation

With respect to the frequency of interaction with different institutions related to wine industry development in Chile, the surveyed firms stated that they mainly interact with people from the Ministry of Agriculture (33%) and Wines of Chile Trade Association (29%) (see table 5.8). The interactions with Wines of Chile Trade Association are of particular interest as the Association was founded and is financed by the private firms and it has no public resources. This same association represents the interests of large and medium-sized firms, and developed the current generic international marketing strategy of the industry.

Interactions occur on both a monthly and an annual basis (33%), and at both formal and informal levels (24%). Answers to the question of whether the institutions help with the process of innovation are mixed, with 48% respondents saying than they do not help, and 29% saying yes, they do help. This may mean that the wine cluster in Chile needs stronger public policies and coordination for the development of innovation processes and networking among actors, and this may lead to inter-firm co-operation to continue reaching competitiveness,

Table 5.9
Type of interaction with key networks/associations

	Formal	Informal	Both
Ministry of Agriculture	29%	24%	24%
Wines of Chile	29%	24%	33%
Universidad Catolica	33%	19%	24%
Universidad Talca	29%	19%	29%

Table 5.10
Main areas for innovation

Marketing	48%
Information systems	48%
Fermentation	43%
Training	43%
Other	19%
Genetics	14%
Sales	10%
Finance	10%

especially in new export markets. Currently support institutions like the Wines of Chile Trade Association (see www.winesofchile.cl), collaborate on generic international marketing campaigns but not on technological upgrading as the industry seems to be mature and because of the dominance of large and medium-sized firms; meanwhile universities are more willing to produce research that may help particular wine firms (if funding is provided) or the whole industry (mainly with the Fund for the Promotion of Scientific and Technological Development, FONDEF).

Most of the firms (81%) declared that they have noticed an improvement in product innovation during the last two years. Moreover, the production process has "improved a lot" (52%). These improvements in productivity and processes were mainly done in the marketing (48%), information systems (48%) and training (43%) areas. Marketing may have improved as all the exporting firms may have contributed to improving their marketing performance by aiming for a coherent new generic international marketing strategy with the clear goal of becoming the most important wine producer and exporter from the New World.

The ways in which firms and institutions interact needs further investigation in future studies. An important issue in this industry is how the different and diverse firms can maintain quality consistency and a sustainable international competitive advantage over time. These elements are fundamental for the new international marketing strategy and positioning of the industry. Marketing innovation seems to be particularly relevant in the Chilean wine cluster.

Recent research conducted by Felzensztein and Deans (2013) studied the factors that influence the development of inter-firm co-operation in marketing in the Chilean wine industry. The results confirmed that location is an important aspect that determines the quality and features of the product and its resulting appeal to foreign markets. Further to this, it was found that location benefits associated with collaboration and access to information and technologies are rarely considered compared to the specific benefits associated with terroir. Results also provide evidence of a focus of co-operation with firms that are located close to the focal firm, and mainly with those directly involved in its value chain. The results highlighted firms co-operating in marketing activities designed to attract new customers and to strengthen relationships with them.

This same research also shows that managers perceive that the most important benefits of being geographically co-located in a specific wine region are related to co-operation in joint marketing delegations (M=3.72), joint trade fairs participation (M=2.90), and joint trade missions to new markets (M=2.83). These results also show a propensity of firms to develop co-operation in activities designed to open new markets. Similarly, the perceived benefits of being located in a specific region of the country for facilitating opportunities for co-operation in marketing with trade associations show that managers perceive that the most important benefits are related to joint trade fair participation (M=3.24), joint market information research (M=3.14), and joint marketing delegations (M=2.97).

Felzensztein and Deans's (2013) results also show that firms that develop any inter-firm co-operation in marketing activities tend to co-operate with firms located outside the district/local area though still in Chile (M=3.52) and with firms located in the same district/local area (M=3.46). Additionally, results show that this co-operation is done mainly with buyers (M=3.52) and with local producers (M=2.70). These results provide evidence of a focus of co-operation

Table 5.11
Sources of funding for innovation

Own resources	43%
Banks	24%
Regional government	10%
Private and risk capital	5%
National government	5%

with firms that are located close to the focal firm, and mainly with those directly involved in its value chain. Implications of these results seem to be that supply chains are the main sources of marketing innovation in the Chilean wine industry.

There is no doubt that the most important actor for the innovation process in the Chilean wine clusters is the own firm (65%), followed by trade fairs (30%), and interactions with customers (25%). Funding for the innovation process comes from the firms' own financial resources (43%) and other funding from private banks (24%), while very little came from the national (5%) or regional government (10%). This is in line with the private ownership of the Chilean industry, having little or no public policy funding at national or regional levels, as may be the case in other countries like New Zealand.

Surveyed firms that did not perform innovation reported it was not done mainly because it was too expensive (45%), or because of a lack of information (45%). Other reasons were a lack of qualified human resources (27%), and a lack of technological information (27%). Firm training is done both internally and externally (81%).

Respondents also stated that wine tourism is key for the development of their firm and industry (48%). However, wine tourism must be developed further to be successful and imitate successful initiatives of wine tourism that are found in New Zealand and Australia, or example.

CONCLUSIONS

Based on our research questions – what does the Chilean wine cluster case tell us about the challenges to competitiveness in the wine industry? How is Chile attempting to be one of the top producers and exporters of wine in the world, and what can be learned from this experience? And, what are the relationships of different actors in this industry and how do they influence competitiveness? – we can draw several conclusions.

First, the Chilean wine cluster has learned from the experience of other top wine-producing and exporting countries like France and Australia. Chilean firms learned from their experience during the 1980s and 1990s, got technology upgrading and public support (e.g. from public-private partnerships like Fundación Chile), and acquired managers and winemakers who were trained abroad, mainly in France, Australia, and New Zealand. From the beginning of 2000, wine companies started exporting more to key international markets, learning consumers' preferences and adapting international marketing strategies to each of their foreign markets (e.g. the UK and SA). Some large Chilean wine firms also started to open sales offices in foreign markets, from 2001 to the present. This helped not only to open new distribution channels, but also to have very clear niche marketing strategies in key export markets. One lesson to be learned by other emerging wine clusters, such as those in Canada and other countries, is that it is necessary to have a sophisticated market demand at local or international levels. This helps the upgrading of an industry not only in technological terms, but also in advanced international marketing strategies for achieving a clear positioning.

Second, as sizes of firms are mainly medium to large and mainly vertically integrated, relationships between competing firms seem to be weak. One of the reasons is the fact that medium- and large-sized firms control their own production, quality, product varieties, and marketing activities, constructing independent brands for each market segment. Additionally, there is strong competition among Chilean firms in international markets. Clearly, this is an internationally oriented industry, exporting more than 70% of its production and focusing in international, developed markets (e.g. the UK, USA, and Japan) and emerging markets (e.g. Brazil, China, and Russia). On the contrary small firms focus on international niche marketing strategies, mainly in the premium market segment, aiming for and working to achieve long-term profitability and positioning. Communication between small and large firms seems to be weak, and the former face problems such as difficulties with technical upgrading and marketing knowledge. It is possible to conclude that there is a need for a new trade association that represents the interests and problems of these small firms, but with the ability to communicate with the Wines of Chile Trade Association, aiming to have synergies for joint marketing activities and a coordinated national and regional wine tourism strategy. These strategies can be learned from Australia and New Zealand, where wine tourism is well developed and coordinated.

Finally, it is important to recognise that an internationally oriented industry depends on international and external factors, such as exchange rates, trade barriers, international economic environment, new consumption patterns, and international competition, among others. Chilean wine producers and exporters need to be aware of these factors. Exchange rates affect international competitiveness and profits of the industry, particularly as the Chilean peso has appreciated against the US dollar. This means that production costs are increasing. Apart from that, other competitor countries like Argentina need to be watched as the country of origin effect of Argentina can be stronger than that of Chile (for example, consider the influence of "brands" such as Tango! Andes, Patagonia, football player Maradona, and Evita Peron). Lastly, it should not be forgotten that well-defined international marketing strategies and clear positioning of the industry are key for maintaining and gaining a sustainable competitive advantage in foreign markets.

ACKNOWLEDGMENTS

This study is part of the activities of the Research Center for International Competitiveness (Conicyt SOC1105) and Fondecyt project 1120336.

REFERENCES

Björk, I. 2005. "Spillover Effects of FDI in the Manufacturing Sector in Chile." Unpublished Masters thesis, School of Economics and Management, Lund University.

Felzensztein, C. 2011. "The Chilean Wine Industry: New International Strategies for 2020." *Emerald Emerging Markets Case Studies.* http://www.emeraldinsight.com/case_studies.htm?issn=2045-0621 &articleid=1917158&show=abstract

Felzensztein, C. and K. Deans. 2013. "Marketing Practices in Wine Clusters:

Insights from Chile." *Journal of Business and Industrial Marketing* 28(4): 357–67.

Felzensztein, C. and K. Dinnie. 2005. "The Effects of Country Origin on UK Consumers' Perception of Imported Wine." *Journal of Food Products Marketing* 11 (4): 109–17.

Kahn, K. and E. McDonough. 1997. "An Empirical Study of the Relationships between Co-location, Integration, Performance and Satisfaction." *Journal of Product Innovation Management* 14 (3): 161–78.

Knowles, T and L. Sharples. 2002. "The History and Development of Chilean Wines." *International Journal of Wine Marketing* 14: 7–16.

Kunc, M. 2008. "A Survey of Managerial Practices in the Chilean Wine Industry." *Journal of Wine Research* 18: 113–19.

La Tercera. 2010. "Viñas Apuestan a Duplicar Envíos y a que Chile Sea el Primer Productor Emergente al 2020." http://www.latercera.com/noticia /negocios/2010/09/655-293075-9-vinas-apuestan-a-duplicar-envios-y-a-que-chile-sea-el-primer-productor-emergente.shtml

OIV. 2010. "International Organization of Vine and Wine." Accessed September 2010, www.oiv.int/oiv/cms/index?lang=en.

Wines of Chile. 2010. "Wines of Chile Strategic Plan 2020 – International Market." http://www.winesofchile.org/site/wp-content/uploads/2012/01/ woc-plan-2020-eng.pdf.

6

The Wine Industry in
Bolgheri–Val di Cornia, Italy:
Facing the Crisis with Success

ELISA GIULIANI, ORIANA PERRONE, AND SARA DANIELE

INTRODUCTION

This chapter is based on a 2010–11 study including a survey about the competitiveness of the cluster of Bolgheri-Val di Cornia (BVC) in Italy. Though the BVC cluster has had remarkable success in the past twenty years (see Giuliani 2007a), we focus on what factors are likely to contribute to this growth trend in spite of the current global crisis, which has threatened the competitiveness of this industry. The analysis is based on the application of industrial cluster theory focusing on the four factors laid out in chapter 1: firm adaptability to market evolution; policy interventions; social networks; and coordination of local and global supply chains. The analysis relies upon original data gathered by the authors via interviews and surveys with a sample of winemakers in the Bolgheri and Val di Cornia area from winter 2010 up to summer 2011. The chapter is organised as follows: Section 2 provides an overview of the wine industry in Italy; Section 3 focuses on the historical background of the cluster of BVC, illustrating some of its key characteristics, and Section 4 discusses some of the key competitive factors that explain the success of BVC wineries. Section 5 explains why wineries believe that government policies have played no role in the success of this industry cluster and provide no support for facing the current market crisis. Section 6 looks at the importance of geography and local networks in leveraging wineries' operations, and Section 7 focuses on the connections of cluster firms to extra-cluster sources of knowledge. Section 8 concludes our findings.

THE WINE INDUSTRY IN ITALY

Recent wine industry accounts have shown us that this industry has undergone three key changes in the past three decades (Anderson, Norman, and Wittwer 2003; Giuliani, Morrison, and Rabellotti 2011). First, there has been a shift from quantity-oriented production of bulk wine to quality wines and a subsequent increase of wine value. Second, the growth of new countries such as Australia, Chile, South Africa, etc., as both producers and exporters of quality wines, has challenged traditional producers such as France, Italy, and Spain. Third, there has been recent saturation of the wine market, which is due to two concurrent effects: on the one hand, there is an increase in the number of producing countries and firms, which have made competition fiercer than it was in the 1990s; on the other, the recent global crisis has undermined consumption in general, as widely discussed in chapter 2.

In this changing context, Italian wine producers have increased the quality of their exported wines much more markedly than other countries' producers. Table 6.1 shows the change in the unit value of wine exports over the period 1975–2008. It shows that Italian wineries have increased the value of their exported wines almost six-fold in that period: in the period 1974–79 the unit value of exported wines in Italy was of US$290/tonne, a value that increased in the subsequent years, reaching an average value of $2,410 in 2005–08. This increase has been much more pronounced than in France, for example, which is the leader in wine quality exports with an average value of US$5,560 /tonne for its wines (2005–08).

Tuscany is currently one of the most traditional wine producing regions in Italy, accounting for about 7% of vineyards planted areas in the country. It hosts thirty-six DOC and seven DOCG areas.[1] In 2007, as the global crisis struck wine consumption, the production of DOC/DOCG wines in Tuscany was 1.57 million hectolitres, a reduction of 2.5% compared to 2006. However, not all areas suffered from such a decline. Some of the areas where decline was stronger include renowned and very traditional DOCG wines such as Chianti (–2% to 15,179 hectares), Chianti Classico (–9% to 5,883 hectares), and Brunello

Table 6.1
Unit value of wine exports, 1975–2008 (thousands us$/tonne)

Yearly average	1975–79	1980–84	1985–89	1990–94	1995–99	2000–04	2005–08
France	1.49	1.66	2.32	3.50	3.70	3.83	5.56
Italy	0.42	0.48	0.73	1.13	1.44	1.88	2.41
Spain	0.52	0.57	0.93	1.11	1.46	1.35	1.51
Germany	1.49	1.51	1.49	1.65	1.91	1.76	2.58
Portugal	0.94	1.38	1.87	2.32	2.58	2.33	2.44
USA	1.08	1.09	1.32	1.42	1.93	1.90	2.03
Argentina	0.35	0.54	0.49	0.76	0.91	1.29	1.33
Australia	1.22	1.70	1.86	2.07	3.30	2.87	2.98
South Africa	0.68	0.83	1.11	1.50	1.61	1.65	1.66
Chile	0.79	0.95	1.19	1.36	1.43	1.59	2.08

Source: Cusmano et al. (2011)

di Montalcino (–21% to 1,334 hectares). In contrast, other areas increased their plantation areas, reflecting a growing trend of investment in wine production. These include Rosso di Montepulciano (+47% in 2007) and Bolgheri (+29%). Our study will focus on Bolgheri and its surrounding area (Val di Cornia), as one of the growing areas in Tuscany.

THE CLUSTER OF BOLGHERI-VAL DI CORNIA: HISTORICAL OVERVIEW AND KEY FEATURES

The cluster of Bolgheri and Val di Cornia is located in the Province of Livorno, along the Tyrrhenian coast in Tuscany. The overall area extends for about 40 km from north to south, an important part of which is nowadays dedicated to the production of wine. As the name of the cluster suggests, the area is composed of two contiguous sub-territories – Bolgheri in the northern part and Val di Cornia at the southern end of the cluster – which differ in many respects. Historical antecedents have, in a purely path-dependent way, created the gap between these two sub-areas, as Bolgheri is far more renowned internationally than the Val di Cornia area. In spite of this, the area is considered to be a whole cluster because of the contiguity of the territory, the high density of wineries, and the de facto institutional recognition of them being an integrated cluster.[2]

There is a long tradition of wine production in the area, within the numerous monasteries that have populated the territory since the seventeenth century. At that time, grape growing and wine production were encouraged by the settlement of the noble family Della Gherardesca.[3] The presence of aristocrats has influenced the dual characteristics of wine production in the whole area. Bolgheri became a suitable place to settle for several aristocratic families – Della Gherardesca, followed by Incisa della Rocchetta and Antinori – who had owned (and some still do) large feudal properties for generations. During the nineteenth century, the Val di Cornia area was subject to extensive drainage works and it has subsequently been characterised by extractive and agricultural activities.

Until the first half of the 1900s, wine making in Bolgheri was mainly based on the old, quantity-oriented pattern of production and on the use of autochthon vine varieties (typically, the Sangiovese). In the 1960s, while most Tuscan wine areas suffered from severe crises,[4] Bolgheri gained momentum thanks to a local aristocrat, Mario Incisa della Rocchetta, who, being a great fan of the fine red wines of Bordeaux, decided to make a red wine using French grapes and techniques (Mansson, 1996). The introduction of new methods of production spurred a renovation of wine-waking techniques, somewhat akin to a technological breakthrough, characterised by the introduction of French vines (typically Merlot and Cabernet), and by the adoption of controlled fermentation and the use of 60-gallon barrels (barriques) for aging. The famous Sassicaia, first launched in 1968, was the outcome of a new way of making wine in the area. These changes were followed with interest, not only by most wine critics, but also by other wine producers in the Bolgheri area. In the late 1970s, a few small producers began aiming at producing high quality wines, and in the 1980s, new firms were established in the area of Bolgheri, with an orientation to quality (see figure 6.1).

The 1980s was a period in which, in the nearby contiguous area of Val di Cornia, long-established farmers started to focus their efforts on wine production. Slowly, a process of renewal started to take place in this sub-area. This was concurrent with the de-industrialisation phase of the coastal area south of Livorno, which carried high unemployment rates and local economic crises. Part of this unemployment was absorbed by the emerging business of wine-making. This suggests that this type of activity is relatively recent in the area. It was about the

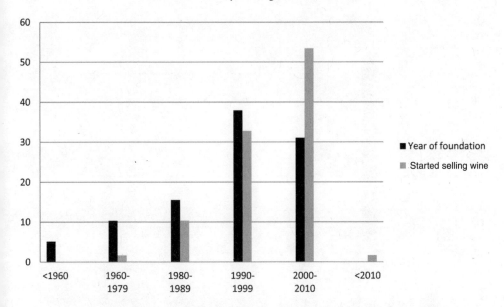

Figure 6.1   Distribution based on year of companies' foundation and year in which first wine was launched

mid 1990s, in fact, when Val di Cornia started to emerge with a few quality-oriented wine producers, as also reflected by the high number of firms being founded in the 1990s (figure 6.1).

Compared to other international contexts, firms in BVC are extremely small, with more than 80% of the firms in the area having less than 50 hectares of planted vines (figure 6.2)[5] and with almost 90% of the firms employing less than ten employees (figure 6.3). Only about a fifth of the firms (17%) belong to a holding or a larger industrial group. These cases include wineries that are part of large-scale wine producing firms with operations in different parts of Italy and/or abroad, such as Marchesi Antinori Ltd., and Angelo Gaja, the undisputed king of Barbaresco who has set up a modern state-of-the-art winery in Bolgheri (Virbila 2003). In another few cases, wineries are part of diversified industrial groups which invested in the wine industry when market opportunities were on the rise. Apart from these cases, the vast majority (83%) of wineries in the cluster are family businesses. Family business is very common in Italy (Corbetta 1995) hence it should not be seen as a peculiarity of the wine industry. What strikes

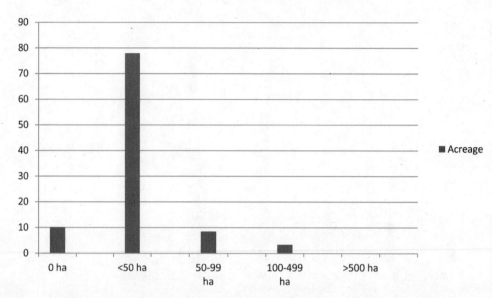

Figure 6.2   Distribution of firms by hectares of vineyard

us is that even small wineries have managed to take advantage of the booming wine demand and have become competitive in the domestic and international markets. Small-sized family businesses have exploited two advantages to grow: on the one hand, some of them had accumulated experience in wine production prior to the 1990s, and they have exploited this experience when wine demand started to boom. Given the fact that the terroir in BVC is highly suited to wine production, even the least sophisticated family businesses have managed to benefit from the market bonanza and have found their own niche, either in the domestic or international markets or both. On the other hand, some other small firms have made investments in the direction of upgrading the quality of their wines by adopting new international methods of vine management and wine making, and by re-investing the profits of the 1990s into building skills and modernizing the wineries.

There are examples of very small firms that have managed to obtain extraordinarily high quality standards in their wines, which became internationally renowned. A case in point in Val di Cornia is the firm Tua Rita, which has twenty-five hectares and nine employees, and reached 100 points in *Wine Spectator* (WS)'s international ranking sys-

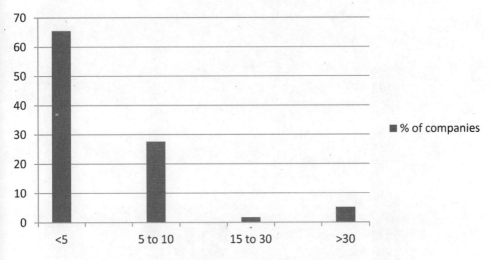

Figure 6.3   Distribution of firms by number of employees

tem (www.winespectator.com) with a 2007 Redigaffi, a Merlot-based wine. This shows that bvc is not just the seedbed of the most famous Sassicaia; from this territory, other superb wines are being produced. Figure 6.4 shows the distribution of wineries' highest rankings, according to *Wine Spectator*'s 100-point scale. While about 40% of the wineries' wines are not ranked in ws, probably signalling poor quality, the remaining 60% reach an average maximum score of 92.65 points. In the section that follows, we will discuss how the firms in the cluster manage to be internationally competitive.

FIRM ADAPTABILITY TO MARKET EVOLUTION

About a decade ago everyone would agree that the key to competitiveness was the quality of wines. Quality was generally understood as the combination of good terroir, capable technological management of the grapes, and the wine-making process. Technological management meant knowledge about how to improve grapes' quality, not simply by choosing the right chemical products for the vineyard or the right machinery, but more importantly by developing and applying new techniques of production – from soil and canopy management, to fermentations and ageing for improving wine taste (Giuliani 2007b). It was clear that good wine was no longer a matter of being

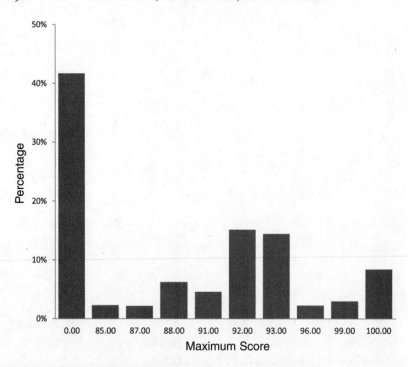

Figure 6.4   Distribution of *Wine Spectator* ratings for BVC wines

traditional but of merging tradition with technology. Over the 1990s wineries in the BVC, and more broadly in Italy, learned how to combine these two dimensions and produced great wines. But so did other countries around the world (Giuliani, Morrison, and Rabellotti 2011). The survey we undertook for this research reveals that competitiveness is now resting on other pillars. Wine quality is a *sine qua non* prerequisite, especially for high-end markets, but it may not suffice in the face of the current global slowdown of wine demand. As shown in table 6.2, branding, exporting, and more broadly having access to market channels (distribution, agents), are considered by our respondents as key elements of competitiveness, along with new product development. Other more "technological" factors such as training, improvements in the production process, and access to information are much less relevant nowadays. As mentioned earlier, this is not because they are not important aspects, but because these were achieved in the 1990s, and these aspects are now considered to be

Table 6.2
Drivers of competitive advantage

Firms' Reliance For Competitive Advantage (from 1 to 5)	Average
Exporting	3.6
Branding	3.4
Marketing	2.9
Production process continual improvement	2.6
Agents	2.6
Market placement at appr. price points	2.5
Distribution channels	2.5
New product development	2.2
Product differentiation	2.0
Employee training	1.9
Access to latest winemaking and Viticultural info	1.7

business-as-usual. Instead, it becomes clear from the interviews that a consolidated brand name and control of distribution channels are very important assets for facing the growing competition in the wine market. In his blog, Francesco Zonin, the owner of one of the largest wine distributing companies in Italy, Casa Vinicola Zonin, suggests that the key challenge of wine producers is no longer production but access to market and distribution, which is becoming increasingly more complex and difficult to achieve (Zonin 2010).

Some of the firms we interviewed told us that all their wines are already fully booked one or even two years before the product is ready to be sold. If we look at the trend in revenues over the past twelve months, we find that around 17% of the firms suffered from a decrease in revenues, while about 57% managed to increase their revenues in a period of crisis. The remaining 26% maintained their level of revenues as compared to the previous year. Prices have remained largely unchanged over the twelve months (since the interviews in 2010–11) for most firms (60.3%), with some of the firms (29.3%) increasing average prices, and a minority of firms (10.4%) had to cut prices to be able to sell their wines. All in all, around 20% of the firms in the cluster are struggling to survive in the market, whereas the vast majority of firms have maintained or even improved their level of competitiveness in spite of the crisis (table 6.3).

Table 6.3
Variation in revenues, prices, and volumes of wines in the past twelve months.

Changes in (last 12 months)	% companies	Mean variation
REVENUES	% companies	
Decreased	17.2%	− 18.8%
Increased	56.9%	+ 20%
Unvaried	25.9%	
PRICES	% companies	
Decreased	10.4%	
Increased	29.3%	
Unvaried	60.3%	
WINE VOLUME SOLD	% companies	
Decreased	18.9%	
Increased	50%	
Unvaried	31.1%	

Table 6.4
Innovation areas over past two years

Innovation Areas Over Past 2 Years	% of respondents
Retail/sales	45.8
Marketing	47.5
Finance	11.9
Plant Breeding	10.2
Use of Genetics	3.4
Vineyard management and investments	45.8
Fermentation	25.4
Information Systems	20.3
Other	6.8

Qualitative evidence suggests that firms in the BVC that have a strong brand name and consolidated distribution channels have not themselves suffered from the crisis, but they are aware of the fact that other firms in the cluster struggle to reach international markets. In fact, many firms in this study seek access to international markets through the strengthening of distribution networks. The importance of market access is also reflected in table 6.4, which reports the functional areas in which firms invested the most over the past two years.

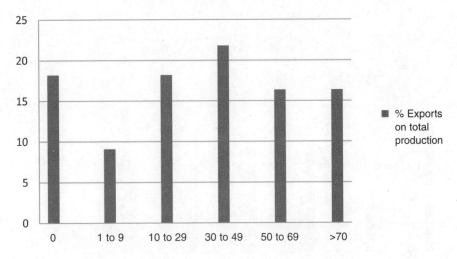

Figure 6.5   Export features

Distribution channels for retail sales (46%) and marketing (47%) are, together with vineyard investments (46%), the most important areas of innovation. These data show that firms continue to invest in the quality of wines, but push strongly on commercial functions and activities.

Access to foreign markets is seen as the most important driver of competitiveness. In our sample about 20% of the firms sell only to the local and domestic markets (figure 6.5), while 33% of the firms export more than half of their production, which indicates that strong export-orientation is still an objective to be achieved by many firms in the cluster. As shown in figure 6.6, firms that belong to large family groups or holdings have less difficulty in exporting: they, on average, export 55% of their production, while individual family businesses exports less, the difference possibly being due to the former economies of scale in distribution. However, there is a wide heterogeneity between individual wineries (black bars), some 50% exporting nothing or very little, and the rest having export patterns similar to those of wineries belonging to larger groups or holdings (grey bars).

Innovation in training is not an area where firms have invested in the past two years. However, more than half of the firms interviewed have declared that their employees undergo periodic training ses-

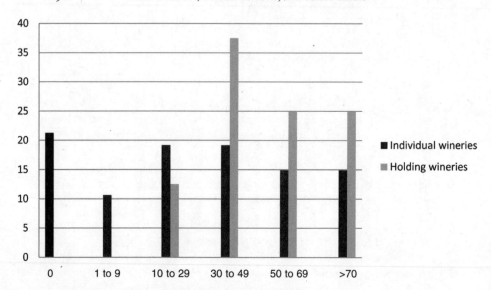

Figure 6.6   Exports (individual vs holding wineries)

sions, which are in the majority of cases offered by external actors, such as suppliers of materials or technologies (table 6.5).

The introduction of innovations is generally considered not to be a problem in the BVC, with most of the firms innovating in one way or another. However, when asked about why they might have decided not to introduce further innovations, the motivations are either that the company does not need to introduce further innovations beyond those already adopted (36% of respondents) or that introductions of innovations have not been undertaken as they are considered to be too costly (59%). Other interpretations are possible but they are marginal, as shown in table 6.6.

ROLE OF POLICY

The general perception of respondents to our survey is that the Italian government has had no role in sustaining the sector, including in the post-crisis period. The Ministry of Agriculture has changed three times in the past three years, during the same Berlusconi government, with the former minister, Saverio Romano, being under investigation for

Table 6.5
Training

How Training Is Provided (Y/N)	%
Yes 69.5 A) In-house training	4.9
B) External provision of training, of which:	95.1
B1) University	17.9
B2) Consultants	48.7
B3) Other (corporate)	58.9
No 30.5	

Table 6.6
Reasons for not innovating

Reasons for not innovating	%
Not needed by the company	35.9
Too expensive	59.0
Lack of human resources	7.7
Lack of information on technology	2.6
Lack of information on potential markets	2.6
Difficulty in finding co-operative partners	7.7
Lack of adequate or clear regulatory framework	10.3
Unaware of what's available	0.0

Mafia crimes. The new Monti government has appointed another Minister of Agriculture, Mario Catania, and he has just recently taken on the Ministry's mandate. At the time when interviews took place, all respondents, with one exception, were extremely critical and even denounced the fact that the government was not simply unsupportive, but in many cases was a burden, as procedures and bureaucracy have not been simplified over the years. In effect, these perceptions are confirmed by the Ministry's anti-crisis agenda, in which interventions have been directed only to targeted wines and wine areas (to some Piedmont wines, for example), and not generally to the whole industry. Even in those cases, there is no apparent strategic vision for the wine industry, and no meaningful policy initiative has been set up to sustain and promote the competitiveness of this industry worldwide. Some respondents highlighted the marginal role of the EU and of the

Table 6.7
Importance of funding sources for innovation

Importance Of Funding Sources For Innovation (1–5)	Average
Private (firm-level) funding (self-funding)	4.5
Commercial Bank/credit union	2.6
Venture Capitalists	0.7
Government	1.4
Provincial Government	1.5
Local or Regional Government	1.2
European funding	1.5

regional governments. Hence, policies in this sector seem to be entirely lacking. This evidence is somewhat at odds with the expected impact of the 2009 EU CAP reform on the wine market (European Union 2008), which, among other things (such as the suppression of the least efficient segments of the industry), was meant to revitalise industry exports and to promote competitiveness. It is possible that impacts of this reform are yet to come, hopefully along with higher stability within the ministry in charge. This perceived lack of policies for the sector is also at odds with the contexts in other countries such as Chile (chapter 5) and Australia (chapter 7), where wine production is considered to be much more strategic for the country-development process. In Italy, however, there has been a generalised lack of attention by the current government to the sustenance of the industry; hence, what we observe for the wine industry is in line with what has occurred to other more strategic manufacturing activities. It is not just that the wine industry is not a strategic activity for this country, but also that the former government was unable or unwilling to design and implement any kind of industrial policy (Onida 2011), which also partially explains poor GDP growth rates in Italy.

The lack of policies for Italian viticulture is also reflected in table 6.7, which is about the major sources of funding for innovation. The table clearly shows that the national government, along with the provincial or regional governments, receive very low scoring (around 1.5 on a 1–5 scale). Most of the investments in innovation are undertaken almost entirely through internal funding, while banks are the second most important source of funding, through loans. Even banks, however, score very low compared to private funding. Venture capitalists are virtually non-existent in this context, scoring a mere 0.7.

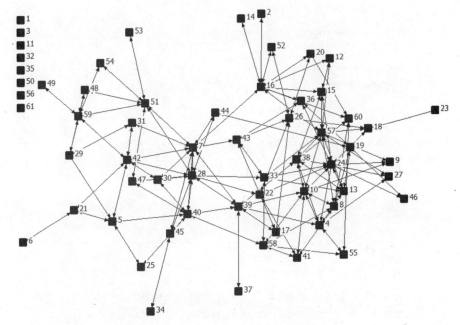

Figure 6.7   The local network in Bolgheri–Val di Cornia

GEOGRAPHY AND LOCAL NETWORKS

Geographic proximity is considered by around 86% of our sample firms to be an important or critical aspect of competitiveness. Only 13% of the firms consider it marginally important, while no firm considers it of no impact or even a disadvantage. There is extensive literature on the importance of local networks for the competitiveness of clusters and their firms. In the case of BVC, wineries have few commercial linkages, with only about 13% of them buying grapes from other wine producers. However, being part of the same territory permits both the joint development of wine-related initiatives such as the consortium or the wine trail, as well as the construction of a local territorial identity, which is generally considered to be a key element of success, especially for firms being part of the DOC Bolgheri. Another advantage of firms' geographical proximity is that it permits the formation of informal linkages among agronomists and enologists, who connect to each other to exchange advice and technical expertise (see Giuliani and Bell 2005 and Giuliani 2007a for a discussion on this matter). Figure 6.7 illustrates the network of local ties in BVC. This network represents the

Table 6.8
Importance of following factors for innovation

Importance of Following Factors for Innovation (1–5)	Average
Intra-firm knowledge	4.1
Suppliers	1.8
Clients	2.8
Other wineries in Bolgheri-Val di Cornia	1.9
Other wineries outside Bolgheri-Val di Cornia	1.9
Universities	1.8
Consultants	3.0
Fairs and Conferences	2.3
Press (Magazines, Specialized Journals)	2.2
Internet	2.2
Other sources	0.3

informal linkages that bind firms together, essentially through the interactions of the agronomists and oenologists of the local wineries.

COORDINATION OF CLUSTER
AND EXTRA-CLUSTER NETWORKS

Connections to extra-cluster networks are vital for competitiveness (Bell and Albu 1999). Concerning external sources of innovation, firms in bvc consider clients and consultants to be the most important external actors (table 6.8). Clients are important gateways to information about forthcoming market trends and consumption patterns. Consultants are channels through which new methods of production or new techniques are introduced in the vineyard. They are essentially ways through which wineries maintain contact with frontier market knowledge and production techniques. Other sources of innovation are valued by our respondents, but much less than the consultants and the clients, as indicated in table 6.8.

Evidence of firms' external connections is also reported in table 6.9, where different types of relationships are analysed in greater depth. The table names organisations and institutions that play a role in fostering innovation. Within the list of institutions, the faculties of agricultural sciences of several regional and national universities seem to be considered, on average, the most important ones (2.3 on a 1–5 scale). Interactions are mostly based on annual or monthly relationships and they tend to be both formal and informal types of ties. Relationships with these specific actors are deemed to be important for innovation by all of the respondents who have such relationships. In this context, university-industry (UI) linkages are generally based on the common interest in understanding and solving a problem, but they do not often translate into a direct competitive advantage. Universities undertake basic and applied research that is useful to wineries (for instance, understanding how a given pest manifests in a given soil and how to deal with it), but, as with any university research, its results are highly uncertain, may require years to materialise and may help to understand something that is relevant for the firm (e.g. how to deal with a technical problem), but that is not necessarily directly associated with a tangible product or innovation. For this reason, universities do not, in absolute terms, score very high when firms are asked about contribution to innovation; universities' research contributions are subtle and their effects are less immediate. Nevertheless, universities do normally undertake research in areas in which firms have no expertise or no interest in undertaking research, so their work is highly complementary to what firms can undertake internally.

The second most important institutional actors are local associations. These are located in the cluster but play an important role in marketing the cluster beyond the local territory. Associations of this type (Consorzio di Bolgheri, Gran Cru Costa Tuscany Association, etc.) are not critical for technical innovation but they are instead important for territorial promotion activities and for attracting oeno-tourists to the local area. Other institutions have connections to firms in the cluster, but they are considered of very little importance for introducing changes at the firm level.

CONCLUSION

This chapter illustrates the case of a wine-producing area in Tuscany, Bolgheri-Val di Cornia, and it examines some of the key aspects that could drive wineries' competitiveness. After a long period of growth and bonanza in the wine market, which went from approximately the end of the 1980s to the beginning of the twenty-first century, the cluster is now going through a challenging period as the wine industry has become exceedingly competitive and the international economic sce-

Table 6.9
Linkages with extra-cluster institutional actors

Importance and Frequency of Interactions	Average Importance (1–5)	Frequency (A,M,W,D) %				Relation			Useful for Innovation
		Annually	Monthly	Weekly	Daily	Formal	Informal	Both	
Ministry of Agriculture, Food, & Fisheries	1.19	100	0	0	0	100	0	0	8.33
ARSIA	0.49	39	15	46	0	0	100	0	33.33
Faculty of Agricultural Sciences (University of Pisa, Florence, Milan, Piacenza, Bologna, Siena)	2.37	71	24	5	0	0	16	84	100
Faculty on Enology of Asti University	0.14	100	0	0	0	0	0	100	100
National Research Centre (CNR)	1.09	100	0	0	0	0	34	66	66.67
Local Grapegrowers Association (Consorzio Bolgheri, Unione Agricoltori of Livorno, Costa degli Etruschi)	1.19	19	57	24	0	83	0	17	0
Gran Cru Costa Tuscany Association	0.39	50	50	0	0	100	0	0	0
Confagricoltura	0.76	3	67	30	0	66	0	33	0
Coldiretti	0.31	0	82	18	0	85	0	15	0
Journalists and Wine Guide	0.96	14	70	16	0	22	11	67	0
Other (Consultant)	1.86	0	24	64	12	9	0	9	0

nario is undergoing a severe crisis. Different from other country contexts (see, for example, the cases of Chile or Australia in this book), Italy's national and local governments have not played a positive role in sustaining competitiveness or in helping firms to face this tough period. This is potentially due to two factors. First, in Italy the wine industry is not a leading industry and subsequently it is not a target of competitiveness policies. Second, and more important, is that one of the acknowledged weaknesses of the former Berlusconi government was its incapacity to promote the industry and the agricultural sectors through fully-fledged industrial and agricultural policies, which could have boosted the country's competitive situation. The combination of these two aspects explains in broader terms why the government is perceived as not having played a key role in the development and success of this cluster.

The success of this cluster has to be found elsewhere. It is primarily a story of firm-level entrepreneurship, with some firms such as Tenuta San Guido, the producer of the famous Sassicaia and Tua Rita, mentioned earlier, having been pioneers in introducing new techniques and models for producing high quality wines back in the 1970–1980s. As suggested by Sanderson (2011), "it may be that Bolgheri's initial success came at least partly because of its use of such "international" varietals, perhaps despite the fact that those early wines were made with little experience, and spotty success." Over the years, with the advantage of an ideal terroir and a growing wine market, the area has attracted investments, also from other Italian wineries – a case in point being Piedmont's Angelo Gaja. The 1990s have been a period of generalised modernisation of wine production in Italy. Wineries started to convert their production from quantity to quality and wine production became more knowledge-intensive and open to international novelties (Giuliani 2007b). Wineries in BVC aligned themselves to this new trend, although there have been profound differences across them. Some firms, either belonging to large national groups or being family businesses, have managed to become competitive and to achieve a certain level of wine quality and brand awareness that allow them to be successful even in this period of generalised slowdown of wine demand. Others, typically firms that have either entered the market too late (at the end of the 1990s or beginning of the twenty-first century), or that have not invested in the improvement of their methods of production and skills in the 1990s, are now suffering from the crisis, not being able to access the markets as they did in the past. However, BVC wineries have not done it all on their own. Connections with local as well as distant actors have been vital for enhancing firm-level capabilities, especially on the production side. For instance, linkages to domestic and international consultants are important for keeping pace with new trends and technological opportunities, and linkages with regional and other national university departments are relatively important for finding solutions to fundamental problems in both the agronomic and chemical fields. Next, stable connections to clients and exporting agents are growing in importance. At the local level, wineries in BVC have created a dense network of informal ties through their technical workers; the transfer of technical advice is common in BVC and it contributes to building up social capital in the area. Local connections are also important to the promotion of cluster oenotourism, which many firms see as an alternative opportunity for selling their wines.

Of course it is hard to tell, with this current analysis, what is the relative importance of each of these influential factors. We can exclude the idea that policies have played a significant role in the growth and success of this cluster. And we can speculate on the fact that a combination of firm-level entrepreneurship, market opportunities, and an excellent terroir for wine production have been essential ingredients in this story.

NOTES

1   "Denominazione di Origine Controllata" (DOC) refers to a geographical indication on the label of fine wines that meet the requirements set out by specific production regulations and national and community legislation. This Italian wine classification system was created in 1963 and has greatly increased the quality of wine exports from Italy. The DOC indicates the geographical location wine must be produced in, standards of grape variety, colour, flavour, aroma, acidity, alcohol content, period of aging, and maximum yield that the producer must adhere to. Only wine adhering to these precise regulations can be labelled with the DOC geographical indication. DOCG ("Denominazione di Originel Controllata and Garantita") is a more restrictive selective classification. DOCG include wines such as Brunello di Montalcino, Chianti, Chianti Classico, and Vino nobile di Montepulciano.

2   As an example, the two sub-areas have a common wine trail, Strada del Vino
    Costa degli Etruschi; see http://www.lastradadelvino.com/it/
    default.aspx (Last accessed 21 March 2012).
3   Ugolino della Gherardesca (1220–0–1289) was Count of Donoratico, a vil-
    lage in the cluster of Bolgheri/Val di Cornia, and head of the noble family
    Della Gherardesca.
4   The crises were due to a fall in prices, to the old-fashioned production regu-
    lations of the DOC, and to a lack of research on clone selection. See
    www.lastradadelvino.com/bg.
5   The average size of wineries in Italy is estimated at 0.9 ha. See
    http://learnitalianwines.wordpress.com/2010/06/04/wine-statistics-in-italy/;
    last accessed 18 June 2011.

ACKNOWLEDGMENTS

The authors would like to express their gratitude to Anil Hira for his sug-
gestions on a draft of this chapter, and to Stefano Di Batte for his support
in data gathering. Special thanks go also to the several oenologists, agronomists, and farmers we interviewed in the area in 2010 and 2011. Financial
support provided by the Genome Canada Research Project (Grape and
Wine Genomics) is gratefully acknowledged. All errors and omissions are
our responsibility.

REFERENCES

Anderson, K., D. Norman and G. Wittwer. 2003. "Globalisation of the
    World's Wine Markets." *The World Economy* 26 (5): 659–87.
Bell M., and M. Albu. 1999. "Knowledge Systems and Technological
    Dynamism in Industrial Clusters in Developing Countries." *World Devel-
    opment* 27 (9): 1715–34.
Corbetta, G. 1995. "Patterns of Development of Family Businesses in Italy."
    Family Business Review 8: 255–265.
Cusmano L., and A. Morrison. 2011. "Catching up Trajectories in the Wine
    Sector." In *Innovation and Technological Catch-Up: The Changing Geography
    of Wine Production,* edited by E. Giuliani, A. Morrison, and R. Rabellotti.
    Cheltenham: Edward Elgar.
European Union. 2008. "Council Regulation (EC) No 479/2008 on the
    Common Organisation of the Market in Wine." *Official Journal of the
    European Union* L 148/1, 6.6.

Giuliani, E. 2007a. "The Selective Nature of Knowledge Networks in Clusters: Evidence from the Wine Industry." *Journal of Economic Geography* 7: 139–68.

– 2007b. "The Wine Industry: Persistence of Tacit Knowledge or Increased Codification? Some Implications for Catching-up Countries." *International Journal of Technology and Globalisation* 3(2/3): 138–54.

Giuliani E., and M. Bell. 2005. "The Micro-Determinants of Meso-Level Learning and Innovation: Evidence from a Chilean Wine Cluster." *Research Policy* 34 (1): 47–68.

Giuliani E., A. Morrison, and R. Rabellotti, eds. 2011. *Innovation and Technological Catch-Up: The Changing Geography of Wine Production*. Cheltenham: Edward Elgar.

Mansson, P.-H. 1996. "Italian Stallion. Tasting 25 Vintages of Sassicaia, the Heavyweight Vino da Tavola." *Wine Spectator*. July 31. www.winespectator.com

Onida F. 2011. "Politica Industriale non Pervenuta." *Il Sole 24 Ore*, April 5, http://www.ilsole24ore.com/art/commenti-e-idee/2011-04-05/politica-industriale-pervenuta-063917.shtml?uuid=Aa9F1GMD.

Sanderson B. 2011. "Impressions of Bolgheri." *Wine Spectator* Bruce Sanderson Decanter Blog. Accessed September 30, 2011, http://www.winespectator.com/blogs/show/id/44925.

Virbila S.I. 2003. 2000. "Angelo Gaja Ca' Marcanda Magari." *Los Angeles Times*. Accessed September 30 2011, http://articles.latimes.com/2003/aug/13/food/fo-wow13.

Zonin F. 2010. "Il Mercato Internazionale del Vino: Crisi, Evoluzione o Rivoluzione?" *Wine is Love*. Accessed October 4, 2011, http://www.wineislove.it.

7

Competitiveness in the Australian Wine Industry: A Story of Loss and Renewal

DAVID AYLWARD

ABSTRACT

This chapter will provide historical and empirical contexts for an exploration of competitiveness within the Australian wine industry. It will trace the evolution of this competitiveness and the structural and policy frameworks that have changed its meaning and its application. Most importantly, the chapter will highlight the three distinct phases of competitiveness: technological advantage, price advantage, and the current attempt at product advantage. The success or failure of each of these phases is examined using empirical data and against an international background of rapidly shifting wine landscapes. Specifically, the author will focus on historical developments, firm responses to market changes, policy responses and implications, and the role that clusters have played in the evolution of industry-wide competitiveness.

AUSTRALIAN WINE – A BRIEF HISTORY

The Australian wine industry, like many in the New World, had rather humble beginnings. Australia's first governor, Arthur Phillip, introduced grapes to the colony in the early 1790s with plantings undertaken in Parramatta, or Western Sydney (Beeston 1994). In 1795, he celebrated the production of approximately 400 litres of wine from the colony's first vineyard, but it was not until James Busby started his

Hunter Valley ventures in 1832, that attempts were made at systematic plantings on a scale that could cater to the larger colony (Beeston 1994).

Vineyard development in Victoria, South Australia, Tasmania, and Western Australia followed over the next two decades and the Australian wine landscape began its slow evolution towards a cottage industry (Aylward 2006a). South Australia's own wine leaders – John Reynell and Richard Hamilton – pioneered substantial vineyard development in 1837, as did John Hack, planting along the prestigious Adelaide Hills between 1839 and 1842, before falling victim to creditors and passing his legacy on (Beeston 1994). The birth of Victoria as a wine region can be traced to 1854 when de Castella established 100 acres planted with 20,000 Cabernet Sauvignon cuttings from the iconic French estate, Chateau Lafite. By 1860 Yarra Valley was entrenched as a major vineyard site in Victoria (Beeston 1994).

Nationally, the passing of various acts for land selection from 1860 allowed for a dramatic escalation in vineyard holdings, with area under vines rising from 2,500 hectares to over 6,800 hectares within twelve years, and by 1863, 145,000 litres a year was being exported (Australian Government Culture Portal 2011). Following Busby, the new leadership of the industry – men such as Alexander Hamilton, Thomas Hardy, John Reynell, Ernst Seppelt, and Dr Alexander Kelly – were providing the vision and practical competence that any nascent industry requires. These figures represented a core of decision makers who forged practice and strategy for others to follow. The fact that all members of this leadership group resided in South Australia meant that it would not be long before that state surpassed New South Wales as the leading wine producer, and in fact, became the epicentre of the industry by the mid-twentieth century (Aylward 2005).

Already, however, the fledgling wine industry knew that with such a small domestic population it could not remain focused on its own fickle and fluctuating markets. It needed to look outward to international markets, particularly Britain, in order to provide growth for the growing vineyard production. This understanding has been continuous throughout the industry's history (Beeston 1994; Faith 2002).

This first transformation took time. For the next four decades, the still rather loose collective of winemakers struggled to provide a foundation of certainty and optimism for their product. State borders and restrictive domestic trade implications stifled entrepreneurship and national vision. Industry leaders spent most of their efforts resisting local parochialism and lobbying their respective state governors for more liberal trade and collaboration laws that they knew were essential ingredients to a successful exporting regime (Faith 2002).

It was Australian Federation in 1901, therefore, that was the defining trigger for this quest. Its legislation allowed for the removal of debilitating trade barriers between states and, as importantly, gave winemakers a collective identity for marketing their product on the international stage. In a practical sense, the reduction in taxes and other levies also meant that for the first time in half a century, their product was seen as sustainable. A formalised exporting regime, a national approach to certain quality standards, the emergence of associated coopers, bottle makers, and cork importers, as well as a collective, albeit anaemic, culture of learning and collaboration gave substance to a long-held optimism (Beeston 1994; Faith 2002).

The early twentieth century was a time of expansion in the Australian wine industry. Capitalising on the economic and collaborative benefits brought about by Federation, the largest winemakers, led by Seppelts, Penfolds, Thomas Hardy, and Lindemans, moved into new regions within Victoria, South Australia, and Western Australia. But it was not only a geographic expansion. The range of varieties was greatly expanded, including an Australian version of champagne. Most importantly, however, there was an expansion of the Australian wine vision. People were thinking differently and on a much grander scale about Australian wine. Science had come to the industry in the form of a young Maurice O'Shea, another of the great visionaries who helped transform the industry. In 1925 O'Shea, a Bordeaux-trained vigneron, moved into the Hunter Valley in New South Wales and together with other established Hunter winemakers such as the Draytons, Tullochs, and Tyrrells, and the McWilliams family, led the industry on a course from which it would never look back (Mattinson 2006). Confronting a range of diseases in the vineyard that had plagued Hunter winemakers for decades and removing guesswork from harvesting, fermentation, acidity control, and ageing through the application of scientific principles, O'Shea ushered in the first of the industry's revolutions (Mattinson 2006).

Transformations continued to take place and in 1955 the "scientific revolution" was epitomised by the establishment of the Australian Wine Research Institute in Adelaide, South Australia. This was commonly seen as the pinnacle of the wine industry's achievements to date and represented a "coming of age." It also firmly established the scientific paradigm within and across Australian winemaking for the next sixty years, a paradigm that the industry is only now struggling to reconfigure and to some extent, justify.

Both O'Shea and Penfolds were followed by other great leaders such as Max Shubert, Evans, Knappstein, Jim Barry, and Max Lake, from the Hunter. These men continued the tradition of experimentation, risk, and learning that had become entrenched in Australia's winemaking psyche and would reach a climax by the late 1970s. It was also an era that witnessed the popular swing towards table wine (Faith 2002). The increase in international travel, relaxation of drinking regulations, and the postwar influx of immigrants brought a greater demand for quality and emulation of wine experiences elsewhere around the globe (Faith 2002). Australia's penchant for experimentation was about to be taken to a whole new level in terms of variety and quality (Croser 2010).

But while these innovations were taking place at home the rest of the world remained largely oblivious to the Australian wine landscape. International markets were enamoured with Bordeaux, Tuscany, Rioja, and Mosel. Within the global memory, Australia was still viewed very much as a colony that had not long escaped penal settlement and one which produced little of value for world markets, including wine. In fact, the common view was that Australia produced bulk wine for the working classes.

POPULARITY

It was not until the 1980s and 1990s that a different view of Australian wine emerged. The industry was now at the forefront of a "democratised" and vastly more accessible wine landscape that became synonymous with New World wines, whether they were from Australia, Canada, South Africa, Argentina, Chile, or New Zealand. These countries were creating technically faultless wines that were fruit driven, approachable, young, and "good value for money" (GWRDC 2001; Aylward 2004). They were the party wines, the wines with which new and irregular drinkers chose to celebrate, to dine out at local cafés, and to introduce themselves to the wonders of a non-beer beverage. Australia, along with its New World peers, had sacrificed tradition and terroir for technical innovation and growth, and in the globalized fashion of the late 1980s and 1990s, their recipe was working.

As a result of this new-found success, Australian wine transformed itself from what was seen as a cottage industry into a leading exporter, ranked fourth internationally in 2009, with sales of AUD$2.271 billion. The industry had approximately 2500 wineries, with 162,550 hectares under vine, and produced 1.171 million litres a year (Winetitles 2010). The growth was indeed impressive, at least in volume. But what type of structure allowed for this growth? How did the industry organise itself?

POLICY FRAMEWORK – STRUCTURAL REORGANISATION OF THE INDUSTRY, 1980S TO 2000

In order to attain the scale required for servicing international markets and for putting the industry on the growth path outlined by its national associations, a centralisation of resources, regulations, and R&D was required. Under the auspices of the Grape and Wine Research and Development Corporation (GWRDC), the Winemakers' Federation of Australia (WFA), the Australian Wine and Brandy Corporation (AWBC), and the Cooperative Research Centre for Viticulture (CRCV) – all newly established national entities – resources would be concentrated to reflect to a degree the parallel wine industry clusters already emerging.

Under their guidance, national standards for exporting wine (under the National Wine Export Council) would be established and strictly enforced. A total of fourteen national industry associations would emerge to regulate grape-growing and wine-making practices. And coordination of the industry's R&D policies, as well as extension and funding, would be controlled by the GWRDC in Adelaide, South Australia (GWRDC 1999; Winetitles 2010). Such control gave the GWRDC enormous power in determining research priorities, research practices, and strategic investment. The in-house entity, which carried out more than 85% of the GWRDC-directed research, was the Australian Wine Research Institute (AWRI), also located in Adelaide. It was a relationship model that closely followed that of the Californian associations and their in-house University of California–Davis wine institute (Aylward 2004).

Research and Development

This new research and development regime quickly began to exert both implicit and explicit influence on structures within many other aspects of the industry, particularly export approvals and extension practices. It was setting new standards, new expectations, and a new way of thinking about the size and scope of what could be achieved. The industry's R&D was to be funded through a matching of levies and government dollars, with the initial levy of AUD$2 per tonne crushed, rising to AUD$3, and later AUD$5 per tonne. This allowed for an unprecedented program of R&D, planning, and implementation that would eventually create world-leading technical expertise in both vineyard management and oenological practices.

The GWRDC and its attendant wine research institute rapidly established themselves as the hub of a new, well-funded, scientific distribution point, servicing Australia's wine R&D needs. And the scientific approach was overt. The mandate of the GWRDC and the AWRI was to apply scientific and technical efficiency to all aspects of Australian wine production. There was a deliberate decision to set the industry on a very different pathway from that of its Old World peers. The active rejection of French, Italian, German, and some Spanish methods meant that the focus would be on uniform, technically faultless vintages year after year regardless of weather and even region. Winemaking would move from the vineyard to the laboratory. Natural and cultural influences of region, terroir, tradition, artisanship, and minimal intervention would give way to the pursuit of wine recipes. They were recipes that required standardisation of flavour and alcohol content and were based on the desire for full fruit, boldness, and approachability. As Terry Theise (2010) would say, "they were wines that made statements rather than asked questions."

The GWRDC and AWRI effectively controlled the research agenda for this industry, the methods by which the research would be undertaken, and the way in which the outcomes would be applied. If a winery did not accept and comply with this scientific approach, it would remain on the cultural periphery of the industry's strategic direction. Some wineries chose to remain on the periphery and pursue their own styles of winemaking and retain their own integrity of approach. Most, however, would follow the large corporations into a multi-region harvesting, standardisation, and production of commodity wines for the growing beverage markets of the world (below AUD $12) (Aylward 2004).

Export Guidelines

These trends were both reinforced and legitimated through the emerging export benchmarks that were being applied. From the late 1980s and particularly through the 1990s the AWBC and the export councils were enforcing an increasingly rigorous set of standards (in terms of sterility) to any wine exported from Australia. Non-compliance meant no international sales. These standards, together with a centralised R&D framework, provided a fertile landscape for large-scale, formula-driven winemaking. It was a style promoted by the large multinationals because of its cost-efficiencies and it was also the safest way to comply with export requirements of cleanliness and quality control. There were simply less variables involved and therefore less compliance issues. But it was a style that would alter the identity of Australian wine for decades to come, and eventually lead to insurmountable problems.

WINE INDUSTRY NETWORKS
AND CLUSTER DEVELOPMENT

As the industry began to transform itself in the 1980s the spontaneous cluster development that had been taking shape in Australian wine over the past century gained definition. Hubs of activity in South Australia around the Barossa Valley, McLaren Vale, and the Adelaide Hills; in Victoria around the Yarra Valley, Heathcote, and Rutherglen; in New South Wales around the Hunter Valley, Mudgee, and Southern Highlands; and belatedly in Western Australia around Margaret River, and Swan Valley, grew rapidly.

In broad terms, this cluster development could be divided into three distinct categories, as outlined by Mytelka and Farinelli (2003) in their ground-breaking cluster analysis.

The first would be an embryonic cluster, which was apparent in geographic regions such as Swan Valley (WA), Mudgee (NSW), and Southern Highlands (NSW), as well as lesser-known regions in Queensland and Tasmania. This cluster model commonly involves local winemakers and grape-growers, local or regional associations, a very limited number of suppliers restricted to the regional geographic area, and, if any, perhaps a local technical education college providing a diploma in vineyard management. If one were to view it on a landscape, it might resemble a small country town. There would often be intense interaction between winemakers and grape-growers but relative isolation from other stakeholders. There would be a level of insularity although channels of communication and distribution would exist. Exports would be growing slowly but the bulk of sales would be domestic and the majority of these within the indigenous region. The labour force would be relatively unskilled by wine industry standards and many operations would be boutique to small, run by a husband and wife team with perhaps one employee. Use of the AWRI's technical services would be sporadic, and the employment of contract winemakers would be relatively high, to compensate for lower than average skilled labour in the region. Tourism would be a growing force within the cluster and would be encouraging greater interaction and a greater focus on client desires (Aylward 2007c).

The second cluster model can be labelled as "organized." The model could be applied to wine industry clusters in Yarra Valley, Rutherglen, Hunter Valley, and Margaret River. From the air, this might resemble a small regional city. The numbers of actors would be higher than those of the embryonic cluster, with a critical mass of small and medium winemakers and grape-growers. There would also be some large winemaking groups or subsidiaries in the vicinity. The interaction would be generally higher across all stakeholder groups, with the entrenched integration of supplier organisations.

This type of cluster would enjoy relatively high levels of technology transfer and uptake, with an increasing usage of the AWRI's technical consultancy. Information flows would be well developed and the cluster would have formal pathways between local and regional, even national grape-growing and winemaker associations. The clusters, however, would not host the national associations and would remain peripheral to the centralised decision-making processes. Although not generally co-located, the cluster participants would have access to relevant vocational and tertiary education and the employee skill level would be generally higher than that of embryonic cluster participants. As a result, more of the wineries would employ their own full-time winemakers, although at least 30% of winemakers would still be on contract from another operation.

The third cluster model is that of the "innovative cluster," which might resemble a large city with associated infrastructure and communication networks. In Australia, the innovative wine cluster model is found only in South Australia, the state at the very centre, both geographically and culturally, of the Australian wine industry. The state's heritage dates back to the 1850s and the grandfather of the South Australian wine industry, Thomas Hardy. The company that bears his name, BRL Hardy, was one of Australia's largest and most successful until its takeover by the US giant, Constellation Wines.

As the state's wine regions proliferated throughout the late nineteenth century, regions such as the Barossa Valley, Adelaide Hills, Clare Valley, McLaren Vale, and Coonawarra, with the quality of their soils and grape-growing climate, attracted more and more serious winemakers. As they came, the reputation of the regions grew until, as a group, they represented a magnet for all those associated in the wine supply chain. By the 1970s, South Australia was universally accepted as the premier wine state of Australia. It was effectively serviced by the University of Adelaide and its Waite campus, it had the very prestigious Roseworthy College from where winemakers graduated with world class qualifications, it was of course home to the GWRDC and the AWRI, and would eventually host all fourteen of the industry's national wine associations.

Such a centrifugal force is evident in industry data. For example, while South Australia hosts 26% of the nation's wineries, it produces 48% of the country's wine and controls more than 60% of exports (Winetitles 2008; Winefacts 2010). The four largest multinationals operating within the Australian wine industry have their headquarters in South Australia, and their influence on the industry's direction is vast. The top four operators account for almost 70% of production and their ability to direct national policy and practice is weighted accordingly. Figures 7.1 and 7.2 highlight the core differences between "organized" and "innovative" clusters in the Australian wine industry.

A cluster comparison survey by the author in 2007 (Aylward 2007c), drawing interview and survey data from 100 SME wine firms, further demonstrated the connectedness of the South Australian cluster. According to the survey sample there was a clear indication that higher levels of R&D, an increase in technical and technological uptake, and enhanced participant integration positively influenced export partici-

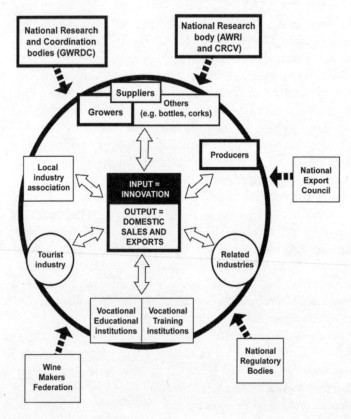

Figure 7.1   Other states' clusters
Source: Aylward 2004, Prometheus, Vol. 22, No. 4, pp. 423–37

pation. Also, greater export participation in turn enhanced the innovativeness and networking of the cluster, as international standards and requirements created the need for continuous improvement among suppliers and greater collaboration among participants. The scenario is explained by Saimee, Walters, and DuBois (1993), who draw attention to the close relationship between innovation and export activity among leading firms.

In terms of export intensity (export sales as a percentage of total sales), "Victorian and New South Wales cluster firms averaged 26.5% and 27.3% respectively, while firms within the South Australian cluster averaged 41%" (Aylward 2004, 2007a). The export intensity and its distribution between different cluster types aligns with the analyses of

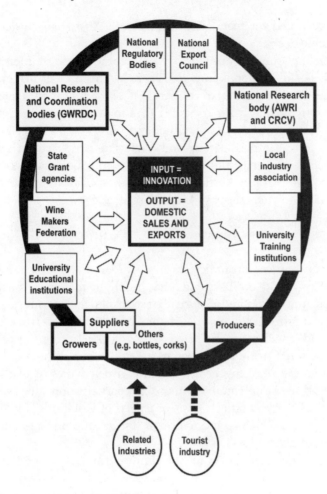

Figure 7.2   South Australian clusters
Source: Aylward 2004, Prometheus, Vol. 22, No. 4, pp. 423–37

Mytelka and Farinelli (2003), and Roper and Love (2001). Reinforcing these trends was the increase in exports over time, another key indicator of a cluster's innovative capacity. An average of 56% of NSW and Victorian firms recorded increases in exports over the past three years. This compared with 66% of firms within the South Australian cluster. In addition, the percentage increase of exports varied between different cluster types. Exports within NSW and Victorian clusters experienced an average annual increase of 14.8% in volume, compared to

32.2% recorded for firms within the South Australian cluster (Aylward 2004; 2007a).

When analysing the number and geographic spread of international markets, similar trends emerged. There had been a national increase in wine firms' export markets between 1997 and 2007, increasing from approximately 3.2 markets per firm to 6.4 markets per firm, but when these figures are disaggregated, we see an even clearer picture. Over a ten year period NSW and Victorian firms within clusters increased their average number of markets from 3.05 markets to 5.15 markets, while South Australian firms increased from an average of 3.3 markets to 7.66 markets (Aylward 2004; 2007a).

INNOVATION AND TRAINING

Using core innovation indicators in a similar study (Aylward 2004), the author found similar trends that highlight the close association between innovation and exports. For example, in accessing research services, approximately twice as many South Australian firms as Victorian and NSW firms participated (68% vs 32%). In terms of collaboration between firms, an average of 44% of NSW and Victorian firms stated that they had engaged in collaborative activities regularly over the past three years compared to a 64% participation rate in South Australia. The trend reflects positive aspects of Dobkins's (1996) spillover theory in which co-located firms "bleed" into one another (Aylward 2004; 2007a).

Using related activities of technical innovation, product differentiation, marketing innovation, and branding that had been undertaken regularly over a three year period, South Australian firms, showed significant leadership again (table 7.1) (Aylward 2004).

A subsequent 2007 study by the author (Aylward 2007a) involving 165 small and medium firms arrived at similar results. With regard to innovation intensity, results reflected the 2004 study and discussion by Mytelka and Farinelli (2003), Roper and Love (2001), and Rosenfeld (2005). When asked where the most intense innovation was occurring within the Australian wine industry 88% of respondents nominated the South Australian cluster. For new product development, process improvement, employee education levels, and training, South Australian firms again ranked as more innovative then their NSW and Victorian counterparts (Aylward 2007a).

Table 7.1
Responses to innovation indicators

Indicator	South Australian firms (%)	VIC/NSW firms (%)
Technical innovation	22	8
Product differentiation	54	54
Marketing innovation	34	18
Branding	40	32
Increase in domestic market share	76	58

Source: Aylward, 2004 study

Table 7.2
Comparative performance in core indicators of innovation

Indicator	NSW	South Australia	Victoria	Western Australia	SA lead over av. %
Innovation uptake	134	162	118	126	28.5
Marketing	148	195	162	136	30.9
Product Differentiation	154	192	161	140	27.2
New product development	163	193	153	149	24.5
Employee training	140	145	120	124	13.3
Process improvement	125	157	113	119	31.9
Distribution	151	164	122	127	23.3
Agents	132	186	139	150	32.9
Exporting	121	158	113	129	30.6

Source: Aylward, 2007

Furthermore, over 82% of South Australian wine firms believed that innovation intensity within their cluster benefitted their firm, while 41% (average) of other cluster firms believed these benefits could be attributed to their own cluster (Aylward 2007a). These responses align with the "competitive advantage" model put forward by Maskell and Malmberg (1999) and Lorentzen (2003). In table 7.2, cumulative scores based on activity, collaboration, and dedicated resources were awarded to firms based on their involvement in associated innovative activities. Although the spread of indicators was larger the trends were similar to those in the 2004 study (Aylward 2004; 2007a).

When firms were questioned about export and innovation advantages of operating within industry clusters, they confirmed the figures.

There was consensus that proximity to large and successful exporters, appropriate industry associations, and suppliers, and the sharing of knowledge between firms contributed to competitive advantage over-all. Many claimed they had been exposed to export markets through their associations and their knowledge sharing with other firms (Aylward 2007a).

Training

As we can see from table 7.2, there is also an association between cluster development and training levels. In the case of South Australia's innovative cluster, training levels in all formats were higher and more sophisticated. For example, significant in-house training is undertaken within the large firms and multinationals, usually with their own programs but also using external contractors. These are run on a continuous basis and all employees are required to under-take some form of in-house training. In terms of tertiary education providers, the prestigious Roseworthy College (University of Adelaide) sits at the heart of the South Australian cluster. It offers under-graduate and post-graduate courses in both viticulture and oenology, as well as associated courses in general agriculture and chemistry. It supplies a large percentage of the educated wine workforce across the country and the associated Waite Institute hosts much of the practical application. There are not only more tertiary graduates in the South Australian wine cluster than the industry in general, but they tend to be better trained and with a higher percentage having post-graduate qualifications.

Supply Chains

Vertical integration with South Australia's innovative cluster is sub-stantially higher than is the case for other clusters or the industry in general. Supply chains, therefore, are necessarily more cohesive. In addition, national suppliers tend to be co-located within this cluster and in many cases coordinate with subsidiaries of international suppliers. Because of the national supplier presence and head office proximity, supply chains of bottles, barrels, fertilizers, vineyard trellises, irrigation systems, and storage containers are notably more seamless in operation than is experienced by the wider industry. Proximity also reduces cost to producers. In cases where grapes are brought in from other suppliers, the vast majority of those supply vineyards are co-located within the cluster, so supply time and costs are minimised. A number of the largest firms have their own exclusively contracted suppliers on retainers. This adds a new and more complex dimension to supply networks, and one that is not obvious in other wine clusters.

A DISTORTED LANDSCAPE?

An intense cluster such as that of South Australia, operating within a centralised industry framework, will always create fundamental con-tours in the landscape. Perceptions among sampled wineries substantiate industry data, and as in the case of a major city and its regional satellites, indications are that there is a real distortion in services, priorities, and activity. When a particular region dominates in numbers of participants, volume of production, and export reputation, then it also begins to dominate the strategic thinking of the overall industry. The geographical proximity of the fourteen industry associations and specifically the close physical and cultural link between the primary R&D bodies (GWRDC, AWRI, and CRCV) and the South Australian wineries (including the largest corporations) forged an unconscious alliance of priorities. In terms of soil evaluation, disease testing and resistance, micro-climate assessment, and localised pest control, these research bodies naturally used their local clients as test cases and developed templates based on their needs (Cabus 2001).

Wineries in regions outside the South Australian cluster – regions in New South Wales, Western Australia, Victoria, and Tasmania – became more and more peripheral to central priorities. Their generic needs were serviced in an ad-hoc, secondary manner that often provided inadequate and unsuitable support. As wineries in a 2008 (Aylward) study indicated, the lack of region-specific research and localised decision-making often meant that firms outside the South Australian wine cluster were provided with South Australian-specific solutions. This had the effect of homogenizing not only R&D support, but also R&D requests. Non-generic solutions were increasingly expensive, particularly for small firms with a limited budget, with the natural consequence being a one-size-fits-all R&D approach that standardised techniques and reduced experimentation. The call for targeted R&D extension programs that acknowledged regional differences and tailored services to those differences was largely ignored. Small firms in peripheral regions did not warrant the additional expense of personnel for delivering specific solutions to specific problems.

At this level there was a very conscious decision to prioritise those clients whose levy dollars overwhelmingly provided the life-blood of these R&D bodies – the large multinational operators, also headquartered in South Australia. This dependency ensured that research around winery requirements, such as fermentation techniques, ageing, flavour manipulation, yeast culture, micro-oxygenation, and standardisation of processes were increasingly tailored to the needs of these larger stakeholders. Critically, for the direction of the industry as a whole, it was a strategy that culminated in the majority of smaller wineries emulating the vineyard and winemaking behaviour of their largest peers in order to access this same expertise and sponsored support (Aylward 2008).

It was also a strategy that has left a legacy of price competitiveness and unsustainable financial practices for the SME wine producer. Lured by the apparent and perhaps transient success of their larger peers in exports, the typical small wine producer effectively forfeited their notions of uniqueness to embrace the "Brand Australia" approach. Their natural attributes of small scale production of a differentiated product that encapsulated a sense of place was subsumed within the standardised Australian offering of value. As a result, they replaced a product-competitive approach with a price-competitive one – an approach that dissolved their comparative advantage. Throughout the first decade of the new millennium Australia's two largest wine markets – the UK and the USA – were becoming saturated with the New World's standardised, "value" wine. There was little to differentiate these products except price and the more saturated markets became, the more intense the price competition became, ultimately reducing profit margins to unsustainable levels (Aylward 2009; Odorici and Corrado 2004).

What had presented itself as a hub of competitive advantage throughout the 1980s and 1990s – the innovative wine cluster – had, due to policy mismanagement and forfeited opportunities, sown the seeds of severe disadvantage in the following decade. Other New World wine producers had adopted Australia's technology, could also produce fault-free wine, and because of cheaper labour, could provide better value for money. Australia's innovative wine clusters had certainly provided a critical mass, inter-firm networking, technology transfer, and easy access to education providers. But because of the industry's adherence to

"Brand Australia" and its focus on standardisation of product, these clusters were now generating far more volume but relatively less value. Their competitive advantage was being diminished by an industry that had become dislocated from consumer needs and traditional wine-making values (Aylward 2010).

THE MASS-PRODUCER MINDSET IN PRACTICE

Compounding the industry's already deteriorating market position and reputation among consumers and critics alike was a continuing reinforcement of bad practices in the vineyard and the winery. In the vineyard, a "fruit-salad" approach to planting grape varieties was the favoured method as producers chased the latest variety fashion rather than that which was most suited to the terroir. Blending of varieties from vastly different terroirs and regions was also commonplace, a practice that ensured a constant supply of the latest fashion, but which also undermined any real quality control of growing conditions and fruit selection. Such a multi-vineyard approach also weakened the sense of identity and place that accompanies wine quality reputation. There could be no intimate story or experience in which a particular wine reflected its geographic and cultural surroundings. There could be no historical setting for the wine or its maker and no differentiation between one site and another (Tuten 2005).

This mindset invaded other elements within vineyard management as well. By rejecting the notion of terroir, many if not most producers practiced wide-scale and heavy irrigation, were relatively free in using pesticides and herbicides, and sought large yields per hectare to boost sales volume. There was largely indiscriminate machine harvesting, so that grape ripeness tended to feature as a secondary concern to cost when deciding on harvest times. In the winery, the high-volume-low-cost mindset continued. Industrial crushers, continuous-screw fermenters, and oak chips replaced more subtle, high quality, and higher cost techniques. Micro-oxygenation was a common feature of wineries as the speed of maturation played an increasingly important role in final distribution. Flavour manipulation and artificial yeasts were also common accessories in what was to many a scientifically devised production line of standardised products.

These processes certainly illustrate the technical expertise and high volume capacity of the modern Australian wine industry, but they also provide an insight into the thinking and culture that had come to dominate winemaking in Australia. A noticeable disconnection had emerged between terroir and the vineyard, and similarly between the vineyard and the winery.

The Terroir and the Vineyard

In 2009, the Australian and New Zealand Wine Industry Directory (2009) listed 53% of Australia's wineries as employing contract wine-makers. A similar number brought in grapes from other vineyards often across multiple regions and even states. Such a situation poses a number of critical issues.

First, buying grapes from other sources and regions undermines the notion of terroir and its connection to vineyard practices quite simply because these sourced grapes are mixed with "home" grapes in a blend that removes the identity of each parcel and the way in which it has been nurtured. Additionally, each batch of grapes will have been tended by different people with different management approaches, different philosophies and different ideas about the connection between terroir and vineyard. There will usually be significantly different standards of quality control. As a result, the wine will not represent "somewhere" but will more accurately represent "nowhere."

Second, the employment of contract winemakers further exacerbates the disconnection between terroir and vineyard and then vineyard and winery by introducing another external element into the process. These contractors have little feel for the specific terroir in which they are working, have little or no knowledge of the vineyard and its management, and often produce a wine that does not represent the site on which it is produced. Further, many of these contractors service up to ten or twelve different wineries, so there is a tendency for uniformity of style and technique and a further standardisation of the product.

The Vineyard and the Winery

With the increasing use of contractors and externally sourced grapes, even among wineries with their own grapes and winemakers, there has been a growing disconnection between activities within the vineyard and those of the winery. As one winery owner recently stated, "I know of many wineries around here where the winemaker never ventures into the vineyard and has no idea about what happens there" (Aylward 2010). For many, the grape-growing/winemaking process has been atomized. Rather than winemakers acting as custodians of the grape, ensuring that it retains its integrity from the vineyard to the bottle, they have come to see their role as one of manipulation in order to achieve a certain taste and style. As with any assembly line, the modern Australian winemaker's role has been to attach the final elements to the product before it hits the supermarket shelves. And as with an assembly line, each attendant believes their role has little to do with any other and is only affected minimally by what has taken place before the product reaches their station. Assembly lines atomize the process so that the product story and experience becomes fragmented.

A FINANCIALLY UNSUSTAINABLE MINDSET

The late twentieth century Australian wine mindset, therefore, was firmly entrenched within a scientific and cost-reduction paradigm. Winemakers came to see their product simply as a saleable commodity, as with all mass-produced products, which could be turned out in ever-increasing volume (Anderson, Norman, and Wittwer 2001). There was little attachment to and respect for a fruit that is imbued with the cultural and physical elements of its site, its region, and its varietal heritage.

By 2011, the mindset was proving unsustainable both at a financial level and in terms of reputation. In the past twelve months, the Australian wine industry has experienced a continuing wine glut in excess of 40 million cases and heavy discounting has so far failed to reduce this surplus (Winetitles 2011). Although winery numbers continue to grow – there are now over 2,500, and their numbers are increasing by approximately 5% per year – the dollar value of domestic and export wines maintains a worrying decline. For example, in 2000, the export value per litre was AUD$4.78; a decade later it was $2.97 (62% less); and in the previous twelve months alone the industry experienced a value-per-litre fall of almost 16% (Winetitles 2010, 2011). Yet in those same twelve months, export volumes have increased by 9%, which means Australia is selling more wine for less return. Even more serious is the fact that in the country's two largest export markets – the UK and the USA – export value-per-litre fell by 21.8% (Winetitles 2010; Aylward

Table 7.3
Further indicators – export approvals to selected wine markets, 2010

Market	Volume 07–08	Value 07–08 $mil.	Volume 09–10	Value 09–10 $mil.	% increase in volume	% decrease in Value
UK	267.9	888.1	271.9	584.6	1.5	–34.2
USA	182.6	745.5	222.9	623.6	22.0	–16.3
Canada	46.1	259.9	51.7	202.3	12.1	–22.1
NZ	22.1	85.9	26.6	70.6	20.3	–17.8
Global	708.9	2,683.2	776.6	2,167.2	9.6	–19.2

Source: Australian Government – Winefacts AWBC 2010

2011a). Australia's domestic markets show similar signs of stress. While the nation's wine drinkers are consuming less overall, their share of imported wine is increasing. In 2009, domestic wine sales fell by 5.5%, while the value of imported wine increased by 16.7% (Aylward 2010; Winetitles 2010). And, according to the Australian Agricultural and Resource Economics Society (2012), the oversupply that has plagued the Australian wine industry for the past decade is expected to remain a long-term malaise. Table 7.3 shows the dramatic decline in export value in Australia's key wine markets.

The figures in the table above are compounded to a greater degree when the increased volumes and lower values are converted into the common value-per-litre measure.

In fact, similar measures were tested at a micro-level in a 2006/7 study on differentiation and competitive advantage within the wine Australian industry (Aylward 2007b). The results were just as clear. Table 7.4 shows the financial impact of the then grape surplus on wineries using the average price-points into which their wines were sold. Data is summarised from one hundred SME wineries across major wine regions, showing an inverse association between price-points and the degree to which wineries were affected financially. Wineries that are most vulnerable to financial stress are those selling into the lowest price-points. Wineries selling into the highest price-points are least vulnerable. These price-points were examined over a three-year period and in the case of the wineries selling into the highest price-points, levels had either remained stable or risen, despite an industry-wide grape surplus (Aylward 2007b).

Table 7.4
Association between impact of wine surplus and export price points

Financial impact of current wine-grape surplus	Average FOB price per case
No Impact	$212
Slight Negative Impact	$114
Moderate Negative Impact	$109
Significant negative Impact	$ 92
Threatening Survival	$ 84

Source: Aylward, 2007 study

Domestically and internationally, Australians need to develop a new approach to wine production and adopt a different way of thinking about their product. As Mackey and Barney (2005) might say, the mass-production mindset of the late twentieth century no longer aligns with a consumer who is after differentiation, a sense of place, and a truly unique wine experience (Marks 2011; Aylward 2010). Winemakers and industry associations need to view their wine product as a cultural asset that represents the very best of artisanal qualities and attitudes. And it is this cultural asset approach that, globally, is providing the foundations for competitive advantage – the creation of product-competitive rather than price-competitive markets where difference creates advantage. As will be demonstrated in the following section, there are still significant exceptions within the Australian wine industry that operate according to this cultural asset philosophy. They are exceptions that, based on their significant and long-term success, should provide a template for the Australian wine industry over the next decades of its evolution.

DEFINING A SUSTAINABLE FUTURE
FOR AUSTRALIAN WINE

What type of landscape will the Australian wine industry traverse in the future? Will it continue along a homogeneous, bland landscape with few defining features, or will the industry instead navigate the contours of differentiation and uniqueness?

Globally in 2011, producer and consumer expectations of wine and what it is meant to represent are fundamentally different from those of even a decade ago. Today's wine consumers have experienced the 1990s transition from region and terroir to variety and brand. They have experienced two decades of wine commodification – the standardised, easy-drinking, fruit-driven wines designed for immediate consumption with little or no challenge to the senses. And, they have witnessed the shift from small artisanal operations to large conglomerates that focus on economies of scale and global distribution (Patchell 2008; Rosenthal 2009).

But just as abruptly as this transition began, it is ending. Today, the wine world is transforming itself once again from the homogeneity of New World, large-scale production to the heterogeneous diaspora of wine experiences. Globalisation has, somewhat perversely, created innumerable portals of localised artisanship, as a consumer bored with bland offerings is demanding a sense of place and meaningful stories. Throughout countries such as Australia, New Zealand, South Africa, Chile, Argentina, and the USA, wine production is slowly returning to its traditional roots. Artisanal wine production methods that were once ridiculed as dated and out of touch with the market are being enthusiastically embraced by producers attempting to differentiate their styles from those of their peers. And so the simplistic economic and cultural divisions of New and Old World are being replaced by more nuanced divisions predicated on an intimate connection between producer and consumer.

From a myriad of styles, terroirs, and philosophies, now come wines that speak in many languages to many different audiences. Apart from creating heterogeneity, they are creating meaning and an environment in which experimentation and exploration can once again be rewarded. They have also brought the localisation of wine back into sharp focus as a reference point for quality and artisanship, and established "place" as a central feature in the wine journey. Today's wine consumer does not just purchase a drink. S/he buys into a whole experience in which the actual wine is the narrative. For that narrative to be interesting, it must relate to history, to place, to community, and to a winemaking philosophy that bestows its product with the artistic and aesthetic qualities that set it apart from the more ordinary (Theise 2010; Rosenthal 2009).

WHAT DOES THIS MEAN
FOR COMPETITION AND AUSTRALIA?

Many wineries throughout France, Italy, Germany, and Spain are well equipped to respond to the new consumer demand. In fact, they have been integral contributors to this particular wine experience for generations. Their often micro operations, their absolute attachment to the local community and a specific terroir, and their reluctance to move beyond local networks, workers, and suppliers has insulated them from much of the ubiquity that global brands have created. For the premium, quality-oriented producers among these, competitive advantage over rivals is at its highest level. They have retained their authenticity, they have sustained price levels, and refused to join the "race to the bottom." Furthermore, they have continued to build trust and loyalty with their customer base, and have attracted new devotees (Nossiter 2009; Theise 2010). These producers have always competed on product differentiation rather than price, and are now enjoying the appreciation of the market, the inflated profit margins, and the sustainability that differentiation fosters. For example, in the midst of the wine oversupply in 2008–09, as well as the global financial crisis, Bordeaux First Growths and France's famous champagne houses could barely keep up with demand, with prices reaching their highest levels in decades. For them, as for a number of iconic producers, there was simply no oversupply. As one Australian iconic winery owner stated: "What surplus? There is certainly no surplus at the prices points I sell at. I'm struggling to meet the demand. Business has never been better" (Aylward 2007a; Kramer 2010).

It was the type of competitive advantage and business model that is now compelling to the rest of the wine world. Despite years of being the butt of New World jokes about an arrogant denial of market trends, these producers were able to ignore the worst wine over-supply in history and continue to strengthen their brands and balance sheets. As with prestige brands such as Aston Martin or Gucci, the attraction lies in the product story, its hand-crafting, its enduring quality, its intellectual property protection, and not insignificantly, its exclusivity. The more international markets are flooded with beverage-style, globalised wine, the more these iconic wine brands can differentiate themselves and increase the consumer migration (Kramer 2010).

The Competitive Advantage of Intellectual Property

In addition, the French particularly have identified value in the intellectual property of wine production. The Bordeaux 1855 classification of terroirs and regions, for example, was every bit as much about attaching intellectual property rights to estates, and individual terroirs as it was about guaranteeing quality. The 1855 classification has been critical to the invention, implementation, and sustaining of reputation. Medoc, Saint Emilion, Graves, Pomerol, and Fronsac are household names throughout much of the wine world, with the wines from these regions being revered among discerning consumers. Within Bordeaux we also have estate names such as Chateau Lafite, Chateau Latour, Chateau Haut-Brion, Chateau Margaux, and Chateau Mouton Rothschild that have been classified as the five First Growths of Bordeaux and as such, command extraordinary prices regardless of vintage and financial climate. Their reputations are now so entrenched that producers and consumers alike use their wines as benchmarks by which to measure the quality of all others.

But probably the best example of the link between intellectual property and reputation is that of Champagne. Such is the rigour of Champagne's intellectual property that the region's wineries are the only ones allowed to use the name. Such is the power of the wine's reputation that it is synonymous the world over with celebration (Mazzeo 2008). For centuries the champagne houses of France have collaborated in creating and maintaining one of the world's most recognisable brands. It is a collaboration that involved a network of ideas and practices – the rigorous enforcement of geographical boundaries, the tight intellectual property rules, the creation of often mythical but very appealing champagne stories, and the careful crafting of identity and drinking experience (Kladstrup 2006; Nossiter 2009).

More than two centuries after its birth, Champagne remains a powerful enigma. It is a global brand that has invaded every market on earth, but perhaps more than ever, symbolizes exclusivity and prestige. Even the very largest champagne houses still project an image of the niche producer, creating a select product for a select consumer.

How is this achieved? It is managed through the strict adherence to terroir and the legal protection of that terroir; it is managed through the maintenance of a primarily hand-crafted production process (even if on a large scale); it involves a carefully crafted image of perfection;

but perhaps just as importantly, it draws upon the centuries of reputation, heritage, and nurtured status that enable Champagne to rise above
other wines as an object of desire, an object with which people want to
associate. In this context, Champagne symbolises success and reward
and something to which not everyone has access (Kladstrup 2006).

Applying a "champagne template" to the Australian wine industry
may not be practical, at least in the medium future, but there are steps
that can be taken to institutionalise a culture of quality definition,
demarcation, and geographic markers. In a recent study, the author
(Aylward 2012) devised a dynamic model of quality demarcation that
focused on practices and values adhered to by Australia's twelve most
recognised iconic wineries and the development of the embryonic
geographic indicator (GI) model emerging within the industry.

Policy Recommendations for Competitiveness

If the Australian wine industry is to regain a degree of competitive
advantage it must develop a multi-pronged approach which includes:

- understanding the advantages and disadvantages of geographic
  clustering;
- ensuring that these clusters are serviced through a decentralised,
  region-specific approach;
- decentralising the R&D extension programs to focus on region-
  specific requirements, using regionally sourced levy funds;
- redefining domestic and international target markets;
- dismantling "Brand Australia" to focus on regional and local
  identities;
- transitioning from mass production to localised niche production;
- creating an international reputation for the pursuit of quality
  rather than "value-for-money"; and
- establishing formal and appropriate terroir classifications with
  requisite intellectual property codes.

CONCLUSION

The Australian wine industry, like a number of New World wine
industries that followed, rode the wave of innovation and experimentation through the 1980s and 1990s. The emphasis was on newness, an

absence of tradition, and scientific formulas for creating standardised, "clean," fruit-driven wine. It was a movement that generated enormous excitement and boosterism among producers and consumers alike, and in fact, changed the wine landscape in a dramatic way. Old World producers from France, Italy, Germany, Portugal, and Spain were challenged and were being called upon by the wine community to defend their methods and, often, their entire way of life. And, for almost two decades they were left with dwindling market share and reputation as consumers swapped tradition and terroir for new varieties and big, bold brands.

But the New World wine craze proved to be unsustainable. In Australia's case, the industry allowed, even encouraged the dominance by global wine corporations, whose interests were very much aligned with global production and distribution. These requirements were in stark contrast to those of the small, local producer attempting to produce wines of distinction and identity. In addition, the innovative processes that were being developed were reliant on a scientific paradigm and the application of standardised, large-scale technologies, technologies that could be easily copied and exported.

As such, the competitive advantages of Australia and its New World wine peers were quickly forfeited. The new production regimes were copied and improved upon and the style of wine, ubiquitous in its universality, became too standardised and too bland. As Theise (2010) writes, it came from "nowhere" and meant "nothing." Consumers were returning to traditional producers who created authentic wines with their own stories and identities, wines that could be traced back to a starting point and unveil their own histories. Many New World producers are now struggling to reach these consumers. They are suffering under the intense pressures of price competition, as their supply becomes a wine lake that is attracting little custom. Having locked their reputations and expertise into the commodity sector of the market (under AUD$10) they do not have the reputation or tradition of differentiated wines to attract consumers into higher price-points. The boosterism of the late twentieth century has left a very sour legacy of destructive discounting and bankruptcies.

Renewal will require substantial reconfiguration. The wine clusters that once provided competitive advantage through a critical mass and knowledge sharing, will help define a new landscape of local and regional identities. These clusters will no longer act purely as hubs of activity and connection within a centralised industry framework. Rather, they will need to assume the characteristics of regional production and branding enclaves that link to global markets but deliver wines of distinctiveness and localised identity. Instead of being subsumed within a "Brand Australia" approach, they must present themselves first as independent regions of unique terroirs, and only secondarily as Australian. In short, each cluster will become a hub of communal wine-making practices and philosophies that gain competitive advantage through the matching of terroirs and approaches, a matching that the market can differentiate from other such clusters.

These hubs, serviced by decentralised and region-specific R&D extension programs, using regionally-sourced levy funding, will be released from the generic strategies of the wider industry. The more specific R&D servicing will reinforce regional identities and terroir-specific wines. It will also help in providing a platform from which to redefine national and international marketing. Target markets, and more specifically, price-points within those markets, will link to actual product differentiation, rather than price-sensitive demand. A clearly defined branding of region, terroir, and the wine itself will guide and educate the consumer in differences between and stories embedded within Australia's range of wines.

With a regional and terroir-based emphasis there will necessarily be a welcome transition from mass production to niche and hand-crafted production of wines. An inverse relationship will emerge between a reduction in scale and an increase in quality as more care and attention is devoted to the wine-growing and producing process. This in turn will reinforce a growing reputation for quality rather than quantity, which again, will enhance demand. As demand increases prices will stabilize and then climb. Only when this is achieved will the Australian wine industry's "race to the bottom" (Croser 2004) be over.

REFERENCES

Anderson, K., D. Norman, and G. Wittwer. 2001. "Globalisation and the World's Wine Markets: Overview." Discussion Paper No. 0143, Adelaide University.

Australian Agricultural and Resource Economics Society. 2012. "The Governance of Grapes: The NSW Inquiry into the Wine Grape Market and

Prices, 2010 – An Assessment." Conference paper. 56th AARES annual conference, Fremantle, WA.

Australian Government Culture Portal. 2011. http://australia.gov.au/

Aylward, D. 2012. "Demarcation: A Dynamic Methodology for Quality Grading Within the Australian Wine Industry." *International Journal of Quality and Innovation* 2 (1): 18–36.

– 2011a. "Creative Highways: Cultural Imperatives and Financial Returns in the Wine Industry." *International Journal of Sustainable Strategic Management* 2 (4): 319–34.

– 2011b. "Pursuing the Creative: New Pathways in the 'Economy of Wine.'" *International Journal of Business Excellence* 4 (1): 80–93.

– 2010. "Moving from Creative to Cultural Industries: The Case of the Australian Wine Sector." International Journal of Business and Globalisation 5 (2): 135–46.

– 2008 "Towards a Cultural Economy Paradigm for the Australian Wine Industry." *Prometheus* 26 (4): 373– 85.

– 2007a. "Differentiation or Path Dependency: A Critical Look at the Australian Wine Industry." *Strategic Change* 16: 385–98.

– 2007b. "Innovation and Inertia: The Emerging Dislocation of Imperatives Within the Australian Wine Industry." *International Journal of Technology and Globalization* 3 (2/3): 246–62.

– 2007c. "Fault Lines: Emerging Domains of Inertia within the Australian Wine Industry." *Prometheus* 25 (1): 85–98.

– 2006a. "Innovation Lock-in: Unlocking Research and Development Path Dependency in the Australian Wine Industry." *Strategic Change* 15: 361–72.

– 2006b. "Global Pipelines: Profiling Successful SME Exporters within the Australian Wine Industry." *International Journal of Technology, Policy and Management* 6 (1): 49–65.

– 2005. "Global Landscapes: A Speculative Assessment of Emerging Organizational Structures within the International Wine Industry." *Prometheus* 23 (4): 421–36.

– 2004. "Innovation-Export Linkages within Different Cluster Models: A Case Study from the Australian Wine Industry." *Prometheus* 22 (4): 423–37.

Aylward, D. and G. Carey. 2009. "High-Value Niche Production: What Australian Wineries Might Learn from a Bordeaux First Growth." *International Journal of Technology, Policy and Management* 9 (4): 342–57.

Beeston, J. 1994. *A Concise History of Australian Wine*. London: Allen & Unwin.

Cabus, P. 2001. "The Meaning of Local in a Global Economy: The Region's Advocacy of Local Interests as a Necessary Component of Current Global/Local Theories." *European Planning Studies* 9 (8): 102–20.

Croser, B. 2004. "Brand or Authenticity." *The Australian and New Zealand Wine Industry Journal* 19 (2): 12–19.

– 2010. "Prospects for Australian Smaller 'Fine Wine' Producers." Paper presented at The World's Wine Markets by 2030: Terroir, Climate Change, R&D and Globalisation, AARES Conference, 7–9 February, Adelaide.

Dobkins, L.H. 1996. "Location, Innovation and Trade: The Role of Localization and Nation-Based Externalities." *Regional Science and Urban Economics* 26: 591–612.

Faith, N. 2002. *Liquid Gold: The Story of Australian Wine and Its Makers*. Sydney: Pan MacMillan.

GWRDC. 1999. *Annual Report*. Adelaide: Australian Government Printers.

– 2001. *Annual Report*. Adelaide: Australian Government Printers.

Kladstrup, D. and P. 2006. *Champagne*. New York: Harper Collins.

Kramer, M. 2010. *Matt Kramer on Wine*. New York: Sterling Epicure.

Lorentzen, A. 2003. "Local and Global Knowledge Sourcing in the Learning Process of Polish Companies." Paper presented at Regional Studies Association Conference: Reinventing Regions in the Global Economy, Pisa, Italy.

Mackey, A. and J.B. Barney. 2005. "Developing Multi-level Theory in Strategic Management: The Case of Managerial Talent and Competitive Advantage." *Multi-level Issues in Strategy and Methods (Research in Multi Level Issues)* 4: 163–75.

Marks, D. 2011. "Competitiveness and the Market for Central and Eastern European Wines: A Cultural Good in the Global Wine Market." *Journal of Wine Research* 22 (3): 245–63.

Maskell, P. and A. Malmberg. 1999. "Localised Learning and Industrial Competitiveness." *Cambridge Journal of Economics* 13 (1): 5–25.

Mattinson, C. 2006. *Wine Hunter: The Story of Maurice O'Shea, the Greatest Vigneron in Australia*. Australia: Hachette.

Mazzeo, T.J. 2008. *The Widow Clicquot: The Story of a Champagne Empire and the Woman Who Ruled It*. New York: Collins.

Mytelka, L and F. Farinelli. 2003. "From Local Clusters to Innovation Systems." In *Systems of Innovation and Development – Evidence from Brazil*, edited by J.E. Casssiolato, H.M.M. Lastres and M.L. Maciel, 249–72. London: Edward Elgar.

Nossiter, J. 2009. *Liquid Memory: Why Wine Matters*. New York: Farrar, Straus and Giroux.

Odorici, V. and R. Corrado 2004. "Between Supply and Demand: Intermediaries, Social Networks and the Construction of Quality in the Italian Wine Industry." *Journal of Management and Governance* 8:149–71.

Patchell, J. 2008. "Collectivity and Differentiation: A Tale of Two Wine Territories." *Environment and Planning* 40: 2,364–83.

Roper, S. and J.H. Love. 2001. "Innovation and Export Performance: Evidence from the UK and German Manufacturing Plants." *Research Policy* 31: 1087–102.

Rosenfeld, S. 2005. "Industry Clusters: Business Choice, Policy Outcome or Branding Strategy." *Journal of New Business Ideas and Trends* 3 (2): 4–13.

Rosenthal, N. 2009. *Reflections of a Wine Merchant, On a Lifetime in the Vineyards and Cellars of France and Italy*. New York: Farrar, Straus, and Giroux.

Saimee, S., P. Walters, and F. DuBois. 1993. "Exporting as an Innovative Behaviour: An Empirical Investigation." *International Marketing* 10 (3): 5–21.

Theise, T. 2010. *Reading Between the Wines*. Los Angeles: University of California Press.

Tuten, J. 2005. "Liquid Assets: Madeira Wine and Cultural Capital among Lowcountry Planters, 1735–1900." *American Nineteenth Century History* 6 (2): 173–88.

Winetitles. 2011. *The Australian and New Zealand Wine Industry Directory*. Adelaide: Winetitles.

– 2010. *The Australian and New Zealand Wine Industry Directory*. Adelaide: Winetitles.

– 2009. *The Australian and New Zealand Wine Industry Directory*. Adelaide: Winetitles.

– 2008. *The Australian and New Zealand Wine Industry Directory*. Adelaide: Winetitles.

8

Summary of Findings
and Policy Lessons

ANIL HIRA

INTRODUCTION

In this book, we have sought to bring out the best of both worlds in terms of research design – to systematically examine sources of competitiveness while also appreciating the differences between cases. This approach is vital, as we recognise that wine in particular is an industry that cultivates differentiation and depends on tacit knowledge, on the one hand, while also being subject to scientific and organised efforts to develop industry, on the other. We can see the representations of both approaches, generally speaking in the Old World stalwarts such as France vs the newer approaches of California, Australia, and New Zealand. In contrast to Old World producers, newer industries use a different approach in which there is a strong presence of multinational brands, and a reliance on scientific and concerted efforts at improvement through collective action in wine-making techniques and marketing. Yet, wine remains an unusual industry in that smaller players can continue to capture and gain market share through claims of differentiation, and once that market share is consolidated through an established reputation for consistent and high quality of a particular type, even the largest multinationals will struggle to recreate the formula. In this chapter, we draw together some of the insights from our cases about how to reconcile these two views in order to develop a better set of policies for the industry.

LESSONS FOR WINE CLUSTER POLICY

As we discussed in chapter 1, cluster theory is a widely accepted conceptual approach that lacks consensus around causal or actor relationships or measurements that allow for precise testing whether a cluster exists (and what are its boundaries), let alone how effective it is. This has led to the policy conundrum of recognising the potential importance of clusters for improvements in economic wellbeing on the one hand, while being left in the dark about how to promote them on the other. Indeed, the basic trends of globalisation, such as the outsourcing of software from Silicon Valley to South India, raise the question about whether such policies can have an effect. The wine industry, being by nature geographically concentrated in suitable production areas, is a natural fit for testing these questions out. Here are some observations from our study about clusters:

Terroir Is Only Part of the Game

If we simply examine the number of potential production areas around the globe for wine, we see vast areas that are underperforming, such as North Africa and Eastern Europe. We also see more obviously that even in the same terroir the quality of the wine can vary dramatically across space and time, however, generally firms that figure out how to produce high quality wine are more able to continue doing so. Therefore, knowledge and learning matter, which in turn suggests the possible role of institutions for helping to spread and instil a culture of innovation.

Timing Matters and Policy Should Adjust to It

What we also see is that timing matters greatly. The centuries-old techniques of producing Champagne or Beaujolais are not easily reproduced elsewhere. More importantly, brand reputation and marketing, as illustrated by the Tuscan wineries, becomes more important once a certain quality standard is achieved and recognised. Thus, we see an evolutionary cycle to policy, whereby heavier intervention and perhaps even protection may be warranted at the infant industry stage, but, as the industry matures, a lighter touch is warranted. What we see in British Columbia (BC) is that without the protection that began primarily with the replanting policies of the 1990s, the industry would not exist, as openly acknowledged by the industry. However, infant industry protection becomes a stagnant policy after a while, favouring incumbents who wish to maintain shelf space at the expense of newcomers who face not only a more crowded field but also higher input costs. The industry then moves towards regulatory capture, which leads to an inability to move to the next logical step, to level the playing field with imports and seek out external markets after a process of improvement.

Institutions Matter, But Need to Adapt to Lateness and Local Conditions

For latecomers such as Chile and Australia, more concerted institutional and policy efforts are needed to catch up to incumbents such as Tuscany. In both cases, a strong concerted effort by industry associations, universities (which also figure largely in Tuscany), and governments play a role in improving quality and promoting a notion of brand. In Extremadura, Spain, the lack of coordination inhibits the improvement of quality, as does the fragmented nature of the industry (also seen in BC). It appears that late successful cases have a more uneven topography of firms. While Tuscany has relatively nimble, medium-sized, family-origin firms, both Chile and Australia have strong differentiation between larger and smaller firms, and across regions. As suggested in other studies of late development (Amsden 1989), some consolidation as well as greater coordination with the state may be needed to overcome the advantages of incumbents. Yet, even across these two latecomers, the differences are significant. Whereas Australia has a strong scientific tradition built around formidable public-private-academic partnerships as reflected in the Grape and Wine Research Development Corporation, Chile's institutional structure is more dominated by the private sector. This reinforces the idea that successful institutions are appropriate architectures to respond to the global market environment if they are also tailored for local conditions. By architectures, we refer to the configuration of institutions in such a manner that each one is designed optimally for their particular function, and that the overall design optimizes interaction towards common policy goals.

Exports and Varietal Specialisation Help to Create Collective Action

In the two cases of areas struggling with saturation, BC and Extremadura, we note a lack of coordination among wineries, as well as between them and support institutions, whereas in Tuscany, Chile, and Australia, we see a rather more concerted action. This action appears to be premised upon two key features. The first is the identification of a region's production with a varietal type, such as Italy's "Super Tuscans," Chile's Cabernet and Carménere, and Australia's Shiraz, whereas BC and Extremadura suffer from trying to be good at many different types of wine. Specialising means that each winery has a collective interest to keep up the quality of their output so that the regional brand will benefit. Moreover, knowledge can become more specialised and deeper in the particular techniques that will benefit the cultivation and processing of a particular varietal. Regional branding thus gives wineries the best of both worlds – an immediate quality reputation as well as the ability to differentiate their particular version of that varietal. The second is that wineries no longer see each other as direct competition. Rather, the flexible specialisation model of cluster theory – competition through niche differentiation – begins to take hold (Piore and Sable 1984). Lastly, export creates a policy space in which all the triple helix parties (researchers, industry, and government) as well as firms of different sizes and inclinations, can work towards a common, and just as importantly, measureable aim, to gain market share. The contrast in terms of motivation for co-operation with BC could not be more stark. Under export orientation, policies turn toward establishing regional brands, promoting regional product differentiation through increasingly deeper and specialised knowledge, and creating forums where tacit knowledge transfer can take place.

Globalisation is Perfectly Compatible with Cluster Policy

As Giuliani, Morrison and Rabellotti have pointed out, external ties are as important as internal ones for knowledge transfer. Appreciating the role of consultants in upgrading in BC, with numerous graduates from New Zealand and Australia helping wineries, is vital to understanding improvements in quality. Similarly, the exchanges between Australian and Chilean researchers with Old World counterparts have vastly accelerated the learning process. More fundamentally, as in the case of BC and Chile, early investments by Old World investors helped to initiate the know how behind cluster success. However, that knowledge still needs to be adapted by local researchers and institutions for local conditions. Thus, the role of agricultural extension via active university researchers, consultants, and training appears to be quite important to Australian, Chilean, and Tuscan success. The lack of such efforts is notable, by contrast, in the struggling cases of BC and Extremadura. Similarly, the relationship between grape growers and wineries appears to be key to quality-upgrading efforts.

One surprising finding of our research is the lack of evidence for agglomeration effects on suppliers. We find no evidence in the new clusters that the development of the wine industry also spurs on the creation of new supplier networks as cluster theory would predict. Rather, in the new clusters much of the equipment is still imported, principally from Europe. This suggests that the same evolutionary cycle forces and advantages of incumbency hold in the wine equipment business.

Even Success Requires Adjustments

The evolutionary perspective on competitiveness is reinforced in another way. In Chile and Australia, the strong brands of the larger companies were accompanied by the carving out of new areas in the global wine market. Australia's penetration of the middle class New World markets, following California's example, beginning with UK supermarkets in the 1980s opened the way for New Zealand, Chile, Argentina, and South Africa to compete against the Old World through a different type of wine designed for an emerging market of new wine consumers who had less concern with reputation and subtlety. The emerging middle class market was developed through marketing exposure as much as it discovered these wines on its own. And the more scientific approach of the New World lends itself to the creation of wines that offer great value and consistency. Ironically, the success of the New World has crowded the marketplace as well as captured market share from the Old World. The end result is that New World producers such as California and Australia are being squeezed out of the low-medium price market by lower-cost competitors such as Chile, Argentina, and South Africa. The situation may get even worse if other potential competitors such as North Africa and Eastern Europe adopt their strategy. The upshot, as relayed in our chapter on Australia, is that they ironically have to move towards some of the more idiosyncratic nuanced production strategies of the Old World in order to move up in price points. This suggests the need again for a new evolution in wine institutions, one that is presently underway in the early New World producers.

Table 8.1 summarises some of our survey findings and reinforces the points made above. See the appendix for the survey document. The

Table 8.1
Synthesis of findings table

Country	n, approx. response rate	Acreage (Ave)	% firms reporting revenue increases in past year	Grapes Purchased Off Estate	% who Export	Geography Critical or Important (%)	Top 3 Sources of Competitive Advantage (at least 4/5 scale exc. Chile)	Top Areas for Innovation	Top Sources of Innovation (1–5 scale)	Top Sources of Training	Key Network Contacts (1-5 or % 4-5)	Importance of Tourism (ave)
BC	33, 30%	77.6	52	47.9 (% average)	0	74.19	Branding (4.4); Price (4.4); Marketing (4.2)	Marketing (67%); Fermentation (64%); Education (61%); soil adaptation (55%)	Internal (4.5); Internet (3.8); Suppliers/trade journals (3.7)	In House (88%); Consultants (43%); External (42%)	BC Wine Institute (3.5); Ok. Wine Fest. Society (3.4)	4.6
Chile	110, 30%	3530	74 (by > 10%)	22% purchase 31% or > off estate	96	Previous research indicates v. strong importance, (% 4 or 5) esp. for reputation; higher still for small firms	Exports (83%); Price (71%); Distribution (54%)	Marketing (48%); Information systems (48%); Fermentation (43%); Training (43%)	Internal (4.6); Internet (3.45); Suppliers (3.37); Consultants (3.35)	Consultants (76%); In House (71%); External (48%)	Min of Agric (33%); Wines of Chile (29%); University of Talca (19%)	71.4% say important

Italy (Tuscany)	32, 85	17.95	49	2%	70	84	Exports (3.3); Branding (3.2)	Marketing (46%); Soil Adaptation (38%); Retail Sales (35%)	Internal (4.1); Consultants (2.9); Clients (2.6)	External (62%); Consultants (34%); In House (24%)	Consultants (4.15); Ast Univ Enology (3.67); Universities (3.2); ARSIA (3.0);	3.9
Spain (Extre-madura)	30,?	1673.9	47	83.30%	39.8	60	Exports (4.2); Price (4.0); Production improvement (3.9)	Fermentation (73%); Marketing (67%); Information sys (63%); Edu (60%)	Internal (3.8); Clients (3.6); Internet (3); Suppliers (2.8)	In House (77%); External (73%); Consultants (37%) U of Extremadura	Almendralejo Wine Inst (2.55); Regulatory Council of DOC (2.53);	3.3
Extremaduran										(23%)	Ag Council (2.52)	

Notes: Because of poor response, Australia is not included in this table. ARSIA (Italy) is a regional agricultural innovation and extension agency.

answers to the question about geography indicate that firms themselves agree it is important, thus supporting the most basic foundation for cluster theory. Note in the table that averages are used, and in terms of questions of importance, a 1–5 scale was used, with 1 being not important; 2 slightly; 3 neutral; 4 somewhat; and 5 extremely important.

CONCLUSION

Overall, we find that the four aspects of our theoretical framework explain well the dynamics of firm and state responses to market demands by cluster actors. Evolution is an apt metaphor for depicting the need for industries to continually adapt to changing circumstances. Key events, such as the replanting policies in BC, spurred by the free trade agreement with the US, can have profound and unpredictable long-term effects, creating path dependencies. Yet, we have also demonstrated that adaptable, collectively oriented policy frameworks are as crucial to success as terroir, timing, and firm strength.

It is interesting to note how often policies, institutional support, and university research support are not considered by firms as being part of their success, despite overwhelming evidence to the contrary. BC's wine industry would not exist without the early leadership of the BC Wine Institute, yet it is not considered highly. In Tuscany and Chile, universities are not cited in surveys as important sources of innovation, yet informal ties with them are clearly important to competitive advantage. Perhaps this is part of the business culture, to claim self-reliance and credit for all good things that happen, and to blame policies and institutions for bad ones. If so, it speaks to the reasons why opportunities to use cluster policies to improve conditions for industries are often ignored or botched.

Our study reveals that, at least in the wine industry, the cluster approach continues to be very relevant, perhaps even more so as a collective response, in an age of globalisation. Inter-firm ties are important to each of the successful cases, and the lack of them in BC and Extremadura reflect problems for a large number of struggling small and medium-sized firms. If we extend the network perspective to supply chains, we find two interesting results. The first is that there is no evidence that clusters lead to local supply chains. Thus, globalisation analysts such as Sturgeon are right that vertical integration in this sense does not seem optimal. However, in terms of controlling grape supply, it still is. In the cases of BC and Extremadura, as opposed to

Tuscany, Chile, and Australia, an inability to upgrade is closely linked with the outsourcing of grape supplies. As an example, BC respondents noted that when they had sought to invest time into helping grape growers develop new techniques, they sometimes found the growers sold their supplies to higher bidders or went into the wine business themselves. Similarly, R&D institutes including important roles for local universities, are central to the successful cases. More than just R&D, the cases point to the need for agricultural extension and tacit learning. In Tuscany, there are close ties between firms and universities, and universities provide important research help that is complementary to firms' efforts, but the relationships tend to be more informal. Thus, the social network behind strong institutions and strands of clusters is upheld well by our study. These networks extend to global partners, who are as crucial to the learning and upgrading process as export promotion efforts.

Rather than seeing them as separate, we find that the four aspects of transforming knowledge into competitive production are tightly interwoven, with networks of actors helping to shape state policy, and those networks changing membership, shape, and power over time based on market and regulatory changes. Timing does matter, and institutional capacity and flexibility figure large in both short- and long-term responses. Thus, structure and agency are closely intertwined with environmental (market) changes much of the time leading networks, but occasionally being shaped in turn by proactive efforts of state and cluster policies. Our cases reveal a wide variety of changing configurations of networks; in fact, the co-existence of different architectures of networks within the same clusters seems clear. In the case of BC and Spain, there are concentrations of large firms co-existing with smaller firms. In both cases, the larger firms seem to be more viable over the long run, however, smaller firms also add a variety and richness that are important for the overall identification of the cluster by customers (its larger cultural value, driving demand for wine from that specific region). Smaller firms seem more willing to take entrepreneurial risks in terms of identifying underserved niches, yet they struggle to bring forward adequate resources for systematic improvement. Thus, there is a level of symbiotic sharing between smaller and larger firms. The development of co-operatives, as in the case of Spain, in theory offers the best of both worlds, however, as that chapter demonstrates, this organisational form brings with it other challenges. Tuscany points out that small to medium sized firms are also important for the health of industrial ecosystems, just as having large enterprises early on that have some degree of vertical control and global reach helps the infant industry to gain a foothold. A complex industrial ecology must be healthy not just to improve tourist trade, but also to spur innovation and competition through differentiation (nimbleness) in the sector.

The exact nature and relationships of the key institutions must be adapted to the idiosyncratic conditions and developments over time, as we have seen from our cases. What remains to be seen in future research is whether patterns or prototypes of architecture, policies, and networks can be discerned to build up a theory of institutional effectiveness and learning in terms of industrial competitiveness. This requires further systematic comparative research across clusters, controlling for industry. Can we find patterns across industrial ecosystems, in terms of identifying institutional and industry firm architectural archetypes for different stages of evolution? Of course, such patterns will need to be adapted to local conditions (the local ecosystem). If such patterns exist, as our study suggests, then the even bigger question looms, which is to understand how the dynamic elements of creation, maintenance, learning, and adaptation can be cultivated through the use of policy tools appropriate for the particular stage of an industry's evolution.

REFERENCES

Amsden, Alice H. 1989. *Asia's Next Giant: South Korea and Late Industrialization.* New York: Oxford University Press.

Giuliani, Elisa, Andrea Morrison, and Roberta Rabelloti, eds. 2011. *Innovation and Technological Catch-Up: The Changing Geography of Wine Production.* Northampton, MA: Edward Elgar.

Piore, M.J. and C.F. Sabel. 1984. *The Second Industrial Divide: Possibilities for Prosperity.* New York: Basic Books.

Sturgeon, Timothy J. 2009. "From Commodity Chains to Value Chains: Interdisciplinary Theory Building in an Age of Globalization." In *Frontiers of Commodity Chain Research,* edited by Jennifer Bair, 110–35. Stanford: Stanford University Press.

—. 2005. "The Future of Manufacturing: The Implications of Global Production for Environmental Policy and Activism." In *Environmentalism & the Technologies of Tomorrow: Shaping the Next Industrial Revolution,* edited by Robert Olson and David Rejeski, 71–9. Washington: Island Press.

Survey Document (BC Example)
BC Wine Survey

ANIL HIRA AND DAVID AYLWARD

I. BASIC FIRM AND INDUSTRY-LEVEL INFORMATION

1. FIRM IDENTIFICATION AS OF MAY 2010
a. Name
b. Address
c. Acreage
d. Region
e. Year founded
f. Number of employees
g. Tonnes crushed or litres/cases sold
h. When did you start selling wine?   Date:

2. REVENUES
a. Have your revenues increased/decreased in the past 12 months?
b. By what percentage?
c. Has the volume of wine sold increased/decreased? By what percentage?
d. What price points are you currently targeting?
e. Have these increased/decreased over the past 12 months?

3. IS YOUR COMPANY PART OF A LARGER ENTERPRISE GROUP?
Yes
No

4. IS YOUR COMPANY CANADIAN OR FOREIGN OWNED? FAMILY OWNED? (Y/N)
Canadian
Foreign
Family Owned?

5. WHAT PERCENTAGE OF THE GRAPES THAT YOUR COMPANY USES IS PUR-
CHASED FROM GROWERS OFF YOUR ESTATE? EXACT NUMBER OR ESTIMATE
PERCENTAGE

6. IF YOU PURCHASE, WHAT PERCENTAGE OF YOUR GRAPES ARE BC, CANA-
DA, OR INTERNATIONAL?
BC/Local
RoCanada
International

7. WHAT PERCENTAGE OF YOUR WINE IS SOLD WITHIN? (LAST 3 YEARS)
BC?
Canada?
Exported?
What percentage of your wine is currently surplus to demand?

8. HOW WOULD YOU RATE YOUR FIRM'S RELIANCE ON THE FOLLOWING
FOR COMPETITIVE ADVANTAGE

1–5 scale with 1 = not important, 2 = slightly important,
3 = neutral, 4 = somewhat important, and 5 = extremely
important

Access to latest winemaking and viticultural information
Market placement at appropriate price-points (price competitive-
ness)
Marketing
Branding
New product development
Product differentiation
Employee training
Production process continual improvement
Distribution channels
Agents
Exporting

II. NETWORKING

9. GIVE THE RELATIVE IMPORTANCE AND FREQUENCY OF INTERACTIONS WITH THE FOLLOWING
1–5 scale with 1 = not important, 2 = slightly important, 3 = neutral, 4 = somewhat important, and 5 = extremely important (Annually, Monthly; Weekly; Daily; and Formal/ Informal or Both)
Did they help you with innovation?

	Importance (1–5)	Frequency (A,Q,M, W,D)	Formal/ Informal/ Both	Innovation Help? (Y/N)
Ministry of Agric, Food, & Fisheries				
PARC				
Okanagan University-UBC				
UBC Wine Research Centre				
BC Wine Grape Council				
BC Grapegrowers Association				
BC Wine Institute				
BC Wine Authority				
Association of BC Winegrowers				
Okanagan Wine Festivals Society				
Okanagan College				
Other (specify)				

10. GIVE THE RELATIVE IMPORTANCE AND FREQUENCY OF INTERACTIONS WITH THE FOLLOWING OTHER WINERIES IN THE OKANAGAN VALLEY (OR OTHER REGION STUDIED); ** They can see list of wineries on survey PO.
1–5 scale with 1 = not important, 2 = slightly important, 3 = neutral, 4 = somewhat important, and 5 = extremely important

	Importance (1–5)	Frequency (A,Q,M,W,D)	Formal/ Informal/ Both
8th Generation Vineyard			
Antelope Ridge			
Arrowleaf Cellars			
Beaumont			
Black Hills Estate Winery			

	Importance (1–5)	Frequency (A,Q,M,W,D)	Formal/ Informal/ Both
Black Widow			
Blasted Church Vineyards			
Blue Mountain Vineyard and Cellars			
Burrowing Owl Estate Winery			
Calona, Sandhill, Peller Vineyards			
Camelot			
Cedar Creek Estate Winery			
Chandra Estate Winery			
Crowsnest Vineyards			
D'Angelo Estate Winery			
Deep Creek/Hainle Vineyards Estate			
Desert Hills Estate Winery			
Dirty Laundry Vineyard			
Dunham & Froese Estate Winery			
Elephant Island Orchard			
ExNihlo			
Fairview			
Forbidden Fruit Winery			
Gehringer Bros			
Golden Beaver			
Granite Creek			
Gray Monk Estate Winery			
Greata Ranch Vineyards			
Hawthorne Mountain Vineyards			
Herder Winery & Vineyards			
Hester Creek Estate Winery			
Hijas Bonitas			
Hillside Estate Winery			
Hollywood & Wine			
Howling Bluff			
House of Rose Vineyards			
Inniskillin Okanagan Vineyards			
Jackson-Triggs			
K Mountain			
Kalala Organic			
Kettle Valley Winery			

	Importance (1–5)	Frequency (A,Q,M,W,D)	Formal/ Informal/ Both
La Frenz Winery			
Lake Breeze Vineyards			
Lang Vineyards			
Larch Hills			
Laughing Stock Vineyards			
Le Vieux Pin (oliver)/La Stella (osoyoos)			
Little Straw Vineyards			
Mission Hill Family Estate Winery			
Mistral Estate Winery			
Mt. Boucherie Estate Winery			
Nichol Vineyard & Estate Winery			
Nk'Mip			
Noble Ridge Vineyard & Winery			
Oliver Twist			
Orofino Vineyards			
Pentage Winery			
Poplar Grove Winery			
Quails' Gate Estate Winery			
Quinta Ferreira			
Raven Ridge			
Recline Ridge			
Red Rooster Winery			
Road 13 (Golden Mile) Cellars			
Robin Ridge			
Rollingdale Winery			
Ruby Tuesday			
Rustic Roots			
See Ya Later @HMV			
Seven Stones			
Silk Scarf			
Silver Sage Winery			
Soaring Eagle			
Sonoran Estate Winery			
Spiller Estates			
Stag's Hollow Winery			
St. Hubertus			

	Importance (1–5)	Frequency (A,Q,M,W,D)	Formal/ Informal/ Both
St. Lazlo			
Stoneboat Vineyards			
Stonehill Estate Winery			
Stone Mountain			
Sumac Ridge Estate Winery			
Summerhill Pyramid Winery			
Tangled Vines			
Tantalus Vineyards			
Therapy Vineyards			
Thornhaven Estates			
Tinhorn Creek Vineyards			
Township 7 Vineyards & Winery			
Twisted Tree			
Van Westen Vineyards			
Volcanic Hills			
Wild Goose Vineyards			
Zero Balance			
Other (specify)			

I I. HOW WOULD YOU RATE THE IMPORTANCE OF GEOGRAPHICAL
PROXIMITY TO OTHER FIRMS & INDUSTRY BODIES?
Critical
Important
Marginally important
No impact
A disadvantage

III. INNOVATION

12. INNOVATIVE ACTIVITIES
a. How many new products (brands or lines) have you developed
over the past 2 yrs?
b. Have you seen significant product improvement over that period?
Y/N
c. To what extent have you improved production processes over this
time not much, a little, or a lot

13. ARE THERE ANY PARTICULAR COMPANIES YOU SEE AS LEADERS IN
INNOVATION?
List companies

14. IN WHICH AREAS HAS INNOVATION OCCURED OVER THE PAST THREE
YEARS IN YOUR COMPANY? (select all that apply)
Retail Sales
Marketing
Finance
Plant Breeding
Use of Genetics
Soil Adaptation
Fermentation
Information Systems
Education/Training
Other, please specify

15. How important were the following actors to innovation activities
your company was involved in over the past three years?
(select all that apply) 1–5 scale with 1 = not important, 2 = slightly
important, 3 = neutral, 4 = somewhat important, and 5 = extremely
important

Level of Importance (1–5)

Internal Company Sources
Suppliers of equipment, materials, components or software
Clients or customers
Joint research with Other BC Wineries
Wineries outside of BC
Consultants
Conferences, trade fairs, exhibitions
Trade magazines or journals
Internet
Other (list)

16. HOW IMPORTANT WERE THE FOLLOWING SOURCES OF FUNDING FOR THESE INNOVATIONS?
1–5 scale with 1 = not important, 2 = slightly important, 3 = neutral, 4 = somewhat important and 5 = extremely important
Personal Finances
Commercial Bank/credit union
Venture Capitalists
Federal Government
Provincial Government
Local or Regional Government

17. IF YOUR COMPANY HAS NOT BEEN INVOLVED IN UTILIZING MAJOR INNOVATION, WHY IS THIS THE CASE?
(check all that apply)
Not needed by the company
Too expensive
Lack of human resources
Lack of information on technology
Lack of information on potential markets
Difficulty in finding co-operative partners
Lack of adequate or clear regulatory framework
Unaware of what's available

18. HOW IS TRAINING GIVEN IN YOUR COMPANY? Y/N FOR EACH
In-house training
External provision of training
via UBC Okanagan
Consultants
via Okanagan College
Other, please specify

19. NUMBER OF TRAINED EMPLOYEES AS PERCENTAGE OF TOTAL EMPLOYEES?

20. HOW IMPORTANT IS WINE TOURISM FOR YOUR STRATEGY?
1–5 scale with 1 = not important, 2 = slightly important, 3 = neutral, 4 = somewhat important, and 5 = extremely important

IV. STRATEGY (PERSONAL INTERVIEWS)

- How do you target markets for your wine? How do you identify the appropriate price points and types of product that will sell?
- What are the tradeoffs between being a small independent producer and part of a larger global enterprise?
- Do you believe exporting (if applicable) has made your firm more competitive? In which ways?
- How do you see the role of government in terms of the industry? How do you see industry associations?
  What else could governments or industry associations do to enhance the industry's competitiveness?
- To what extent are you able to rely upon local suppliers for equipment? Has this changed over time?
- Do you take a scientific or artisan approach or both? Do you see wine more as a commodity or cultural asset? How important is terroir to the value of your product? How important is the local identification ot the sale of your product?
- What role does the success of the wine cluster have in terms of the overall identity and culture of this province and of the country?
  Do your suppliers tend to be local or global?
  Do your buyers tend to be local or global?
- Do you primarily take an artisan or scientific approach to winemaking?
  Reasons?
  What role do you think the concept of terroir plays in the value and perceived value of your product?
  What value do your buyers place on local identity?
  Do you view your wine as a commodity or more of a cultural asset?

Contributors

DAVID AYLWARD is research manager for the Faculty of Arts and Social Sciences at the University of Technology, Sydney (UTS). He is a founding member and co-director of the UTS Research Strength – Creative Practices and Cultural Economy. David has studied and written extensively on the international wine industry, particularly innovation systems, knowledge diffusion, and organisational structures within the wine industry. David is editor-in-chief of the international journal *Arts and Social Sciences*. He is also on the editorial board of two other international journals and a regular reviewer for nine international journals.

SARA DANIELE graduated in economics from the Faculty of Economics of Pisa. She is now a student of the masters program in strategy and corporate governance of the University of Pisa.

CHRISTIAN FELZENSZTEIN, PhD International Marketing, University of Strathclyde, Glasgow, UK, is currently a professor of international marketing and director of the Research Center for International Competitiveness at Universidad Adolfo Ibañez, Chile. He has conducted international research on regional clusters in different countries. His research appears in different journals such as *Long Range Planning*, *Entrepreneurship Theory and Practice*, *Industrial Marketing Management*, and *Small Business Economics*, among others. He is the founding director of ClusterInnovation.com, a think tank focussed on industry clusters, and STEINbc.com, a specialized consultancy firm in international marketing strategy.
E-mail: c.felzensztein@uai.cl

SARAH GIEST is a PhD candidate at Simon Fraser University in the Department of Political Science. She holds a degree in society, science, and technology studies from Aalborg and Lund University, and a degree in political science from the University of Bonn. Her research focuses on the effectiveness of network management for cluster development and policies.
Email: sgiest@sfu.ca

ELISA GIULIANI, PhD Sussex University, is associate professor of management at the University of Pisa. Her research focuses on the impact of the private sector on processes of socio-economic development. She has carried out extensive research on the wine industry and her research has been published in several international journals such as the *Journal of Economic Geography*, *Research Policy*, *Regional Studies*, and *World Development*. She has served as consultant to the Inter-American Development Bank and the UN Economic Commission of Latin America and the Caribbean.

ANIL HIRA, PhD in political science from Claremont Graduate University, is professor of political science at Simon Fraser University in Vancouver, British Columbia, Canada. His research examines global competitiveness from the point of view of industrial policy and institutional effectiveness. Much of his work is focused on the developing world.
E-mail: ahira@sfu.ca

HUSAM GABRELDAR is a research economist with a masters degree in economics from the University of Missouri – Kansas City and an MBA from Emporia State University. His main research is focused on the economics of oil and natural gas and issues in developing countries.

MICHAEL HOWLETT is Burnaby Mountain Chair in the Department of Political Science at Simon Fraser University. He specializes in public policy analysis, political economy, and resource and environmental policy. He is the author of *Canadian Public Policy* (2012) and *Designing Public Policy* (2011), and co-author of *The Public Policy Primer* (2010), *Integrated Policymaking for Sustainable Development* (2009), *Studying Public Policy* (2009, 2003, 1995), *In Search of Sustainability* (2001), *The*

Political Economy of Canada (1999 & 1992) and *Canadian Natural Resource and Environmental Policy* (1997, 2005).

FRANCISCO J. MESÍAS is an agricultural engineer and holds a PhD in economics. He is a senior lecturer in the Department of Economics, University of Extremadura. His main research focuses on the study of consumer preferences for food and on farm management. He has been the leader of several competitive research projects on the topic of analysis of consumer preferences. His research in consumer preferences and farm management has been published in various academic journals, such as *Ecological Economics, Meat Science, Journal of the Science of Food*, and *Agriculture or Livestock Science*. He has also published several books and book chapters with Spanish and international publishers.

ORIANA PERRONE, PhD in management – innovation, competitiveness, and sustainability at the Santa Anna School of Advanced Studies and at Bocconi University, is a specialist in sustainability, corporate strategy, and stakeholder engagement. She works in collaboration with universities, companies, and international organizations on studies and research in the areas of development of innovation, new business models, business strategy, and corporate responsibility. She is particularly interested in international policy and strategies, and the impact of business action in the social and environmental fields. Recently, she was an advisor in macroeconomics fields for the Italian mission at the United Nations. Now she works for Bocconi University, at the Center for Research in Organization, Innovation, and Strategy (CRIOS), in the Global Observatory on the Evolution of the Sustainable Enterprise (GOESE). Her areas of expertise include corporate responsibility strategy, social impact assessment, and social development.
E-mail: oriana.perrone@unibocconi.it

FRANCISCO PULIDO is an Agricultural Engineer and holds a PhD in Agricultural Economics. He is a professor in the Department of Economics, University of Extremadura. Since 2008, he has been the dean of the Faculty of Agriculture, University of Extremadura. He is the founder and leader of the research group "Agri-food Economics." His main research focuses on the effect of the Common Agricultural Policy on the agricultural sector and on the management of extensive farms. He has published several books and papers with Spanish and international publishers.

ANGEL F. PULIDO is a PhD student in the Department of Economics, University of Extremadura. His research deals with the development of modeling tools that can be used in decision support systems in agriculture.

Index

Almendralejo Wine Institute (AWI), Spain, 146–7, 162

Amsden, Alice, 16, 21

appellation, wine regions, 71, 74; in Extremadura, Spain, 128, 132

Association of Extremaduran Wine Producers (ASEVEX), 146–9,

Australia, wine industry origins, 207–10

Australian Wine Research Institute, 211–12

"battle of ideas" between state intervention and free markets, 3–4

BC Grape Marketing Board, 89

BC Liquor Distribution Board, 89–90, 103–4

BC Ministry of Agriculture, Forestry, and Fisheries, 94, 118

BC VQA (Vintners' Quality Alliance) program, 92, 104, 112–13

BC Wine Institute, 92–3, 96, 112–13, 122–3

British Columbia (BC): land prices and geographic spread of wineries, 101–2; network ties, 106–9;

number of wineries, 98; provincial policies towards winemaking, historical, 87–91; policies resulting from North American free trade agreements, 91–3; sub-appellations, 109–11

Burt, Ronald, 24, 77

Canada, BC wine market trends, 96–7, 99–100

Cellared in Canada, import blending program, 105

Chile, history of wine industry, 166–7

clusters: definition, 34–5; diagram (of Australia), 216–17; dynamics, 42–3; European initiatives, 37, 39; firm agreement on geographical importance, 242–4; and globalisation, 38, 45; and innovation, 35, 40; meso-case approach, 33; origins, 5, 35–6, 76; (promotional) policy, 5–6; policy failure, 44

competitiveness, national, 11, 16, 19, 38